Music of
the Postwar Era

Music of
the Postwar Era

Don Tyler

American History through Music

GREENWOOD PRESS
Westport, Connecticut • London

Library of Congress Cataloging-in-Publication Data

Tyler, Don.
    Music of the postwar era / Don Tyler.
        p. cm.
    Includes bibliographical references (p.) and index.
    ISBN 978–0–313–34191–5 (alk. paper)
    1. Popular music—United States—History and criticism. 2. Popular
culture—United States—History—20th century. 3. United States—Social
conditions—1945- I. Title.
    ML3477.T85 2008
    781.640973'09045—dc22   2007032817

British Library Cataloguing in Publication Data is available.

Library of Congress Catalog Card Number: 2007032817
ISBN-13: 978–0–313–34191–5

First published in 2008

Greenwood Press, 88 Post Road West, Westport, CT 06881
An imprint of Greenwood Publishing Group, Inc.
www.greenwood.com

Printed in the United States of America

The paper used in this book complies with the
Permanent Paper Standard issued by the National
Information Standards Organization (Z39.48–1984).

10 9 8 7 6 5 4 3 2 1

Contents

Preface

I was honored when Debra Adams, senior acquisitions editor, asked if I'd be interested in writing the Postwar Music volume for Greenwood Press' "American History through Music" series. I was particularly excited because, literally, this is the "music of my life." I was in the first grade when World War II ended, and in high school when Elvis Presley burst into the nation's consciousness. Obviously, as a first grader I was not completely enthralled with the hit songs of the era, but my family was listening to *Your Hit Parade* weekly. And my parents and I were always singing the currently popular hits. Popular music has been an important part of my life as a consumer, performer, and teacher.

I wish musical labels didn't exist because they tend to create barriers. Good music is the music that affects the listener's emotions, whether it is classical or popular, pop or country, jazz or semi-classical, rhythm and blues (R&B) or swing. In order to get an accurate view of any era, we must consider various styles of music to try to determine how they influenced—and were influenced by—the nation's music-listening public.

When it comes to judging the American public's taste in popular music, one must be extremely careful. It does appear, however, that the public chooses commercialism over quality most of the time. A song may be well written but still have no hit potential. If it isn't commercial—if it doesn't appeal to a broad market—it isn't really successful in the eyes of music publishers and record-company executives. Beauty is definitely in the ear of the beholder when it comes to popular music hits, and commercialism defeats quality in most instances.

The starting point for me in the writing process for this book was to look at the various charts that were available between 1945 and 1959. I knew what songs I liked and thought were the best from this time period, but I thought it was extremely important to find some evidence to support or to refute my personal preferences. Some critics may rightfully claim that I have been too chart oriented, but as fallible as the pop charts were, they furnished me with reasonably accurate information as to which songs should be included.

I quickly found that the various charts very seldom agreed with each other, so I decided to combine the available charts to form a more accurate measurement of popularity. The charts available during this era were *Billboard*, *Your Hit Parade*, *Variety*, and *Cash Box*. Joel Whitburn, generally recognized as the *Billboard* guru, has published several books using the *Billboard* charts, but for this book I primarily used *A Century of Pop Music* and *Pop Memories*. I used John R. Williams's *This Was Your Hit Parade* for information on that hit survey. I simply counted the weeks each song spent at number one over the period covered by this book. The tiebreaker was the total number of weeks on the program. *Variety* published a top ten for each year from 1941 through 1980 in its January 14, 1981, edition. I used it as *Variety*'s contribution. There were two potential sources for *Cash Box* information: Frank Hoffmann's *The Cash Box Singles Charts, 1950–1981* and Randy Price's Web site. There were many conflicts of information between these two sources. For instance, Hoffmann's book named "Any Time," "Tell Me Why," and "I'm Yours" the No. 3, No. 7, and No. 8 songs, respectively, in 1952, even though they didn't register at number one for any week of that year. Therefore, I chose to simply count the weeks at number one from Price's Web site and rank them accordingly. The unfortunate result was several ties when songs collected the same number of weeks at the top.

Next, I simply assigned numbers to the corresponding place on the charts. I started with number one equaling 40 points, number two equaling 39 points, etc. Taking each song's rankings, they were added together. For example: "Till the End of Time" in 1945 was number two on *Billboard* (39 points), number one on *Your Hit Parade* (40 points), and number two on *Variety* (39 points), which equals 118. That qualified the song as the top hit of 1945 because no other song collected more points. The *Cash Box* chart began in 1950. *Your Hit Parade* ended on June 7, 1958.

This simple system did necessitate a few arbitrary decisions. In instances when multiple recordings of the same song made it to number one or, for that matter, when multiple versions were in *Billboard*'s year-end top forty, I decided to count only the highest ranking. Some of the charts counted all recorded versions of the song as one, while others ranked each version as a separate entity. In normal circumstances, using all four charts, if a song was number one on all the charts, the total number of possible points would be 160. Using three charts (pre-1950, before *Cash Box* started), the total would be 120. However, in the case of "To Each His Own" (1946), with *Billboard* rankings of No. 4, No. 12, and No. 18, the total, once added to *Your Hit Parade*'s number-one tie and *Variety*'s number two, would be 172, which is 52 points above the maximum allowed when using three charts. The same thing would apply to "Peg o' My Heart" (1947). *Billboard* had three popular versions of it ranked No. 4, No. 5, and No. 7, while *Variety* had two ranked No. 4 and No. 10, and *Your Hit Parade* had the song, not the recording, ranked No. 1. Those rankings added together came to 215 points, 95 points too many. Therefore, I made an executive decision: adding up all the rankings would skew the results far more than provide a clear view of the top songs. I have listed the multiple rankings under each song in the Top Hits of the year so readers can make their own judgment as to relative popularity. The combined charts from 1945 through 1959 are available in the appendix.

In addition to chart hits, I included works from *Songs of the Century* and *Rolling Stone* magazine's "The 500 Greatest Songs of All Time." In 2001, the Recording Industry Association of America (RIAA) and the National Endowment for the Arts (NEA) announced the *Songs of the Century* project, a national education initiative to promote a better understanding of America's musical and cultural heritage in the nation's schools. The songs included were from a variety of genres from country, jazz, Hollywood film music, Broadway musical songs, gospel, rhythm and blues, calypso, and mainstream pop. The December 9, 2004, edition of *Rolling Stone* magazine listed its choices for "The 500 Greatest Songs of All Time." The best thing about their list is that it was not at all chart based. Several songs are included that did not chart particularly high, but were important or historic songs.

I tried to write this book in a reader-friendly style, not to impress some imaginary music critic, but as I would want someone to write for me to read. I do not pretend to be a popular-music scholar. My goal is to play the role of guide for those reminiscing readers, or for those too young to remember, but who want to learn about the popular music of the postwar era. I sincerely hope that the reader enjoys reading this book as much as I enjoyed researching and writing it.

Acknowledgments

Debra Adams, Greenwood Press, Senior Acquisitions Editor

Grover C. Baker III, Librarian, Center for Popular Music, Middle Tennessee State University, Murfreesboro, TN

Paige Carter, Belmont University Library, Nashville, TN

John Rumble, Senior Historian, Country Music Hall of Fame and Museum, Nashville, TN

Doris Tyler, my wife, who was very helpful, especially in the proofing and indexing of the book

Charting the Hits

How does one determine the most popular hits of any particular era? One needs quantitative data concerning record and sheet-music sales, radio and television airings, the number of jukebox plays, and public performances of songs.

YOUR HIT PARADE

The first attempt at charting the hits began in the mid-thirties. When *Your Hit Parade* premiered over the NBC radio network, the show's producers hired an advertising agency—Batton, Barton, Durstine, and Osburn—to survey weekly record and sheet-music sales by contacting various unnamed music shops around the country, questioning some unnamed bandleaders concerning the songs their audiences most requested, and noting what songs were played on certain radio broadcasts. Introducing an early broadcast, the announcer explained the process, "Once again the voice of the people has spoken. New Yorkers and Californians, Northerners and Southerners, Republicans, Democrats, men, women, and children—120 million of you have told us what songs you want to hear this Saturday night. You've told us by your purchases of sheet music and records, by your requests to orchestra leaders in the places you've danced, by the tunes you listen to on your favorite radio programs. That's why the *Hit Parade* is your own program." There was no mention of jukebox play among the sources of data, but that was also supposedly checked weekly. Although the exact methodology behind this survey was never revealed, most audience members were willing to accept the tabulations without question. This rather unscientific poll tended to produce skewed results. For instance, even though the surveyors consulted some unidentified bandleaders, the poll often ignored strictly instrumental songs. Amazingly, one of the biggest big-band hits, Glenn Miller's "In the Mood," made one appearance on their survey of hits at No. 9. The show was very vocally oriented. If it wasn't singable, the producers, or some other authority, seemingly ignored its popularity. The show also completely ignored big-band hits like "Rhythm Is Our Business" (1935) and "Let's Swing It" (1935), film songs like "Warsaw Concerto" (1943) and "High Noon (Do Not Forsake Me)" (1952), country and western crossover hits like "Smoke! Smoke! Smoke! (That Cigarette)" (1947), and early rhythm and blues hits like "Earth Angel" (1955).

Your Hit Parade started on July 20, 1935, with the top fifteen songs of the week as determined by a nationwide survey. The songs were played in a random order. The first show was an hour long and featured several guest stars, such as W. C. Fields, who had nothing to do with popular music.

The show was sponsored by Lucky Strike Cigarettes, a product of the American Tobacco Company, during its twenty-five year run.

The singers on the first broadcast were Gogo DeLys, Johnny Hauser, Charles Carlisle, and Kay Thompson. Other famous singers connected with the program over the years (with the month and year they started and ended their Hit Parade stint) included Buddy Clark (May 1936–June 1937); Fredda Gibson, better known later as Georgia Gibbs (May 1937–December 1938); Bea Wain (August 1939–May 1941); Bonnie Baker (January 1940–September 1940); Johnny Mercer (February 1946–May 1946); Dinah Shore (January 1947–February 1947); Ginny Simms (February 1947–May 1947); Martha Tilton (May 1947–July 1947); Pied Pipers (June 1947–July 1947); Dick Haymes (July 1947–August 1947); and Doris Day (September 1947–November 1947); but the most famous alumnus was Frank Sinatra (February 1943–December 1944 and September 1947–May 1949).

The format varied from five to fifteen songs, with the most common number being seven. As a treat, a "Lucky Strike Extra" was often added to the show's lineup. That song was usually a standard that was not currently popular.

The length of the program also varied. The original was one hour, but both 45-minute and 30-minute versions were common at various times, with 30 minutes being the most prominent.

The continuing popularity of certain songs over multiple weeks never seemed to be a problem for the radio version of the program. Regular listeners were willing to hear a repeat performance of songs, perhaps sung by different vocalists to provide variety.

Your Hit Parade became a Saturday night ritual, except for its last season when it was on Friday night. During its peak years, millions of Americans sat in front of their radios each Saturday evening, waiting for the announcement of the top hits in the nation, especially the number-one song. It may be difficult for anyone who did not live during this period to understand the multigenerational appeal of the radio version of *Your Hit Parade*. It was a family institution each Saturday evening.

On July 10, 1950, *Your Hit Parade* premiered on television. It made four appearances that summer, and then regularly, beginning in October of that year, until its demise in April 1959, less than a year after another network bought the program to try to revive it.

For a few years, the program was simulcast on television and radio. The original cast of the television version was Eileen Wilson (November 1948–November 1951), Snooky Lanson (June 1950–August 1957), Dorothy Collins (October 1950–August 1957), and the "Hit Parade Singers and Dancers," of which Gisele MacKenzie (September 1953–August 1957) was part.

The television version attempted to dramatize each song with innovative skits, elaborate sets, and a large entourage of performers. But creating new skits for longer-running popular songs proved much more difficult on television.

During World War II, many of the shows were recorded for broadcast to servicemen abroad by the Armed Forces Radio Services. Many of those commercial-free programs are now available for purchase. Some of the black-and-white television shows are also available.

What killed *Your Hit Parade*? It may have died of old age! With the advent of television, the format of radio changed. Television took over the situation comedies and drama series. After a few years of floundering between its past and what the future might be, radio adopted the disc jockey format. Key disc jockeys in metropolitan areas, especially New York City, soon wielded considerable influence on song popularity. The advent of rock 'n' roll and the electric guitar signaled a radical change in popular music tastes. The rock-era audience wanted to hear only the singer who popularized the song sing it! They hated hearing a Hit Parade singer perform the song with an orchestra when the original had been recorded with a small, amplified guitar ensemble. It just didn't sound right. To the new rock age, the Hit Parade performances were equivalent to "elevator music" (Muzak). The rock music of the fifties was clearly targeted at youth and actually thrived on the disgust of its adult critics. *Your Hit Parade* was simply out of touch with the new music and youth culture. It had run its course.

In the early years, *Your Hit Parade*, even with its less than scientific survey of hits, was considered *the* authority on what music was most popular. The program served as the best available barometer of the nation's taste in popular music until the premier of *Variety*'s and *Billboard*'s more authoritative charts in the early forties.

BILLBOARD

Billboard is a weekly magazine devoted to the music industry. It maintains several internationally recognized music charts that track the most popular songs and albums in various categories on a weekly basis. Its most famous chart, the *Billboard Hot 100*, ranks the top 100 songs regardless of genre and is frequently used as the standard measure for ranking songs in the United States. The *Billboard 200* survey is the corresponding chart for album sales.

Billboard magazine was founded in 1894 as a trade paper for the billposting industry, hence its name. Within a few years of its founding, it began to carry news of outdoor amusements, a major consumer of billboard space. *Billboard* next became the official magazine for circuses, carnivals, amusement parks, fairs, vaudeville, minstrels, whale shows, and other live entertainment.

By the mid 1930s, the magazine began committing more and more space to music coverage. Early in 1936 it introduced a feature called "Chart Line," which listed the most-played songs on the three major radio networks.

Then, in 1940 it introduced the "Record Buying Guide" for jukebox operators and the "Best Sellers Retail Records" chart, considered to be the antecedent of today's *Hot 100 Singles* chart. The first national No. 1 was "I'll Never Smile Again" by Tommy Dorsey and his orchestra with vocals by Frank Sinatra. The "Record Buying Guide" became a chart called "Most-Played in Jukeboxes" in 1944.

The popularity of songs played on the radio was measured separately, ranked for the first time with a 15-position chart on January 27, 1945. The original name of that chart was "Disks With Most Radio Plugs." That name was soon changed to "Records Most-Played On The Air." The airplay chart completed the triad of mainstream music popularity charts: record sales, jukebox plays, and radio airplay. Sheet-music sales evidently were not considered.

Billboard published its first African American music chart in 1942 under the name "Harlem Hit Parade." In 1948, it introduced the "Best Selling Retail Race Records" chart. When the magazine recognized the term "Race Records" might be offensive, Jerry Wexler, a magazine editor who eventually left to be a founding partner in Atlantic Records, coined the term "rhythm and blues" and in early summer 1949 changed the "Race Records" rankings to "Best Selling Retail Rhythm & Blues Records."

Country music also had its own charts. The initial country chart, a jukebox list introduced in 1944, ran under the heading "Folk Records." For a period in 1947, the term "Hillbilly" replaced "Folk." Then in 1949, the name "Country & Western" was introduced for a trio of jukebox, sales, and airplay charts. It wasn't until 1962 that *Billboard* settled on the name "Hot Country Singles."

It was no mistake that *Billboard* veered so heavily into music charting in the forties. By the early part of the decade, radio had made superstars of bandleaders like Tommy and Jimmy Dorsey, Benny Goodman, Harry James, and Artie Shaw. Their tours, nightclub appearances, radio dates, and recording sessions were big news in the entertainment industry. They, and singing stars like Frank Sinatra, were frequently featured on the magazine's cover.

The music business was hot and *Billboard* had begun to dedicate more and more of its pages to music, radio, and jukebox coverage. Then in December 1941 came the shock of war. The magazine often reminded entertainers of their important role in the war effort. Throughout the war, *Billboard* carried page after page of ads promoting the sale of war bonds and articles honoring show business's support for the troops.

After the war, *Billboard* changed with the times. With the arrival of the 45-rpm record and the LP, the music industry was poised for a boom.

The rock 'n' roll revolution was knocking on the door. *The Billboard Book of No. 1 Hits* starts the rock era on July 9, 1955, when Bill Haley His Comets' recording of "(We're Gonna) Rock Around the Clock" hit number one.

In early 1955, the magazine's review of Elvis Presley's "Milk Cow Blues" said he was "one of the slickest talents to come up in the country field in a long, long time." Just over a year later, Elvis achieved his first No. 1 *Billboard* pop hit with "Heartbreak Hotel." Rock 'n' roll was here to stay!

In November 1955, *Billboard* published its first 100-position pop chart, the *Top 100*. The *Hot 100* has been published since 1958, combining sales of singles and radio airplay for the first time. The first number one on the *Hot 100* was "Poor Little Fool" by Ricky Nelson.

Over the years, *Billboard* has become the best-known popular music charting organization.

VARIETY

Variety magazine began in 1905 covering vaudeville, circuses, parks, burlesque, minstrels, and fairs. It soon added the legitimate theater, touring plays and musicals, sheet-music sales, the "talking machine," and nickelodeons.

As other entertainment media became important, the magazine expanded its coverage to include things like radio broadcasting, the "electronized" phonograph, motion pictures, television, and eventually everything else concerning the entertainment industry.

Joel Whitburn, in *A Century of Pop Music,* says that in 1929 *Variety* published the top sellers each month for the major labels. It also added top songs for sheet-music sales in 1934. The weekly record-label best-seller charts continued to run until 1935.

The magazine compiled information for its charts from three major sources—coin machines (jukeboxes), retail record sales, and retail sales of sheet music in the early forties. It published weekly and yearly charts covering sheet-music best sellers, top tunes, and best sellers on coin-machines. Most of the time, those charts were alphabetical and offered no rankings.

In 1947, *Variety* added a new weekly chart measuring the popularity of songs and recorded talent, as reflected by the "most-requested" records reported by a pool of nearly one hundred disc jockeys.

Of particular value to pop-music historians was a group of Top Ten, for each year from 1941 through 1980, that was published in their January 14, 1981, edition. Those charts were ranked 1 through 10 and were used as *Variety*'s Top Ten of each year covered by this book.

When the magazine celebrated its fiftieth anniversary, it presented its Hit Parade of a Half-Century (1905–1955) in the January 4, 1956, issue. Their 50-year Hit Parade is very interesting to lovers of old popular music, but the number of songs varies per year and the listings are alphabetical. In many instances, there are well-known songs listed that did not make the yearly Top Ten charts mentioned above.

CASH BOX

Cash Box magazine was a weekly publication that charted the weekly hits since 1950. They had charted recordings as far back as 1942, but those charts are not available.

According to Frank Hoffmann's *The Cash Box Singles Charts, 1950–1981,* the "Nation's Top 10 Jukebox Tunes" began to be designated with an asterisk beginning with the March 25, 1950, issue. With the July 7 issue of that year, the "Top 10" was extended to include positions 11–20. In May 1951, the "Additional Tunes" section was expanded to include 11–25, then expanded again in May 1953 and re-titled the "Top Ten, Plus the Next 25." On August 4, 1956, "The Cash Box Top 50 Best Selling Records" chart was instituted. That was finally expanded to the "Top 100" in September 1958.

Cash Box combined all currently available recordings of a song into one chart position, with no indication of which version was the biggest seller. The chart was sales-based until the late seventies, when airplay data was first incorporated. Also in the seventies, a "Weeks on the Chart" column was added.

Hoffmann's book is a valuable source, but it offers no explanation as to how the magazine generated its Top 10 for each year. The magazine's name seems to refer to coin machines or jukeboxes, using the term "cash" for "coin" and "box" for "jukebox," but there is no solid evidence to support that supposition.

There are also some incongruities that are not explained. For instance, in one section of the book, the No. 1 singles are listed in order with the number of weeks it appeared at the top of the *Cash Box* chart in parentheses. Even though "My Heart Cries for You" collected six weeks at No. 1 in 1951, it was not a year-end Top 10. Also, according to Hoffmann's charts, songs like "Any Time," "Tell Me Why," and "I'm Yours" were No. 3, No. 7, and No. 8, respectively, in 1952, even though they didn't register any weeks at No. 1.

Randy Price's Web site, "*Cash Box* Top Singles," lists the *Cash Box* No. 1 hits from 1950 through 1996. His dates don't match Hoffmann's. Price has the Top 40 from January 7, 1950, to October 6, 1951; the Top 50 from October 13, 1951, to April 6, 1957; the Top 60 from April 13, 1957, to June 14, 1958; the Top 75 from June 21, 1958, to September 6, 1958; and the Top 100 beginning September 13, 1958.

Neither do Price's No. 1 songs—or the number of weeks at the top—match Hoffmann's figures. Just one example illustrates the discrepancy: Hoffmann's book contends that "*The Third Man* Theme" in 1950 was the No. 2 hit of the year with two weeks at No. 1. Price lists it eleven weeks at the top, from April 22 through July 1.

Hoffmann says "Goodnight, Irene" (1950) and "Because of You" (1951) tied with the most weeks at No. 1, with ten weeks. If Price's listings are correct, "*The Third Man* Theme" collected eleven weeks, besting both of those songs.

When this book begins to add the *Cash Box* chart information to those of *Billboard, Variety,* and *Your Hit Parade* in 1950, Price's figures are used. Weeks at No. 1 were the determining factor for the year's rankings for *Cash Box* figures.

Billboard, Variety, Your Hit Parade, and *Cash Box* do not often agree with each other. In 1946, the three agreed that "The Gypsy" was the year's top hit, but in no other year of the 1945–1959 period was there a consensus by them, or after *Cash Box* was added. Therefore, it is important to consider all of them, even admitting that *Billboard* has become the industry's most famous charting service. The combined hit charts of each year are available in the appendix.

2

How Was Popular Music Dispensed?

RADIO

The Beginnings Through World War II

Commercial broadcast radio has been around since November 2, 1920, when experimental radio station 8XK became KDKA in Pittsburgh, Pennsylvania. In 1921 there were eight stations, but within a couple of years there were 564, and spectrum shortage became a problem. Radio caught on quickly and expanded rapidly. It could disseminate music to hundreds of thousands of listeners and make a song a national hit overnight, but it also shortened the life of songs due to overexposure. Irving Berlin lamented, "Our songs don't live anymore ... Radio has mechanized them all. In the old days Al Jolson sang the same song for years until it meant something ... Today, Paul Whiteman plays a song hit once or twice or a Hollywood hero sings them once in the films and the radio runs them ragged for a couple of weeks—then they're dead" (Bergreen, 328). Perhaps Berlin exaggerated slightly, but only slightly.

Radio was the most important entertainment medium of the Great Depression because people couldn't afford to go out, so they stayed at home and got their entertainment by twirling the radio dial. Therefore, many hit songs were made through exposure on radio programs.

It is estimated that by the mid-thirties, the number of homes with radios was nearly 23 million, and the total audience was around 91 million. This was the "Golden Age of Radio."

In the mid-thirties, radio became particularly important in disseminating swing music to its youthful audience. In Benny Goodman's book, *The Kingdom of Swing*, he tells how, in 1934, the National Biscuit Company hired his band for a program on NBC. Three bands were hired. Goodman's represented the hot band (or swing). The three-hour show, called *Let's Dance*, was broadcast on fifty-three stations. Goodman's was the final feature of each broadcast, making it too late for high school and college students in the Eastern time zone—where listeners were more apt to like Goodman's hot music—to hear these broadcasts.

The 1935 U.S. tour that followed the *Let's Dance* radio show by Goodman and his band wasn't very successful until the group reached the West Coast. Because of the three-hour time difference, the *Let's Dance* broadcasts had been heard by the youth out West. They eagerly anticipated hearing this hot, swing band. Considering the rest of the tour, the band certainly wasn't expecting the reception they experienced. When the kids at the Palomar Ballroom in Los Angeles heard the musicians launch into their hot repertoire, they crowded around the bandstand cheering. Instead of the end, the band experienced the dawn of a new era in American popular-music history.

Soon live radio remotes were regularly featuring this new swing music coast to coast. Nearly all the major hotels in metropolitan areas had a direct feed ("wire") installed for broadcast transmission. In 1938, a young Frank Sinatra was eager to land a job as a singing waiter at the Rustic Cabin, a small-time roadhouse in New Jersey, because it had a direct radio line to WNEW in New York City. Once a week, Harold Arlen's band, with Frank as the singer, was heard on *Saturday Night Dance Parade*. Frank thought there was no better way for him to be heard by some big-time bandleader. And it proved to be true.

As World War II began, many radio broadcasts originated from army bases where the big bands played for United Service Organizations. Some radio shows also featured amateur talent from local army bases.

Radio stations began to play more records and disc jockeys became well-known personalities. Right after the U.S. entered the war, some record companies, particularly Decca, tried to prevent stations from playing their records because the record companies, the recording artists, and the music publishers were not being compensated.

James C. Petrillo, president of the American Federation of Musicians, tried to force radio stations to replace what he called "canned music" with live musicians. Petrillo's efforts were futile because Congress passed the Lea Act (or "Anti-Petrillo Act"), which was later upheld by the U.S. Supreme Court.

Radio After World War II

By 1945 there were 943 AM radio stations, 46 FM stations, and nine TV stations in the United States. There were over 56 million radios and approximately 16,500 television sets in American homes.

Nazi Germany had developed tape recording during the war to broadcast music and propaganda twenty-four hours per day. When the war ended in 1945, some of the tape recorders were recovered and brought back to the United States One of them was demonstrated to Bing Crosby in 1947. Crosby had been looking for a solution to having to perform his radio show multiple times for different time zones. As an experiment, his first show of the new season was recorded and edited entirely on magnetic tape. Bing was so impressed by the quality that he financed the development of an American version of the German machine. By 1948, the result was manufactured and marketed by the Ampex Electric and Manufacturing Company.

Bing Crosby was one of the biggest radio personalities during this era. In the mid-forties he broadcast for ABC, primarily because they would allow him to tape his program, but he returned to his original radio home, CBS, in the late forties. By then, recorded broadcasts had become commonplace. Bing's big-budget primetime show ended May 30, 1954, because TV was drawing the big money away from radio broadcasting.

Another major radio personality was Arthur Godfrey. *Arthur Godfrey's Talent Scouts*, a program not unlike today's *American Idol*, featuring amateur talent, debuted on CBS radio in 1946 and transferred to television in 1948. The show became a national phenomenon and several famous performers got their start there, including Pat Boone, the Chordettes, Tony Bennett, Eddie Fisher, Connie Francis, Al Martino, Rosemary Clooney, Steve Lawrence, Roy Clark, The Diamonds, and Patsy Cline. Interestingly, two who auditioned for the show and whom Godfrey turned down were Buddy Holly and Elvis Presley.

Though the hostilities of World War II came to an end in 1945, the postwar-radio era dates from 1947 because it took some time for the country to return to routine civilian life. Radio continued to grow even with the intrusion of television. In 1948, radio networks grossed more revenue than ever before.

Country music was broadcast by Chicago's *National Barn Dance* from 1928 until 1957; by *The Louisiana Hayride* from Shreveport, Louisiana, from 1948 to 1960; and by Nashville's *Grand Ole Opry* from 1925 to the present. *The Hayride*, broadcast on KWKH, showcased established country stars, but it is also famous for giving talented unknowns, like Elvis Presley, their first national exposure. The *Barn Dance*, broadcast on WLS, covered the Midwest and many of the western states. Perhaps for that reason several western performers, like Rex Allen, Gene Autry, Pat Buttram, and Patsy Montana, were featured on the show.

In the early forties, a Chicago radio station, WSBC, was programing five-and-a-half hours of shows per week aimed at the city's African Americans. But in the late forties, WDIA in Memphis became the first radio station in the country that was programmed entirely by African Americans for African Americans. When *Tan Town Jamboree* first aired in the Fall of 1948, the response was decidedly positive, except for some bomb threats by white segregationists. The station's African American DJs played blues, rhythm and blues, swing and jazz by black bands, and black gospel. WDIA's achievement seems all the more extraordinary because it occurred during a time of strong racial unrest.

Other radio stations around the nation were becoming aware of the economic significance of R&B music now that whites accounted for as much as forty percent of the radio audiences listening to what was formerly called "race music." Many local stations added at least one disc jockey to play R&B music, normally cover recordings by white artists.

Todd Storz is credited with originating the "Top 40" radio format in the early fifties. At that time, typical AM radio programming consisted mostly of dramas and variety shows. Storz got the idea for his radio format when he noted the positive response certain songs got from the record-buying public and compared that with the way certain selections on jukeboxes were played over and over again. Storz owned and operated several radio stations. He gradually converted those stations to an all-hits format and named the result "Top 40." Within a few years, "Top 40" stations appeared all over the country, spurred by the popularity of rock 'n' roll music. The format was based on a continuous rotation of popular songs presented by a disc jockey.

Particularly during the mid-fifties, southern white teenagers, and some from the East and Midwest, were tuning in every evening, often discreetly, to WLAC, a 50,000-watt clear channel radio station in Nashville, which was introducing rhythm and blues to millions of young listeners. At bedtime for many teenagers, if the weather cooperated and the radio's tuner was sensitive enough, these youngsters heard the strange, new, wonderful sounds of authentic R&B for the first time.

One of the unique listening experiences on WLAC was the nightly program sponsored by "The World's Largest Mail Order Phonograph Record Shop"—Randy's Record Shop in Gallatin, Tennessee. Randy's sponsored what may have been the most-listened-to DJ show in the country during this era. The show's host was Gene Nobles, who has as much claim as anyone to being the first to play rhythm and blues records for a racially mixed audience. The "Randy" of Randy's Record Shop was Randy Wood, a successful entrepreneur who boasted that his shop was "The Home of the World's Largest Stock of Recorded Music." He was also President of Dot Records, and it was in this capacity, in 1955, that he was introduced to an aspiring twenty-year-old singer named Pat Boone. Wood signed the young man to a contract, and before the year was gone, Boone had his first hit on Dot: a cover version of Fats Domino's R&B classic, "Ain't That a Shame."

By the early fifties, a few northern stations began playing R&B to satisfy white youth's newfound taste, but they usually spotted the R&B discs between mainline pop songs by white singers or by white cover versions of R&B hits.

Of course, not everyone was happy about white youths' listening to this music. It was definitely threatening to the old order. As the musical tastes of teenagers changed, social change was not far behind. Youth was on the move, with their own spending money, fashions, culture, and ideas about the music they wanted to hear.

Radio station WHB in Kansas City became the first all-rock 'n' roll station in the country in 1958, while some other stations announced they would smash rock records while on the air.

By the end of the fifties, radio was largely the portable variety: transistor radios, an everyday part of the automobile, or a bedside medium, while television became the big piece of entertainment furniture in the family living room.

Disc Jockeys

In the mid-thirties, American radio commentator Walter Winchell coined the term "disc jockey," combining "record disc or disk" with "jockey," as in the operator of a machine, as a description of a radio announcer who plays recordings.

At first, the large U.S. radio networks and the musicians' union were against the use of recordings because it put live musicians out of work. Los Angeles radioman Al Jarvis played records and created the illusion that he was broadcasting from a ballroom. The show, which he called *The World's Largest Make Believe Ballroom*, was basically a disc jockey program. Martin Block took the concept to New York City and had considerable success with his *Make Believe Ballroom* beginning in 1935. Success is quickly imitated, so soon other DJs and stations picked up the idea and the format became established.

The disc jockey program didn't come into its own as a major ingredient of radio programming until after the war, when phonograph record production went spiraling to unprecedented levels. The product was plentiful, the choice was broad, and the artists were abundant. It was time for the platter spinner to emerge as a major factor in making hits. One of the problems, however, was that companies like Columbia Records put key jockeys on their payrolls to plug their current releases. Such practices led to the payola scandal (see below).

Capitol Records was one of the first companies to court disc jockeys with promotion techniques other companies were hesitant to adopt. Capitol executives were smart enough to discern that a large portion of the radio audience was no longer satisfied with the same old music, played or sung in the same old way by the same performers, so they promoted their stable of artists to the disc jockeys and quickly reaped positive results. By 1947, the disc-jockey vogue caused *Variety* to inaugurate the "request" poll in its magazine.

Americans aren't crazy about being told what to like, but they're much more susceptible to suggestion. The typical disc jockey in a major market usually received at least a hundred sample recordings each week to consider. Theoretically speaking, he selected the best from this avalanche of records, packaged them into a cohesive and well-balanced program, and presented them with some pleasing chatter. The DJ was thus subtly "suggesting" to the public the songs destined for popularity. He wielded considerable responsibility as to which songs succeeded and which ones failed.

The shrewdest publishers and record companies marketed their products to the public via the DJs. In the spring of 1950, publisher Howard S. Richmond purchased several thousand copies of the Weavers' recording of "Goodnight, Irene," which he mailed to 1,500 disc jockeys around the country. Because of his well-established contacts with the DJs, "Goodnight,

Irene" received considerable airplay. In the first month, Richmond sold 250,000 sheet-music copies of the song, and the Weavers' recording sold half a million. Richmond's shrewd marketing of his song, his well-cultivated relationship with the disc jockeys, and their willingness to plug his song, certainly helped make the song and the Weavers' disc one of 1950's top hits.

The Birth of BMI

As the forties opened, before the United States entered World War II, record sales soared. That prompted the American Society of Composers, Authors, and Publishers (ASCAP)—the long-established performing rights organization (since 1914)—to propose a new contract with radio stations that demanded an annual fee of $9,000,000, twice the amount the stations had paid under the old contract, for playing music written and published by ASCAP members. Radio executives refused to discuss the proposed contract, which resulted in all ASCAP music being banned from the airwaves until 1941, when ASCAP signed a new five-year contract and with that accepted even less each year than it had received under the previous contract. ASCAP came out of its war with radio seriously battered in both its prestige and its pocketbook.

To protect its interests, radio formed a new performing-rights organization called Broadcast Music Incorporated (BMI), which sought out songwriters and publishers from fields that ASCAP had ignored: foreign music, country and western (then called hillbilly), and from places outside the metropolitan areas of New York City and Los Angeles. Within a decade, BMI was licensing eighty percent of all the music played on radio.

Arrogantly, ASCAP became convinced BMI songs were becoming hits only because DJs were being paid to play BMI songs. It had been proven that the more a specific record was heard over the radio, the more it became imprinted on the listening public, who in turn bought its recordings and sheet music or played the song on jukeboxes. BMI also became the most prominent performing-rights organization for early rock music. So ASCAP asked Congress, specifically House Oversight Subcommittee Chairman Oren Harris, to investigate the recording industry's practice of payola.

Payola

Even though payola had been around in one form or another since the days of vaudeville, congressional probers became determined to bury payola practices, so they began to investigate DJs who took gifts from record companies in return for playing their products on the radio. The investigators found that DJs were not only wined and dined, clothed and even housed, but they were sometimes also partners or stockholders in various musical enterprises. Running scared, record companies began admitting they had given money to specific DJs. Soon twenty-five disc jockeys and radio program directors were named in the scandal.

A central target of the payola crackdown was disc jockey Alan Freed, who is generally given credit for originating the term "rock and roll" in 1951 for his *Moon Dog's Rock and Roll Party* over radio station WWJ in Cleveland. When Freed moved to New York City's WINS in 1954, he became a dominant power via the make-or-break influence of airtime exposure of a song. The disc jockey, and Freed in particular, quickly became a kingpin in the music business.

In addition to his disc jockeying, Freed was listed as cowriter for some songs, like "Sincerely," popularized in 1955 by the R&B group The Moonglows and taken to No. 1 in a cover version by the McGuire Sisters. The question is, did Freed really help Moonglows member Harvey Fuqua write the song, or might Fuqua have been happy to give Freed writing credit so he would help promote the song on his radio show? It very well could have been just another payola scam.

When asked to sign a statement denying involvement in payola, Freed refused and was promptly fired by WINS and WNEW-TV. In 1960, Freed was indicted for accepting $2,500 that he claimed was a token of gratitude and did not affect airplay. He paid a small fine and was released. However, his career faltered, and five years later he died from alcohol abuse at age forty-three. The 1978 film *American Hot Wax* chronicled Freed's career.

Another target of the payola scandal was Dick Clark. As host to the first network television series devoted to rock 'n' roll, *American Bandstand*, Richard "Dick" Clark helped promote the careers of many rock artists of the fifties through the eighties.

In 1952, Clark went to work for WFIL radio and television in Philadelphia. That summer, the radio station decided to follow the new trend of having announcers play records over the air. It proved so successful that soon they tried the same format on television. Bob Horn, a WFIL radio DJ, began broadcasting a show called *Bandstand*. A month after the show's premier, teenagers were invited to the studio to dance while Horn played records. The show became very successful with high school students.

Dick Clark was hosting a similar program on WFIL radio and, in 1955, filled in for Horn during the latter's vacation. After Horn was arrested on a drunk-driving charge in 1956, Clark took over the television show permanently.

After several years of local success, the first national broadcast of *American Bandstand* was on August 5, 1957, on ABC-TV from three to four thirty in the afternoon. A regular group of clean-cut Philadelphia high school students were featured on the show as dancers.

American Bandstand provided the first national exposure of many early rock performers like Chuck Berry, Jerry Lee Lewis, Buddy Holly, and Chubby Checker, but at least initially, Clark's personal taste in music was more big band, as illustrated by his choice of "Bandstand Boogie," by Les Elgart and his orchestra, as the show's theme song.

By 1958, some twenty million fans were watching the show that was carried on sixty-four stations. With such a large viewer base, having a new song played on the show virtually guaranteed the record's success. Records that were played on the air tended to go at least Top Ten.

American Bandstand (ABC). (Courtesy of Photofest)

Some agents who tried to get their artists' recordings on the show became suspicious of the method of choosing artists and songs. It seemed local Philadelphia record-label artists were frequent guests. Agents also complained that Clark had invested in the local record labels Swan and Jamie, and that the records they produced were played more often on the show.

In 1959, as part of the payola scandal, Clark was investigated by the congressional probers. They discovered, he owned partial copyrights to 150 songs and that many of those songs had been played frequently on his show. Also, there were financial ties to thirty-three music-related businesses, mostly in the Philadelphia area.

Despite all this, Clark was only admonished for accepting a fur stole and expensive jewelry from a record-company president. The investigation ended by absolving Clark. However, in 1959 ABC-TV gave Clark the choice of selling his outside businesses or leaving the network. His music-business enterprises proved to be very impressive, including a trio of labels, as many publishing companies, one disc-distribution firm, and one pressing plant. Clark capitulated and sold his "outside" business ventures. He was inducted into the Rock and Roll Hall of Fame in 1993.

Clark survived and thrived, while others, like Freed, had their careers and lives ruined by the payola scandal.

RECORDINGS

The American Federation of Musicians' Strike

Record sales slowly recovered after the Great Depression and were booming again by the early forties. But the prosperity didn't last. Members of the American Federation of Musicians (AFM), the union for instrumentalists, became worried that live musicians were being replaced on radio and in nightclubs by recordings and jukeboxes. The union demanded that the record companies establish a fund for unemployed musicians. From August 1942 to September 1943, AFM initiated a strike against record companies, forbidding any member instrumentalists from participating in recordings. The result was several all-vocal (a cappella) recordings. In November 1944, the record companies agreed to the union's demand for payment of a royalty on each record to be used for the benefit of unemployed members. The passage of the Taft-Hartley Act, however, made the agreement illegal, and a new ban on making recordings was initiated in January 1948. The first ban had caught the major record companies by surprise, but by the second ban they had stockpiled enough recordings to satisfy the market until a new compromise was finally reached fifteen months later. For more on the AFM strike, please see http://www.swingmusic.net/Big_Band_Era_Recording_Ban_Of_1942.html.

During the War

Record production declined during the war because there was a shortage of shellac, which was used in making records. Shellac was produced in India, but because of the war in Asia, trade with India was disrupted. The industry launched a drive, "Records for Our Fighting Men," to get the public to turn in old records that could be melted down and reused. As a result, many rare recordings were lost.

Several recording artists and some record companies tried to prevent radio stations from playing records without paying for the rights. Record labels clearly stated the records were for home use only and were forbidden to broadcasters. However, when Capitol was launched in 1942, they promoted their recordings among DJs and radio stations (see more under **Disc Jockeys** above).

The first gold record ever given was presented to Glenn Miller by RCA Victor for his recording of "Chattanooga Choo Choo," on their Bluebird label. The presentation was made over the Chesterfield radio program on February 10, 1942. The recording had reportedly sold 1.2 million copies by then. At this point, record sales were reported by either the record company or the artist, but the numbers were not always reliable. Therefore, "reportedly" seems an appropriate adverb to qualify sales figures until 1958, when the Recording Industry Association of America (RIAA) began to certify sales figures.

Recorded background music became more prominent during the war years. Research had shown that playing background music in factories and businesses decreased fatigue, raised morale, and increased productivity by as much as twenty-five percent. This revelation had an enormous impact on the history and development of recorded sound.

During the war years, the record company that produced the most hits on *Billboard*'s year-end top forty was Decca, with over forty percent for that four-year period.

The Postwar Years

In the postwar years, more and more Americans had the time and the money to enjoy prerecorded music in their homes. The late forties began a period of both innovation and standardization that changed the technology of prerecorded music and revitalized the record industry. As World War II ended, research facilities could be utilized for peaceful purposes. As a result, sound quality greatly improved.

At the beginning of 1945, the music business looked forward to a sales boom, but no one was ready for the doubling of sales that took place.

The cancellation of all wage and price controls, except on rent, in late 1946, brought on rapid inflation, which also affected the record business. Popular discs went up to seventy-five cents, while classical music recordings cost one dollar.

Several months before it was to take effect, the American Federation of Musicians announced another ban on recordings using AFM members. The ban would take effect on January 1, 1948. Once Columbia and Victor were convinced that AFM was completely serious about another strike, they invested millions of dollars in a down-to-the-wire frenzy of recordings that produced 2,000 masters. The record companies also became worried because of a provision in their contracts with the AFM that voided, in the event of a strike, all existing artist contracts. They were convinced a bidding war for talent would certainly be the result.

In the year that passed before union musicians returned to the studios, the recording industry changed drastically. New recording techniques and equipment initiated the modern age of the art. The announcement in early 1948 that the ABC Radio Network was going "all-tape" for nighttime programming drew new attention to the changes that had taken place since American troops first discovered German tape recorders during their liberation of occupied Europe (see more about this under **Radio** above).

Evidence that the record industry was hurting for talented, charismatic performers and songs with huge sales potential is illustrated by the fact that only one out of every twenty-five popular releases during the late forties enjoyed some measure of success in record stores.

RIAA—Who, What, Why?

The Recording Industry Association of America (RIAA), a nonprofit corporation designed to deal with legislation, the allocation of materials, preparation of industry statistics, and responding to the government's requests for information concerning the industry, was founded in September 1951.

RIAA's initial public statement reported a $200 million national gross sale of 186 million discs in 1951, purchased by the owners of nearly 22 million record players of all types—or one in every three families. For the first time, production of 45-rpm records surpassed 33 1/3-rpm records, almost doubling their sale.

One of RIAA's most visible purposes became certifying Gold, Platinum, Multiplatinum, and Diamond albums and singles. The Gold standard is one million units sold. Platinum is awarded for two million. The first Gold plaque awarded by RIAA went to Perry Como in 1958 for his single "Catch a Falling Star." Four months later, the cast album of *Oklahoma!* became the first official Gold album.

At the end of 1953, RIAA confirmed that the previous all-time sales high of $204 million in 1947 had been surpassed. Resistance to the new 45 and 33 1/3 speeds continued, each with only twenty percent of all sales, with the soon-to-be obsolete 78-speed records accounting for $122.4 million in sales. Despite the recent technological advances in recording and record players, only twenty percent of American households owned a phonograph. With all the sales records, it is surprising to learn that only one recording out of every thirty releases became a hit. A major hit did, however, provide returns far in excess of those in the past. Jo Stafford, who had been recording as a soloist since 1944, had accumulated twenty-five million copies sold as of 1953. The young singer Eddie Fisher, who was attracting some of the same female-teen-age adulation that Frank Sinatra once enjoyed, sold five million records in 1953. It usually took three to five years for a disc to become a million-seller.

The number of million-selling records more than doubled from the end of the war to the beginning of rock 'n' roll. In 1945, twenty-one records that would eventually sell a million copies were released. In 1955, fifty records became million-sellers, and the discs usually reached million-seller status within their first year of release.

Record sales dipped in the late fifties as teens listened to more of their music on portable transistor radios.

R&B Gains

In the early fifties, many of the major record companies formed subsidiary labels to handle R&B music—for example, Okeh by Columbia; Coral, and later Brunswick, by Decca.

Jukebox operators began to notice that white teenagers were playing the original R&B versions of songs on their machines. Then, local record retailers began to catch on. However, they often had difficulty keeping R&B recordings in stock because most companies were in the business for the African American market only.

Cover Versions

The term cover, or cover version, simply means any recording of a song other than the original. Critics decried the cover versions by white performers of rhythm and blues originals, very common in the mid-fifties, claiming the white artists were virtually robbing the original African American performers. The heyday of covers of R&B was basically 1954 through 1956, when the social climate of the times has to be taken into consideration. In most instances, white performers took the original R&B song, cleaned up the lyrics a little to make it more palatable to WASP (white, Anglo-Saxon, Protestant) ears, recorded it, and therefore reached a much larger audience. The social climate of the mid-fifties would never have allowed the original, more risqué version to become a big hit. It just wasn't possible. As unfair as it appears today, the original R&B song most likely would never have become a national hit at all had it not been for the cover version. And the critics were not always consistent. Nobody strenuously objected when Elvis Presley covered Big Mama Thornton's original R&B version of "Hound Dog." (African American singers also covered the work of R&B artists. Chubby Checker's 1959 "The Twist" was a cover of Hank Ballard's original, for instance.)

The same critics who cried foul when R&B songs were covered, never raised an eyebrow, much less their voices, when country songs were covered by mainstream pop singers. That was white artists covering white artists. The trend was particularly active between 1949 and 1957. As country songs were popularized by mainstream pop performers, the residual effect was that authentic country performers crossed over into the pop market with hits. Crossover is a term describing a song or performer that becomes popular in two or more musical genres.

The term cover is not a four-letter word. It only got a bad name during the period when white singers covered R&B, but the practice goes on, and will continue.

Motown Records

Berry Gordy, Jr., launched Detroit's Motown Records in 1959. The company, the first record label owned by an African American, became particularly important in the sixties with its soul music and incredible lineup of recording artists, including Smokey Robinson and the Miracles, the Marvelettes, Martha and the Vandellas, Mary Wells, the Supremes, the Temptations, the Four Tops, Gladys Knight and the Pips, Marvin Gaye, and the Jackson Five, among others.

Albums Become Important

In 1956, stereophonic albums (LPs for "long playing") became available. Most new releases were issued in both monaural (mono) and stereophonic (stereo) versions, but by the end of the sixties mono had been phased out.

In the second half of the fifties, there were five movie-soundtrack LPs, a couple of original-cast recordings from Broadway musicals, and the first classical recording to sell a million copies (at the height of the Cold War, a 23-year-old East Texan, Van Cliburn, won the International Tchaikovsky Piano Competition in Moscow. The recording was of the piece he performed in his prize-winning performance). The calypso craze is evidenced by two Harry Belafonte LPs, and the folk-song trend that was particularly popular in the early sixties is evidenced by two Kingston Trio albums, among the top twenty-five. Johnny Mathis also collected a couple of albums in the top pop albums list. When Columbia Records and Frank Sinatra parted in the early fifties, he had difficulty getting a recording contract with any company. He eventually signed with Capitol and, with the help of arranger-extraordinaire Nelson Riddle, he began his climb back. Long playing records also came along at exactly the right time for Frank; albums became his salvation in the music business because he could build a mood and sustain that feeling with songs that followed a theme as he did in several of his best-selling LPs. He had two LPs in 1958 that ranked among the top twenty-five during this half-decade. Not to be outdone, Elvis Presley had four listed. Henry Mancini wrote the music for the television detective series *Peter Gunn*, and his LP of some of the music from the show also made the list. The series' theme song became particularly well known.

As significant as LPs were becoming, singles were the primary sales medium until the late seventies, when albums overtook singles in sales.

Singles vs. Albums

The changes brought about because of the payola scandal, and the end of the disc jockey's arbitrary power over the music business in the late fifties, came as a punctuation mark to the steep decline in sales of single records. While the record-industry profits had been climbing steadily at an annual growth rate exceeding twenty-five percent for a decade, single sales lost ground and fell to less than one-third of yearly sales in 1959. The slack caused by the singles dip was replaced by rising album sales.

One theory for lagging singles was the ninety-eight-cent price, which many felt was too high compared to a pop album. The LP appeared to the buyers to be a better bargain. Another reason singles buyers, predominantly teenagers, were bypassing the purchase of discs was transistor radios. They could hear their favorite tunes anytime by dialing in a "Top 40" station.

The largest sales increase in 1955 had been in LP records, with only a minor increase in 45s, and a significant decline in 78s, which were now primarily used for rhythm and blues and country and western recordings. Because the old-fashioned 78 record represented one fourth of all sales, but less than twenty percent of dollar volume, and its production costs were climbing, manufacturers were slowly phasing it out and forcing the independent labels to do the same, by increasing its manufacturing costs while making those for 45s more attractive.

Approximately 100 singles were issued each week in the late fifties, enough for a disc jockey on the air sixteen hours a day to play each just once, without touching anything issued in the past. It was a glut that the country's nearly 700 distributors found difficult to handle.

By the end of the fifties, the adult market for pop music had dwindled almost to the vanishing point. If they purchased recordings at all, it tended to be albums that were filled with pop standards, showtunes, or classy background music.

JUKEBOXES

The word "juke" or "jook" most likely originated in West Africa. According to the Columbia dictionary, the word comes from Gullah, a language spoken by African descendents who lived off the coast of Georgia and South Carolina. It originally meant "wicked" or "to live wickedly," but came to be associated with brothels or houses of prostitution. Later, after the word migrated to America with the African slaves, it came to mean dancing in a sexually suggestive manner or the places where those dances were performed. Those dancing places were usually low-class roadhouses or taverns that became known as juke joints. These small juke joints could not afford live bands. So when electric, coin-operated phonograph machines were introduced in the late twenties, they quickly made their way to these establishments. The new machines were like having a band in a box, a juke-band-in-a-box, or "jukebox."

Manufacturers did not call their machines "jukeboxes." They called them *automatic coin-operated phonographs.* They were futilely attempting to disassociate their machines from the lower-class joints that coined the term.

By the late thirties, jukeboxes could be found in nightclubs, lounges, bars, pool halls, restaurants, cafes, hotels, bus stations, ice cream parlors, soda fountains, and even drugstores. They soon became a major factor in the ultimate resurgence of the recording industry.

The records in the nation's jukeboxes required constant change, often as frequently as weekly. By the mid-thirties, over half of all record production in the United States was destined for jukeboxes. Many of the classic jazz and blues records of the thirties were made for them specifically.

The jukebox was at least partially responsible for increases in record sales as the 1940s dawned. When people heard songs they liked on the jukebox, they went out and bought copies of their favorites to experience at home.

For several years during World War II, jukebox production was halted by the U.S. government to conserve labor and materials for the war.

The new postwar jukeboxes, which could hold as many as one hundred or more records, were adapted to the 45-rpm speed and were of considerable assistance in gaining public acceptance for the new speed.

Coin operators were the largest single users of phonograph records, purchasing about fifteen percent, or 50 million discs, annually by the early fifties.

There were very few radio stations that played music such as rhythm and blues, swing, and jazz performed by black bands, or black gospel. For African-Americans the jukebox was the only place to hear their music or their bands and singers until the fifties.

Luckily, the jukebox was color-blind in a segregated world. In the segregated society of the late forties and early fifties, it was not permitted for a Caucasian singer to sing like an African American. And conversely, an African American would have been dubbed an "Uncle Tom," or worse, for daring to sing like whites. However, some whites, particularly the young, were exposed to black artists through the jukebox and either didn't know or didn't care that they were black. Blacks heard some of the early rock performers like Elvis Presley and Carl Perkins—both of whom had been deeply influenced by African American music—and, without seeing them perform in person, may have assumed they were black. For example, Bill Haley and his Comets' recording of "Rock Around the Clock" rose to No. 4 on the all-black rhythm and blues charts, while Chuck Berry, Fats Domino, the Penguins, the Platters, and Little Richard crossed over from rhythm and blues charts to the pop charts.

The importance of the jukebox to country and rockabilly (a blend of R&B and country and western music) artists like Elvis Presley, Jerry Lee Lewis, Carl Perkins, and Johnny Cash at Sun Records cannot be underestimated. Independent record companies, like Sun Records, often had to resort to bribery to get jukebox operators to stock their records.

The customers' choices of recordings could provide valuable information, so jukeboxes were fitted with indicators that displayed which of the discs were most frequently played. The collected data was used for marketing the recordings, but also helped in charting the hits by services such as *Billboard*.

The heyday of the jukebox came to an end as the booming economy of the postwar years allowed many consumers to buy their own phonographs and records.

SHEET MUSIC

The pinnacle of sheet music was the 1890s and early 1900s, when vaudeville was at its height and when families gathered around the parlor piano after the evening meal to sing their favorite songs. Publishers would arrange for their featured song to be used by various vaudeville acts and then have it displayed in music stores. Local department stores usually employed a pianist—often a pretty, young female—to play the songs.

There weren't a great deal of entertainment choices, especially outside the major metropolitan areas. Families were proud of their piano and usually saw to it that at least one person in the family learned to play well enough to accompany the family sing-a longs. However, most of these pianists needed sheet music to play the songs. They did not usually "play by ear."

People tended to gather in the evening to listen to their favorite recordings and broadcasts rather than participate in music-making themselves.

As more and more entertainment options developed, the more the public took the role of spectators rather than participants. With the advent of motion pictures, and especially talking films, if they didn't listen to their favorite radio personalities, many Americans went to the movies.

However, sheet music continued to be a big seller into the twenties. The music publishers branched out to sell their wares in five-and-ten-cent stores across the nation. Many aspiring pianists, composers, and singers got their start by demonstrating songs to potential sheet-music buyers in such establishments.

Sheet-music sales fell off drastically during the Great Depression of the early thirties and never fully recovered. Once the lifeblood of the industry, sheet-music sales became the third, and far less significant, element of hit making, behind record sales and jukebox (coin machine) plays.

From the early forties, *Variety* published weekly and yearly top sheet-music seller charts, but no sales figures were presented.

There was a temporary resurgence of demand for sheet music immediately after World War II, but not to its earlier extent. Publishers were displaying their songs on wire racks that contained the current top twenty or so hits in various businesses to make them accessible to the public. For about a decade, sales of sheet music increased, but with the advent of the LP (album), the resurgence collapsed.

Radio was no longer responsible for large sheet-music sales. Thirteen of 1951's best sheet-music sellers did not appear among the thirty-five most-played songs on radio.

Sheet-music sales declined steadily for several years. The day of the multimillion-seller had faded, and music publishers had to be content with a half-million sale at best.

The first accurate estimate of printed music sales in the United States was commissioned in 1952 by the Music Publishers Association. Only sixteen percent of the $30 million income from printed-music sales came from popular sheet music. The remaining $25.2 million came from classical, religious, and educational music.

Today, sheet-music sales are far smaller than they once were, but the total dollars that a single song earns from all its uses—sheet music, radio and television airplay, recordings, live performances—is certainly greater for the publishers than ever.

TELEVISION

Humble Beginnings

In 1922, a fourteen-year-old farm boy first sketched his idea for television for his science teacher. The boy's name was Philo T. Farnsworth. After many years of experimenting, Farnsworth's first public demonstration of television took place at the Franklin Institute in Philadelphia in the summer of 1935. The new Farnsworth Radio and Television Corporation began business in 1939.

The United States involvement in World War II slowed the development of domestic industries such as television. In 1942, WCBW television cut programming back from fifteen hours per week to four for the duration of the war.

Postwar Television

It wasn't until after the war that television really began to thrive. Around 1946, ABC, NBC, and CBS networks began regular television broadcasts.

By the end of 1947, there were 175,000 TV sets in use, and by the end of the forties, fifty TV stations were broadcasting to 700,000 home television sets with a potential audience of approximately four million. The years between 1948 and 1955 were a period of transition for the network television industry, comparable to the mid-twenties for network radio.

In 1948, Ed Sullivan's *Toast of the Town* debuted and ran until 1971. The name was changed to *The Ed Sullivan Show* in 1955. The CBS Sunday evening show was hosted by former entertainment columnist Ed Sullivan. Virtually every type of entertainment appeared on the show: opera singers, pop music and later rock stars, songwriters, comedians, ballet dancers, and circus acts. It was basically vaudeville for television.

The show enjoyed phenomenal popularity in the fifties and early sixties. It became a family ritual to gather around the television set to watch Ed Sullivan's show. Sullivan was soon regarded as a kingmaker, and performers considered an appearance on his program as a guarantee of stardom. Sullivan introduced more than 10,000 performers throughout his career.

One of the things that distinguished Sullivan from most other variety hosts of the time was his fondness for African American performers, including Bill "Bojangles" Robinson, Ethel Waters, Louis Armstrong, and Diana Ross, as well as his willingness to program them.

Sullivan also had the ability to capitalize on teenage obsession. Even though Elvis Presley's appearance on *The Ed Sullivan Show* in 1956 was not his first TV exposure, it certainly created a national sensation. Sullivan knew how to capture the baby boom generation.

Other popular variety programs were *Ted Mack's Original Amateur Hour*, which also premiered in 1948 on the DuMont network, and Perry Como's first series, *The Chesterfield Supper Club*, which ran on NBC from 1948 through early June 1950. Como's later shows included *The Perry Como Show*, on CBS from 1950 until 1955, and *The Kraft Music Hall*, which lasted into the sixties.

Record sales continued to drop, and company inventories piled up during the late forties. Confused by the speed battle between 45-rpm, 33 1/3-rpm, and the traditional 78s, and bored by recordings that usually seemed without individuality, many Americans were turning to television. During 1949, there was a 400 percent increase in the production of television receivers.

Pat Boone's parents and sisters watch him on TV, from left: Mr. and Mrs. P. A. Boone, Marjorie Boone, Judy Boone. Nashville, TN, Oct. 4, 1957. (Courtesy of Photofest)

During the early fifties, the music business began to look to television for its salvation. Former vaudeville comics who began digging into the past for the songs they had once used at the Palace Theater during their vaudeville days were transforming television into the most popular entertainment medium. Television seemed scared to use songs that had not already proven their audience appeal. Almost overnight, a song's appearance on a popular TV show became worth ten times that of a radio plug.

By 1954, TV had become the favored medium for "breaking" a new song release. Frank Sinatra's "Young at Heart" was launched on the *Colgate Comedy Hour*, but only after Capitol executives and the song's publisher persuaded Sinatra to introduce it on television after he had publicly canceled his appearance. Mercury, the label, held up the release of Patti Page's "Cross Over the Bridge" until Ed Sullivan found a place for her on his *Toast of the Town* television program.

Television began to challenge the supremacy of radio by the mid-fifties. By that time, TV had begun to take over the variety shows, the quiz programs, the soap operas, and the big stars.

Summary

In the immediate postwar years, the most important dispensers of popular music were radio, jukeboxes, single records bought for private consumption, and to a lesser degree, sheet music. By the time rock 'n' roll arrived in the mid-fifties, radio was still important, but it had changed to a disc jockey driven industry. Television became more and more important, jukebox play was more significant for R&B and country music, and sheet-music sales dwindled. Recordings were still very important, but 45-rpm and 33 1/3-rpm records had virtually replaced 78-rpm discs.

3

From Swing to Sing

SETTING THE STAGE

As the twenties began, the country was recovering from "The War to End All Wars" (WWI), and the decade was a reasonably affluent, carefree time characterized by the flapper and her collegiate beau. But by the end of the decade, the nation was plunged into the economic debacle of the Great Depression. By the time the country emerged from the worst years of the Depression, the winds of war were already blowing in Europe. As much as the nation's leaders were committed to neutrality, involvement in the world-wide hostilities was inevitable. And the populace responded. Men were drafted or they enlisted, women worked in munitions factories or enlisted in the women's branches of the various military units. Rationing of goods and services to aid the war effort were instituted at home. Everything, including the entertainment industry, aimed to support American soldiers and to achieve victory.

Music, better than any other art form, can become a working symbol of resistance and inspiration during war times. Music moved out of the concert halls and took up its battle station on the home front and at the war's front lines. The nation needed "war" songs to help the people at home and the soldiers sing and hopefully make their bullets whistle. In addition to war songs, many of the numbers that appealed to both the soldiers and their loved ones were the songs that sang about loneliness, separation, and reunion. War or no war, there will always be love songs. Is it better to laugh or cry in the face of adversity? The answer is debatable, but at least some Americans chose to laugh in Hitler's face with a few comedy songs that came out during the war years.

When the war ended in May 1945 in Europe, and September 1945 in the Pacific, the soldiers began to return home by the millions, only to find that the country had changed in their absence. For example, their wives and sweethearts had become more independent after working outside the home. There was a postwar boom in business and in babies on the horizon.

Musically, the big bands had been the big thing from the mid-thirties into the early years of the forties, but many of the bandleaders and their side-men enlisted or were drafted, making it difficult for the bands to function as before. Many of the dance halls that had featured the bands had closed because musicians and their fans found travel difficult with wartime ration-ing of gasoline and tires.

The new musical trend was toward the singers being the feature, with the bands, those that still existed, accompanying these new singing stars.

With all the changes that had transpired and those that were still in progress, there was also, at least in some circles, a longing for the past and nostalgia for the way things had been before the war.

The world had become smaller. The servicemen and women had experi-enced other cultures around the world. Some of the world's music began to make its way into the American musical marketplace. The mingling of native cultures in the military and in the workplace during the war was responsible for an exchange of musical styles unlike any that had occurred in the past.

MUSICAL STYLES EXCHANGED

During the four years of World War II, many Americans became transi-ents, bringing with them their own folk traditions, culture, and music as they crisscrossed the nation or were shipped overseas as members of the armed forces. For the first time, people became aware of other styles of music in this country because they had access to songs and performers that they had never heard before. The white soldiers from the South shared country and western with their buddies, while African American service-men eagerly introduced rhythm and blues to their comrades-in-arms.

Once people's economic conditions improved, and they were in a position to pay for their own preferences in recorded and printed music, they began to explore these new styles.

WAR-INFLUENCED SONGS

Because the war ended in 1945, there weren't as many topical songs about the war, or military life, during the "Swing to Sing" period (1945–1954) as there had been during the war years. There were a few, however, that were still influenced by the war.

U.S. Navy trousers during World War II were bell-bottoms. Moe Jaffe set new lyrics to a sea chantey for the popular song "Bell Bottom Trousers." There were several recordings of the song that were popular with the public: Guy Lombardo and Tony Pastor's orchestras competed for the most popular version, but Kay Kyser's was extremely close.

"It's Been a Long, Long Time" was introduced on the radio by Phil Brito, but Harry James and his orchestra, with Kitty Kallen's vocal, and Bing Crosby both had top-ranked recordings of the song.

The most famous line of the song is "Kiss me once, then kiss me twice, / Then kiss me once again." Those sentiments were most likely those of every serviceman as they returned from their wartime posts to their loved ones back home.

Mark Twain wrote a book titled *Innocents Abroad* that was published in 1869 about his European travels. In the lyrics of the song "Symphony," the "innocents" are American servicemen in the Riviera who misunderstand the lyrics of a French song.

The song, "C'est Fini" ("It's Over") was written by French lyricist Andr Tabet and Roger Bernstein, with music by Alex Alstone. The song was often sung by Johnny Desmond with Glenn Miller's American Band of the Supreme Allied Command, and it became a hit with our fighting men. Because of the pronunciation of "c'est fini," the GIs mistakenly thought the title and the refrain was "symphony." When the song was brought to the United States, Jack Lawrence wrote English lyrics to fit the misunderstanding. Freddy Martin and his orchestra, with vocals by Clyde Rogers, had the most popular recording of the song on Victor.

"Surrender" was a number-one hit on *Billboard*'s chart with Perry Como's version in 1946. The idea of the song likely came from the end of World War II when Germany and Japan surrendered. Bennie Benjamin and

George Weiss made a connection between that type of surrender and lovers surrendering to each other.

"Far Away Places" was a hit possibly because of servicemen who yearned to return to places they saw during World War II, or because of people at home who had learned about many places they never knew existed from their loved ones who served there or from news reports from war zones. "Far Away Places" was popularized in 1949 in recordings by Bing Crosby with the Ken Darby Choir and by Margaret Whiting with the Crew Chiefs.

"Sound Off" was originally used for close-order drill training by the U.S. armed forces. It was first published in *The Cadence System of Teaching Close Order Drill*, by Colonel Bernard Lentz. In 1951 a recording by Vaughn Monroe propelled the song onto the hit list.

Vera Lynn, a British songstress, had her most famous U.S. hit with "Auf Wiederseh'n Sweetheart" recording on London Records in 1952. Total sales of the 1949 German song reportedly went over the 2 million mark. Eberhard Storch wrote the melody to which English lyrics were added by Britain's Jimmy Phillips (using the pen name John Turner) and Geoffrey Parsons.

During World Wars I and II, there was quite an anti-German bias. Germanic operas were banned, and the language was eliminated from the curriculum of most schools. Such feelings must have abated by the early fifties, allowing a song like "Auf Wiederseh'n Sweetheart" to become a hit. Even though World War II had been over since 1945, this was a song about separated lovers, possibly a wartime romance.

DEMISE OF THE BIG BANDS

As World War II ended, the people of the United States found that the life they had known before the war had vanished. One casualty was the big bands.

The big bands had suffered during the war years because many of the musicians had been drafted or had enlisted in the military services. When the war ended, practically speaking, so did the big bands. Band members returning to civilian life found the popular music scene had changed drastically. Vocalists, not the bands, were now the major hit makers.

Rationing of gasoline and tires during the war had crippled traveling by the bands and their fans. Numerous places where the bands had once played had been forced to close, and a twenty-percent amusement tax, levied on places that allowed dancing, caused many clubs and ballrooms to close their dance floors. Even when some bands re-formed or new bands were organized, their former ballrooms and audiences no longer existed. A few bands stubbornly survived, but they had to find new places to perform and build up a different clientele.

The bands disappeared or they accompanied the singers. Les Brown, Harry James, Sammy Kaye, Frankie Carle, and Woody Herman were the bandleaders who had major hit recordings in 1945, but they often featured their vocalists Doris Day, Nancy Norman, Billy Williams, and Kitty Kallen.

In the space of a few weeks in 1946, several of the country's most popular bands, including those of Tommy Dorsey, Benny Goodman, Woody Herman, Les Brown, and Harry James broke up. Some of the bands reorganized later and continued to operate, but the heyday of the bands was sadly gone.

Tommy Dorsey disbanded his orchestra in 1946, but the release of an "All-Time Hits" album enabled him to reorganize his big band in early 1947. Between 1935 and 1945, Dorsey had collected 174 chart singles on *Billboard*, while he only managed eleven between 1946 and 1953, with none rising higher than number four.

After Benny Goodman disbanded his orchestra, he frequently appeared as clarinet soloist with major classical symphonies and would occasionally put together small jazz ensembles for special-occasion performances. Goodman had 148 chart singles on *Billboard* from the early thirties through 1945, but only collected fifteen more by 1953, with none charting higher than number six.

When Woody Herman was forced to disband his orchestra in 1946, he said it was to spend more time with his wife, who was having problems with alcoholism and a prescription drug addiction. However, in 1947 he organized another band, the "Second Herd," and signed with Columbia Records. Between 1937 and 1945, Herman and his band managed thirty-nine chart singles on Decca. Herman had only fourteen additional chart singles between the years 1946 and 1952 with a recording of Kachaturian's "Sabre Dance" peaking at number three in 1948.

Les Brown reorganized his band and accompanied Bob Hope on radio, stage, and TV for many years, including on eighteen USO tours to entertain American troops around the world. They were also the band for Dean Martin's TV show, which ran ten seasons, and for Steve Allen's show. They also performed with many other famous singers on stage and in recordings. Between 1939 and 1945, Brown collected a dozen chart singles with two number-one hits, but only a revival of Irving Berlin's "I've Got My Love to Keep Me Warm" in 1948 was successful thereafter.

"Sentimental Journey" might be termed *the* song of the mid-forties. Most people who were alive in the immediate postwar years, and especially those who began dating their future spouse while this song was popular, have a special fondness for "Sentimental Journey."

Les Brown's Columbia recording of "Sentimental Journey" was *Variety's* top hit of 1945. Brown's disc was also a number-one hit on *Billboard*, and the song topped *Your Hit Parade*. Brown's recording, with Doris Day as his vocalist, was inducted into the Grammy Hall of Fame in 1998 and was named by RIAA and NEA as one of its *Songs of the Century*. This song and this recording brought Doris Day into prominence and launched her stellar vocal and film careers.

"Sentimental Journey" is one of several songs about traveling by train, including the major hits "Chattanooga Choo Choo" (1941), and "On the Atchison, Topeka and the Santa Fe" (1945). One reason for its popularity might have been people's longing for home immediately after the end of the war. There must have been something romantic about train travel that is not present with other forms of transportation. In this instance, the singer is taking "a sentimental journey to renew old memories." The song was used in the 1946 film *Sentimental Journey* starring John Payne and Maureen O'Hara.

Trumpeter and bandleader Harry James was born into a circus family. It was his father, the circus bandmaster, who taught him to play the trumpet. When the family finally quit the circus, they settled in Beaumont, Texas, where Harry attended school. His first important music job came with drummer and band leader Ben Pollack, who had one of the top pre-swing era bands in 1935. A couple of years later, he became the featured trumpet soloist with Benny Goodman's band. After only a year with Goodman's group, Benny loaned Harry $42,000 to organize his own band. The James orchestra specialized in the blues, boogie-woogie, and, of course, trumpet showpieces. James was elected to the Big Band and Jazz Hall of Fame in 1983.

His first chart single was "One O'Clock Jump" in 1938. James's theme song, the 1898 Italian tune "Ciribiribin," arranged in big-band style with a flashy trumpet solo, was the first chart single on the Columbia label in early 1940. One of his most famous trumpet showpieces was his Variety Record recording of Rimsky-Korsakoff's "The Flight of the Bumble Bee" in 1940. In the early forties, he collected seven number-one hits.

In the mid-forties, Harry James was in top demand among band followers, but he spent most of his time on the West Coast, wouldn't play theaters, and performed only a few one-nighters. James seemed like the best chance to revive interest in the big bands, but he appeared indifferent.

James and his orchestra introduced and popularized "I'm Beginning to See the Light" in 1945. It was one of the first recordings James made after the musicians' strike ended in November of 1944. James's Columbia recording featured the band's vocalist, Kitty Kallen. Four men are listed as the song's cowriters. According to *The Swing Era: 1944–1945*, the tune probably originated with Johnny Hodges, who was Duke Ellington's saxophonist. Hodges took the tune to Ellington for his approval and constructive ideas. Songwriter Don George got the idea for the lyrics from a short being shown at the Paramount Theater in Times Square. The film was about a preacher's congregation in the Deep South getting carried away by the spirit. One large woman in the film shouted, "I'm beginning to see the light." George quickly left the theater with his lyric idea.

Vocalists at different times for the band included Helen Forrest, John McAfee, Frank Sinatra, and Dick Haymes.

James and the band signed a movie contract in the early forties and appeared in several films including *Do You Love Me?* and *If I'm Lucky* in 1946. James married the popular film star Betty Grable in 1943 (his second wife; band vocalist Louise Tobin was the first).

INNOVATIONS IN RECORDING

By the end of the war, several new record companies were in existence, and the recording industry was growing into the giant it is today.

Before the late forties, all records sold were 78-rpm discs. In 1948, Dr. Peter Goldmark of Columbia Records tossed a bombshell into the business by demonstrating the "long-playing" (LP) microgroove phonograph record. A battle of speeds soon developed between the traditional 78-rpm record, the new 33 1/3-rpm Columbia disc, and RCA Victor's 45-rpm version.

The 12-inch, 33 1/3-rpm LP offered more than twenty minutes of playback per side, and was far more durable than 78-rpm records. RCA Victor soon followed with the introduction of the plastic, 7-inch, 45-rpm record, and brought out a new player that played all three speeds. The battle of speeds preoccupied manufacturers and angered consumers for several years. Consumers had to invest in new machines to play the new speeds or purchase converters for their old turntables. The number of home record players doubled between 1945 and 1950. Half of the more than 25 million were capable of playing all three speeds. In the early fifties, the industry agreed to standardize the 33 1/3-rpm speed for albums of pop standards, Broadway musicals, and Hollywood scores, and 45-rpm for singles. Record-industry sales nearly tripled in the fifties thanks to 45s and LPs, but 78s had almost disappeared by 1955. In 1945, six records in *Billboard*'s Top 40 eventually became million-sellers, whereas it used to take three to five years for a disc to reach that level. In 1954, seventeen records in *Billboard*'s Top 40 for the year became million-sellers, and the discs usually reached Gold status within their first year of release.

Although there had been isolated and primitive attempts at multitracking, the person credited with the invention of magnetic audio-tape multitracking was guitarist, composer, and inventor Les Paul. He had been experimenting with overdubbing since the late forties. The first commercially released overdubbed recording was Paul's "Lover" in 1947. It featured him playing eight different electric-guitar parts meshed into a cohesive whole. Early multitrack recordings were made on wax discs. Paul would record one track, then record himself accompanying it with each additional part, repeating the process multiple times. His multitrack recordings took a giant step forward in 1948 when Bing Crosby gave him an Ampex Model 200, the first commercially produced reel-to-reel tape recorder. Within a few hours, Paul had figured out a way to modify the machine by adding more recording and playback heads to allow performers to record a new track while they listened to the playback of a previous track. In 1953, Ampex built the world's first eight-track tape recorder. In 1955, they released the first commercial multitrack recorder. By the 1970s, sixteen-, thirty-two-, and sixty-four-track recorders were available. Multitracking or overdubbing soon became standard procedure in making recordings.

Les Paul made several records with his wife, Mary Ford. The successful duo, with their multitracking (or overdubbing) technique, racked up six million dollars in sales in 1951 with their cuts of "Mockin' Bird Hill," "How High the Moon," "The World Is Waiting for the Sunrise," and other best sellers. The Library of Congress named their recording of "How High the Moon" to its National Recording Registry.

"How High the Moon" was written by lyricist Nancy Hamilton and composer Morgan Lewis for the 1940 revue *Two for the Show,* where it was introduced by Frances Comstock and Alfred Drake. Bandleaders Benny

Goodman and Mitchell Ayres helped popularize the song with 1940 recordings. Jazz great Stan Kenton revived it with some success in 1948. Les Paul
and Mary Ford's 1951 recording of the song was inducted into the Grammy
Hall of Fame in 1979 and was named by RIAA and NEA as one of its *Songs
of the Century*.

Another early recording using overdubbing or multitracking was Patti
Page's "Confess" for Mercury in 1948. Her first hit, "With My Eyes Wide
Open I'm Dreaming" (1950), was billed as the "Patti Page Quartet" because
she sang four different vocal parts on the recording.

IMPORTED HITS

The popular-music industry in the late forties and early fifties imported
several songs from foreign shores, the biggest European invasion since
Columbus. The practice had started during the ASCAP ban in the early forties, and the trend intensified during the war as the Spanish-speaking market replaced the European one. The industry definitely was becoming more
international.

British songwriter and bandleader Billy Reid imported three hits during
this era: "The Gypsy," "A Tree in the Meadow," and "I'm Walking Behind
You." Reid's "The Gypsy" was a big hit in the U.S. in 1946 in recordings by
the Ink Spots on Decca and by Dinah Shore on Columbia. In the lyrics, the
singer is seeking a Gypsy fortune-teller's advice on romance. "A Tree in the
Meadow" became Margaret Whiting's first number-one hit in 1948. Whiting
is the daughter of the famous popular song composer Richard Whiting. The
song's lyrics explain that the "tree in the meadow" is special because her
lover carved "I love you till I die" on that tree. Even though she saw him kissing someone else on "lovers' lane" she wants him to know she loves him.

Two middle-aged British ladies, Eily Beadell and Nell Tollerton, wrote
"Cruising Down the River" in 1945. Their song won a nationwide songwriting contest in Great Britain. Two recordings of the song in 1949 made it to
number one: Russ Morgan and his orchestra's version with the Skylarks on
Decca and Blue Barron and his orchestra's MGM version. "Cruising Down
the River" might be considered a nostalgic hit. In addition to being a waltz,
more associated with songs from the past, the song's lyrics are about a carefree Sunday afternoon spent floating down the river. Such a scene seems
more associated with the 1890s and early 1900s than the late forties. We
must also remember that in 1949 it was the adults, not the youth, who had

the buying power to make hits. Perhaps some adults felt sentimental about a more uncomplicated time. After all, during this period, several songs from the past were being revived into popularity, so nostalgia was very likely an important factor in this song's success.

"You Can't Be True, Dear" was written in 1935 in Germany by Han Otten and Gerhard Ebeler as "Du Kannst Nicht Treu Sein." In 1948 a recording of the song by organist Ken Griffin and vocalist Jerry Wayne was the first one made by overdubbing a voice onto a pre-existing recording. Griffin had recorded his organ version primarily as music to accompany skaters in public ice rinks. The skaters responded so positively that the record company decided to dub a vocal version on top of Griffin's organ version. Vocalist Jerry Wayne waited in the recording studio while Hal Cotton quickly wrote the English lyrics. The dubbed vocal version was released on Rondo Records and became the most popular recording of the song and a number-one hit. Griffin's organ-solo version was also popular enough to chart.

NOSTALGIA

The revival of old songs became a trend during the postwar period. In the years preceding the birth of rock 'n' roll, it almost seemed like the current crop of songwriters' inspiration was running out, so the singers and record companies turned to the past for proven songs to record. *Variety* editor, Abel Green, questioned if it was the established songsmiths that were not attuned to the public's tastes or if the public had its own ideas concerning quality. Green said, "If the public wants nostalgia, then the modern music creators may lack the fresh spark to produce quality songs. Tin Pan Alley songwriters need to take stock of themselves."

Jose Collins introduced lyricist Alfred Bryan and composer Fred Fisher's "Peg o' My Heart" in the *Ziegfeld Follies of 1913* as an interpolation (that is, it was not originally written for the production). The 1913 sheet-music cover pictures Laurette Taylor, who is sitting with a valise on her lap and a dog in her arms. The cover also includes the following dedication: "Written around J. Hartley Manners wonderful character 'Peg' in Oliver Morosco's production of the comedy *Peg o' My Heart* at the Cort Theatre N.Y. Dedicated to the star, Miss Laurette Taylor." Three versions of the 1913 song "Peg o' My Heart" were popular in 1947: Jerry Murad's Harmonicats' instrumental version (a harmonica trio), the Three Suns' instrumental version (a trio consisting of guitar, accordion, and organ), and Buddy Clark's vocal version. The

Harmonicats' recording of "Peg o' My Heart" was inducted into the Grammy Hall of Fame in 1999. In most recordings, it is the chorus that is sung, not the verses. Without explanation, the lyrics changed between the original 1913 version and the 1947 version.

The song can be heard on the soundtracks of the movie musical *Babes on Swing Street* (1944), where it was sung by Ann Blyth, and of *Oh You Beautiful Doll* (1949), the screen biography of composer Fred Fisher.

Disc jockeys became important as hit makers in postwar America. For example, Ted Weems and his orchestra's 1933 recording of "Heartaches" was pulled off the shelf fourteen years later, dusted off, and played by a Charlotte, North Carolina disc jockey. When the DJ got a favorable response from his listeners, he played it again every day for a week. Record dealers began to receive requests for the record, so Victor reissued the Bluebird disc, and Weems's recording of "Heartaches" became a big hit in 1947, eventually selling over two million copies. One of the highlights of Weems's recording was Elmo Tanner's extraordinary whistling. In a 1947 interview Weems said, "We were working in Chicago about fifteen years ago, and the publishers of 'Heartaches' had been begging us to put the tune on the air. So one night we ... played it just the way you hear it on the record, with that corny sort of half-rumba rhythm and with all those effects. After the broadcast, the writers and the publisher called me on the phone and they really let me have it. They claimed I was ruining their song, that we had given it the wrong interpretation ..." (Simon) The popularity of "Heartaches" turned out to be a wonderful dividend for Weems and his career, which, like that of all other band leaders, was declining.

Ragtime music also experienced a revival during the postwar years. The 1914 ragtime classic, "Twelfth Street Rag," was recorded by trombonist and bandleader Pee Wee Hunt in a rousing Dixieland rendition. When it was released in 1948, it became one of the biggest hits Capitol had released to date, reportedly selling a million copies by 1951. This ragtime classic was written by Euday L. Bowman and published as a piano rag in 1914. Lyrics were added to the music in 1916 by James S. Sumner. New lyrics were added by Spencer Williams in 1929 and again by Andy Razaf in 1942. Ragtime started as African American folk music. No one knows exactly where or how it developed. The term "ragtime" first appeared on sheet music in 1897. Although African Americans had played rags for years before the general public became aware of it, its heyday was the first two decades of the twentieth century, with more than 1,800 rags published. One of the first evidences of the music in public was during the Chicago World's Fair of 1893. Scholars aren't even sure why this type of music is called "ragtime." The term was two words until around the late 1890s. Ragtime legend Scott Joplin speculated that the music's "ragged movement" was the genesis of the name, but Joplin was trying to explain a style of music that had been around quite a few years before any of his own rags were published. The rhythm of ragtime is heavily syncopated. Syncopation is the accentuation of a normally unstressed beat. For instance, in common or quadruple meter, the first beat is a strongly accented beat, with the third beat the second-most accented. The second and fourth beats are unaccented. Therefore, accenting the second and fourth beats, as people often do when they clap their hands to music, would create a simple syncopation.

An even more acute syncopation would be felt by accenting a half beat, like placing a rest on the normally strongly accented first beat, and accenting the second half of the beat (in 1 & 2 &, accenting the "&"). Scholars know that ragtime music was, initially, primarily written for the piano. The pianist's left hand kept a steady, march-like rhythm, while the right hand played the melody in a much more syncopated rhythm. The music was often later transcribed for other instruments, for ensembles like military bands, and for banjo players in particular. Kansas City, a major hub for ragtime music, was the inspiration for Euday Bowman's "Twelfth Street Rag." The song's title came from the Kansas City street that was the home of several pawnshops he frequented. The original version was almost impossible to play on the piano with only two hands, so Bowman wrote a new version and sold the rights to J. W. Jenkins Sons Music Company in 1919 for fifty dollars. In 1942, Bowman reacquired the copyright. However, he didn't get to enjoy the fruits of the song's 1948 popularity for long, because he died in 1949.

The ragtime fad died down, like all musical trends eventually do, but experienced several revivals, most notably during the late forties and early fifties, and again in the seventies, then mostly due to the 1973 movie *The Sting*. The film's soundtrack reintroduced this nearly forgotten predecessor of jazz to an entirely new generation of musical connoisseurs. Five recordings of "Twelfth Street Rag," by the All Star Trio, by Earl Fuller's Rector Novelty Orchestra, by Ted Lewis and his Band, by Fats Waller and his Rhythm, and by Paul Whiteman and his orchestra, are available for listening at http://www.redhotjazz.com/bands.html.

An older Broadway musical song became a hit song in 1950. Richard Rodgers and Larry Hart wrote "Bewitched (Bothered and Bewildered)" for the 1940 musical *Pal Joey*. The song was not an immediate hit for a couple of reasons: it could not be played on the radio because of the ASCAP ban, or more likely because of its subject matter, which was a bit questionable for audiences of the era. In the musical, a middle-aged woman was questioning falling in love with a much younger man. Lines like "Couldn't sleep and wouldn't sleep until I could sleep where I shouldn't sleep" and "Horizontally speaking he's at his very best" were too risqué for the moral climate of the early forties. Even the vocal recordings made in the fifties revised the more suggestive lyrics. In 1950, the Bill Snyder Orchestra revived the song into popularity with a recording that became one of the year's biggest hits. It was Snyder's only chart single. The Hollywood version was released in 1957.

In another revival of an oldie from the same period, the duo Gary Crosby and Friend (his father, Bing) recorded Irving Berlin's "Play a Simple Melody" which had originally been introduced in the 1914 Broadway revue *Watch Your Step*. In the story, a couple goes to the theater. Later that evening, the man's girlfriend sings a portion of a sprightly, syncopated tune they had heard that evening. Her male companion complains about "modern" music: "Oh, this new music gives me a pain. Why don't they spring some of the old stuff of the Harrigan and Hart days? That was music!" After this complaint, a charming, ballad-like tune is heard. Then miraculously the two tunes, which at first seemed completely incompatible, are heard together. Berlin, one of popular music's most gifted songwriters, was a musical illiterate, but possessed an extraordinary musical ear. Berlin's pulling off such a complex song was a minor miracle, but he definitely created a musical classic. What he had written was a piece of musical propaganda. The father requests, "Play a simple melody" like those that were popular when he was young. The son requests "a song that is snappy," in other words, ragtime. He then dexterously combined the traditional Stephen Foster–type melody with a ragtime melody, suggesting that the two could blend harmoniously. Berlin claimed the musical part didn't give him as much trouble as writing two lyrics that wouldn't "bump into each other." The Crosby father-and-son disc became a hit in 1950. The song's lyrics perfectly evidence a father and his son's different musical tastes. Originally, Irving Berlin was talking about the musical generation gap that existed in the mid-1910s. Every generation experiences the same musical taste differences. During the roaring twenties, the youth preferred jazz. During the era of the big bands, youth was swing crazy. In the mid-fifties, the teenagers were crazy about rock 'n' roll. And today's teenager prefers the rap or techno styles of the early twenty-first century. The genius of Berlin's song was combining generational melodies to make beautiful contrapuntal harmonies, signifying that different generations and their music can actually coexist.

The next song was not a revival of an oldie, but nevertheless fits into the nostalgia category. There was a time in America when the job of lamplighter was a common occupation. With his matches and ladder, he would make his rounds from lamppost to lamppost, lighting gas lamps at dusk, and putting them out at dawn. Songwriter Charles Tobias got the idea for "The Old Lamplighter" from his memories of boyhood days. Both recordings—by Sammy Kaye and his orchestra with vocalist Billy Williams and the Kaye Choir, and by Kay Kyser and his orchestra with vocalist Michael Douglas—were very successful in 1946. In the song's lyrics, this particular lamplighter makes his nightly rounds, lighting the lamps in the park, but he would leave a lamp unlit near lovers sitting on a park bench, because of his memories of his own loved one from years past.

NOVELTY SONGS

At the turn of the century, novelty songs were called "nut songs," because they were often so nonsensical. But as the nation learned to take popular music more seriously, they began to be termed "novelty songs." A novelty song is a humorous song, a parody of some famous song, or perhaps a comic view of some current event or fad.

New York–based National label anticipated a big seller in its initial recording of "Open the Door, Richard," by Dusty Fletcher, an African American vaudeville performer who had used it in black-only theaters for years. The song became a number-one hit on *Billboard* in two versions: Count Basie's and the Three Flames', a New York rhythm and blues trio. Count Basie and His Orchestra had been one of the nation's premier jazz ensembles since the late thirties. Ironically, their only number-one hit was this novelty song, sung, or rather talked, by trumpeter Harry "Sweets" Edison and trombonist Bill Johnson.

Five other artists released recordings of the song that charted on *Billboard*. There were versions by colyricist "Dusty" Fletcher, by the Charioteers, by Louis Jordan and his Tympany Five, by the Pied Pipers, and by co-composer Jack McVea, whose recording of the song appeared on the soundtrack of the 1998 film *Lolita*.

Was the title phrase a common expression before the song became a hit, or did it become so well known due to the song's popularity that it entered the cliché category? Either way, during the late forties, "Open the door, Richard," became a common expression whenever anyone knocked on a door.

Two novelty songs of 1947 made fun of obesity, something that would be deemed politically incorrect today. Master songwriter, singer, and actor Hoagy Carmichael had his biggest personal hit recording in 1947 with a song he didn't write, the novelty song "Huggin' and Chalkin'." It is about the singer's heavy girlfriend. When he tries to hug her, he needs a piece of chalk to mark where he began so he'll know when he has returned to his starting place. The girl is so fat that he meets another hugger coming around the other way.

The very popular radio star Arthur Godfrey had a popular Columbia recording of another song that poked fun at obesity: "Too Fat Polka (I Don't Want Her, You Can Have Her, She's Too Fat for Me)."

The novelty hit of 1953 was "(How Much Is) That Doggie in the Window?," which Bob Merrill adapted from a well-known Victorian music-hall song. Patti Page's 1953 Mercury recording of it reportedly sold over three million copies during the next fourteen years. Page first recorded the song for a children's album, but there was so much demand by disc jockeys for its release as a single, Mercury Records acquiesced. The song tells about a young woman taking a trip to California to visit her boyfriend. She wants to buy him a dog because she thinks having a pet for company will keep him away from other women.

CHRISTMAS CLASSICS

What did people sing during the Christmas season before the forties? There were the traditional carols like "Silent Night" and a few fun songs like "Jingle Bells" or "Santa Claus Is Coming to Town" (1934), but the period beginning with World War II and extending to the late fifties was a particularly productive period for Christmas songs.

In the early forties, a few all-time Christmas favorites arrived: "White Christmas" from *Holiday Inn* in 1942, "I'll Be Home for Christmas" in 1943, and "Have Yourself a Merry Little Christmas" from *Meet Me in St. Louis* in 1944.

Christmas songs are like money in the bank if they are near the caliber of "White Christmas." By the mid-fifties, that Christmas ballad had topped the eighteen-million mark in record sales, of which Bing Crosby's version accounted for half. Holiday songs return every year and usually sell well for more than fifty years after their publication.

"Let It Snow! Let It Snow! Let It Snow!" was popularized by Vaughn Monroe in 1945. His recording of the song was played on the soundtrack of Bruce Willis's *Die Hard II*. Even though the weather is unbearable outside, the lyrics say, two lovers can keep cozy and warm together by the fire, so why go out?

Songwriter Johnny Marks was the "King of Christmas Songs." He owned the St. Nicholas Music publishing company. His most famous songs are "Rudolph, the Red-Nosed Reindeer" (1949) and "Rockin' Around the Christmas Tree" (1958), but he also wrote "When Santa Claus Gets Your Letter," "I Heard the Bells on Christmas Day," "A Holly Jolly Christmas," and "Silver and Gold." Marks was inducted into the Songwriters Hall of Fame in 1981.

Sales of more than 450 versions of "Rudolph, the Red-Nosed Reindeer" had reached more than 110 million by the end of the seventies, and the song continues to sell more every Christmas. It became Columbia Records' all-time best seller in the early fifties. ASCAP selected Marks's song as one of sixteen songs to appear in its *All-Time Hit Parade* in 1963, and Gene Autry's recording of it was named by RIAA and NEA as one of its *Songs of the Century*. His recording of the song charted at the end of the 1949 Christmas season, and for the next four holiday seasons. A 1964 animated version has continued to be a popular television show every holiday season.

In addition to "Rudolph . . .," Autry is responsible for popularizing two other Christmas classics: "Here Comes Santa Claus," and "Frosty, the Snow Man." His recording of "Here Comes Santa Claus (Down Santa Claus Lane)" charted for three straight Christmas seasons beginning in 1947. It reportedly sold more than eight million copies and was inducted into the Grammy (NARAS) Hall of Fame in 1985. Autry's recording of "Frosty, the Snow Man," with the Cass County Boys and Carl Cotner's Orchestra, charted during the 1950 and 1952 Christmas seasons, eventually amassing more than a million copies sold. "Frosty, the Snow Man" has been kept alive by the 1969 Rankin/Bass animated version, which is replayed annually on television.

Although there are numerous recordings of "The Christmas Song," Nat "King" Cole's became the most well-known version. It charted five times between 1946 and 1954. Cole's recording was inducted into the Grammy (NARAS) Hall of Fame in 1974 and, according to Rhino Records' "Greatest Christmas Hits," it was the number-four Christmas hit between 1935 and 1954. "The Christmas Song" has remained an important seasonal song.

When singer and songwriter Mel Torme visited his lyricist friend Robert Wells one summer day in California, Wells was trying to keep cool by reminiscing about New England winters. Wells had jotted down a few lines as part of his thought process: "Chestnuts roasting ... Jack Frost nipping ... Yuletide carols ... Folks dressed up like Eskimos." In less than an hour, Torme and Wells had converted Wells's jottings into "The Christmas Song." Many people think its title is "Chestnuts Roasting on an Open Fire." When they had completed the song, Wells and Torme drove over to Nat Cole's home to demonstrate their new creation. Cole loved it and cut his recording of the song during his next studio session.

Songwriter Don Gardner's wife, Doris, was a music teacher in a New York elementary school. In 1944, Gardner substituted for his wife one day. When the children laughed at something funny Gardner said, he noticed that most of the students were missing their front teeth. That evening he wrote "All I Want for Christmas Is My Two Front Teeth." However, the song didn't become known until 1948, when the Satisfiers introduced the song on Perry Como's radio show. During the 1948 Christmas season, Spike Jones and his City Slickers had a number-one hit with the song. George Rock, imitating a toothless child, was Spike Jones's vocalist on their recording, which also charted in early 1950.

Jimmy Boyd's recording of "I Saw Mommy Kissing Santa Claus" broke records for Columbia, selling 248,000 copies in one day, 700,000 in ten days in early December, and more than 1 million before Christmas of 1952. Columbia reported total sales exceeded 2.5 million. In the lyrics, a small child has witnessed his mother kissing Santa Claus and thinks it would have been quite a laugh if his daddy had seen them kissing.

"Santa Baby" was written by Joan Javitz and Philip and Tony Springer. The most famous recorded version was Eartha Kitt's 1953 rendition. However, the tune has been covered by many femme fatales both in live performances and in recordings. The song is a Christmas list sung by a woman who wants very extravagant gifts. It was initially considered quite provocative, with its plea for Santa to "hurry down the chimney," suggesting she was Santa's present.

MULTIPLE CHOICES

During the postwar years and previous eras, the record-buying public tended to buy the song—not a definitive recorded version. Every major company had one or more of their artists record songs that had hit potential. The public then chose from their preferred version. By comparison, more modern music fans want to hear what they feel is *the* authoritative version. If Elvis Presley popularized a particular song, the public wants to hear it sung by Elvis and no one else. Such feelings were one of the chief reasons for the demise of the *Your Hit Parade* television show. Their ensemble cast performed the week's top hits, and the public didn't like their interpretations of other singers' hits (they were like cover versions, which had gotten such a bad name during the early years of rock).

In 1945, "It's Been a Long, Long Time" was a number-one hit on *Billboard* for Harry James and his orchestra and for Bing Crosby. In 1946, "The Gypsy" had number-one versions by the Ink Spots and by Dinah Shore; "Oh! What It Seemed to Be" had number one versions by Frankie Carle and his orchestra and by Frank Sinatra; and "To Each His Own" was a top hit for Eddy Howard, Freddy Martin and his orchestra, and the Ink Spots. In 1947, "Peg o' My Heart" was a top hit for the Harmonicats, Buddy Clark, and the Three Suns; "Mam'selle" had two versions reach number one by Art Lund and by Frank Sinatra; and "Open the Door, Richard" was taken to the top by both Count Basie and his orchestra and by the Three Flames.

The trend continued in 1949 with Russ Morgan and the Blue Barron and their orchestras both charting with number-one hits of "Cruising Down the River." In 1950, it was Anton Karas and Guy Lombardo and his Royal Canadians, whose separate recordings of *"The Third Man* Theme" went to the top of the charts. There were also multiple chart versions of "Three Coins in the Fountain," "Sh-Boom," "Mister Sandman," and "Stranger in Paradise" in 1954.

Amazingly, all the top hits of 1953 had only one recording listed in the *Billboard* yearly Top. That doesn't mean there were no other recorded versions on the market, but it does reflect a future trend as rock 'n' roll takes over where one artist tended to have *the* authoritative version.

The practice of multiple recordings didn't completely disappear during the early years of rock, but it slackened considerably, so that after Tab Hunter and Sonny James had popular versions of "Young Love" in 1957, recordings of the same song by various artists that had competed as top hits practically disappeared.

BORROWING FROM THE CLASSICS

Borrowing from the classics was certainly nothing new in the mid-forties. One of the first popular songs to have been borrowed from a classical composition was "I'm Always Chasing Rainbows" in 1918. The source was Frédéric Chopin—a beautiful melody from the middle section of his *Fantasie Impromptu in C-sharp minor.*

Chopin was for 1945 what Pyotr (Peter) Ilyich Tchaikovsky had been for the earlier years of the forties—a classical master on the hit parade. In 1945, there was a very popular Hollywood film about Chopin and his music titled *A Song to Remember.* Buddy Kaye and Ted Mossman were inspired by the film to adapt Chopin's *Polonaise in A-flat* into "Till the End of Time," which Perry Como recorded with the Russ Case orchestra. The song topped the *Your Hit Parade* survey, Como's disc became a number-one hit on the *Billboard* chart and was *Variety's* number-two hit of the year. Perry Como's recording of "Till the End of Time" was inducted into the Grammy Hall of Fame in 1998.

Other popular recordings of "Till the End of Time" were Les Brown's, with Doris Day as his vocalist, and Dick Haymes's version. A rhythmic version of the same polonaise by pianist Carmen Cavallaro and his orchestra was *Variety's* number-ten hit of the year and spent ten weeks at number three on *Billboard.* Concert pianist José Iturbi, who played the piano pieces in *A Song to Remember,* also charted on *Billboard* with the classical version of *Polonaise in A-flat.*

MINI-CALYPSO FAD

The Andrews Sisters' recording of "Rum and Coca-Cola" became one of the major hits of the mid-forties, reportedly selling four million singles. Morey Amsterdam, who later would star with Rose Marie and Dick Van Dyke as writers on *The Dick Van Dyke Show,* heard this calypso-style melody during a USO tour to Trinidad in 1943. He assumed it was a folk melody, therefore public-domain property, so he had Jeri Sullivan and Paul Baron adapt it for American audiences. He then published it with his own lyrics. When the song became famous, it was involved in a plagiarism suit because it was, in fact, not in the public domain but had been written in Trinidad, in 1906 by Lionel Belasco, and titled "L'Annee Pasee." The song's original lyrics were written by Rupert Grant, a calypso musician from Trinidad, who went by the stage name of Lord Invader. After years of litigation, Grant was awarded $150,000 in royalties, and Amsterdam was granted copyright to the song.

According to Grant, "Calypso is the folklore of Trinidad, a style of poetry, telling about current events in song. Back home in the West Indies,

Trinidad, where I'm from ... I noticed since the GIs come over there, ... they drink rum, and they like Coca-Cola as a chaser, so I studied that as an idea of a song."

Amsterdam's version of the song strips it of some of its social commentary. The Lord Invader version was critical of the local island women giving U.S. soldiers "a better price." The original lyrics also lament a new bride running away with a soldier and the husband going "staring mad." Amsterdam's version, of course, takes a decidely different view of the Yankee presence on the island.

The Andrews Sisters apparently gave little thought to the meaning of the lyrics other than they were cute. According to Patty Andrews, the girls got the song the night before a recording session. With a little bit of time left in the session, they decided to record it, so they made up an arrangement on the spot and "just kind of faked it." Maxine Andrews recalled that what attracted them to the song was the rhythm and they never really thought about the lyric, except that it was cute.

The song was controversial enough to be banned by network radio stations because it mentioned an alcoholic beverage and a commercial product—free advertising for the Coca-Cola Company.

FIRST MAJOR HIT BY AN INDEPENDENT LABEL

Bullet Records was started in 1945 by Jim Bulliet and C. V. Hitchcock in Nashville, Tennessee. Bulliet had been an early partner in Sun Records with Sam Phillips in Memphis (that's the company that "discovered" Elvis Presley). The label was primarily known for its country, rhythm and blues, and Southern Gospel releases.

Pianist Francis Craig had organized a band after World War I and had played for more than twenty years at Nashville's Hermitage Hotel. Craig was one of the family that controlled Nashville radio station WSM and the Grand Ole Opry. He was also a staff member at WSM for twenty-five years and was on NBC radio for a dozen years.

Bulliet decided to inaugurate a pop music series to compliment his other releases. One of the first was a recording of Craig's theme song, "Red Rose." When Bulliet reminded Craig that he needed another song for the flip side, Craig selected "Near You," a song Craig had written with lyricist Kermit Goell. Craig had actually already retired from the band business, but he regrouped the band for the recording session. The recording was made in WSM's Studio C and piped by telephone line to the recording studio.

A Georgia disc jockey was the first to flip the record over and play "Near You," sung by Craig's sightless vocalist, Bob Lamm. It became a phenomenal success, the first major hit by an independent label. Craig had to unretire to tour again to promote the record, and at one point, Bullet Records had to hire forty record-pressing plants to try to meet the demand for the disc. Craig's recording was named by RIAA and NEA as one of its *Songs of the Century*.

Bulliet spent so much money attempting to repeat the success of "Near You" that the label was in financial trouble by 1949, so Bulliet sold the company to W. C. "Red" Wortham.

ETHNIC DISCRIMINATION IN SONG

Many ethnic groups have faced discrimination in the United States through popular songs. As far back as the 1870s, stage partners Ned Harrigan and Tony Hart presented a wildly popular series of musical plays that comically dealt with the lives of New York's ethnic groups. The Irish, Germans, and African Americans each had their own chowder-and-marching societies (called "Guards"), and the humor of Harrigan and Hart's plays came in setting these ethnic "Guards" in comic opposition.

In the mid-forties, "Mañana (Is Soon Enough for Me)" was not flattering toward Hispanics. Written by singer Peggy Lee and her then-husband, guitarist Dave Barbour, its lyrics are far too politically incorrect for today, accusing Latin Americans of being procrastinators. However, in 1948 the song was a number-one hit on *Billboard*, *Your Hit Parade*, and *Variety*.

NETWORK RADIO EXPOSURE MAKES HIT

Though disc jockeys were important in the hit-making process by the early fifties, one hit was made by its exposure on a radio network broadcast in 1950. Originating from Chicago's Allerton Hotel, *Don McNeill's Breakfast Club* became a fixture on the ABC radio network from 1933 through 1968. The show was a variety show featuring comedy, live music, conversations with studio audience members, and even a moment of silent prayer. It became an extremely popular show.

For $300, Maurice Wells, an obscure hymn publisher in Chicago, bought "If I Knew You Were Comin' I'd've Baked a Cake" from the song's writers,

Al Hoffman, Bob Merrill, and Al Trace (using the name Clem Watts). He then persuaded some friends to sing it on *The Breakfast Club*. Before the day was over, several publishers were seeking publishing rights to the song. In 1950, Eileen Barton recorded the song, and it became her only number-one hit.

FAMOUS JAZZ CLASSICS FROM THE ERA

Bandleader Bobby Troupe wrote "(Get Your Kicks on) Route 66," as he and his wife traveled across the country to California. Nat "King" Cole's recording of "Route 66" was inducted into the Grammy Hall of Fame in 2002.

The lyrics tell about the highway that "winds from Chicago to L.A. more than 2,000 miles all the way." The lyrics also name many of the towns that drivers saw along the way, like St. Louis (St. Louie), Joplin, Oklahoma City, Amarillo, Gallup, Flagstaff, Winona, Kingman, Barstow, and San Bernardino.

An advertising copywriter called U.S. Highway 66 "America's Main Street," even before the entire highway was completed in 1926. The road became a primary route for poor farmers fleeing the Dust Bowl states that were plagued by drought in the thirties and led them toward what they hoped was the "promised land" of California. One of the road's other famous nicknames was "the Mother Road," which was used by John Steinbeck in his novel *The Grapes of Wrath*.

Jane Powell and Pat Hyatt (dubbing for Ann Todd) performed the song "Route 66" in the film *Three Darling Daughters* (1946). José Iturbi also contributed a boogie-piano solo of the song in the same film. The 2006 Pixar animation movie *Cars* has a lot to do with the highway, and the song is prominently featured in recordings by Chuck Berry and by John Mayer.

"Route 66" has remained a favorite with jazz bands and jazz (scat) vocalists for many years. According to *Missouri Life Magazine*, more than 200 different artists have recorded the song.

Trumpeter Dizzy Gillespie became a major figure in the development of bebop and modern jazz. Gillespie played an unusual trumpet whose bell was bent at a forty-five degree angle. This happened originally by accident, but Gillespie liked the altered tone. His "Salt Peanuts" (1945) was named by RIAA and NEA as one of its *Songs of the Century*.

Jazz legend Charlie Parker's "Ornithology" (1946) was based on the same chord progression as "How High the Moon." Many jazz musicians have combined "Ornithology" and "How High the Moon." "Ornithology" was named by RIAA and NEA as one of its *Songs of the Century*.

One of jazz pianist Thelonious Monk's most famous pieces is "Round Midnight" (1948). Monk is often regarded as one of the founders of the bebop movement in jazz. "Round Midnight" was named by RIAA and NEA as one of its *Songs of the Century*.

4

The Pre-Rock Fifties

INTRODUCTION

Were the early fifties really as innocent, wholesome, and wonderful as they are pictured on television shows like *Father Knows Best*? The answer probably depends on where you lived and your family's economic status, assuming you had been born by then. The early fifties was the time of hula hoops, Frisbees, Davy Crockett caps, 3-D movies, canasta, flying saucers and UFOs, bomb shelters, poodle skirts, ponytails, and pink for men. It was the time when rhythm and blues transitioned to rock 'n' roll. The big bands had faded as the singers became the focal point of musical entertainment. Patti Page, Jo Stafford, Kay Starr, Doris Day, and Peggy Lee were the most productive female vocalists. Perry Como, Eddie Fisher, Frankie Laine, Nat "King" Cole, Bing Crosby, and Frank Sinatra were the male singing stars.

A new medium of entertainment began to challenge the supremacy of radio by the mid-fifties. By the end of the forties, fifty television stations were broadcasting to 700,000 home television sets with a potential audience of approximately four million.

Still, it was not until the last few years of the forties and the first few years of the fifties that radio was seriously threatened. By that time, television had begun to take over the variety shows, the quiz programs, the soap operas, and the big stars.

When TV usurped radio's place in the entertainment world, radio became the disseminator of news and the player of music. Disc jockeys now ruled the radio airwaves. Some of them became quite powerful in the pop music industry, especially in the metropolitan areas. See more about television and radio in the "How Was Popular Music Dispensed?" Chapter 2.

COMEDY CLASSICS

The early fifties should be called the heyday of comic recordings. Between 1950 and 1954 several classic comedy routines were popular recordings.

Classic Comedy Routines of the Early 1950s

- Harry Stewart as Yogi Yorgesson on "The Bees and the Birds" (1950); "I Yust Go Nuts at Christmas" backed by "Yingle Bells" (1952); "The Object of My Affection" (1953); and as Harry Kari on "Yokohama Mama" (1953)
- Andy Griffith's "What It Was, Was Football"; "Romeo and Juliet" (both in 1954)
- Stan Freberg's "John and Marsha" (1951); "Little Blue Riding Hood;" and "St. George and the Dragonet" (both in 1953)
- Johnny Standley's "It's in the Book" (1952)

The two most popular recordings during the period were "It's in the Book" and "St. George and the Dragonet." "It's in the Book" managed to top the *Billboard* chart and was 1952's number-ten hit, according to *Variety*. The disc was Johnny Standley's parody of a fundamentalist sermon based on the nursery rhyme, "Little Bo Peep." Standley wrote the routine in collaboration with Art Thorsen and recorded it with Horace Heidt and his orchestra.

Stan Freberg's comedy routine "St. George and the Dragonet" was a number-one hit on *Billboard* in 1953. Although it is not a song, Walter Schumann's theme music for the television series *Dragnet* was an integral part of the recording. In the routine, Freberg basically tells the classic story of St. George and the Dragon as if it were a *Dragnet* episode.

RELIGIOUS SONG FAD

There was a marked religious song cycle in the early fifties. For many years it was also quite fashionable, especially for country crossover artists like Tennessee Ernie Ford, to close their television shows and personal appearances with a religious number.

Frankie Laine's recording of "I Believe" helped popularize the song to hit status in 1953. It reportedly sold three million copies. According to the Songwriters Hall of Fame Web site, "I Believe" has sold a total of 20 million copies in its various recordings. However, according to cowriter Ervin Drake's Web site, it has sold over 100 million copies. The lyrics to "I Believe" never actually confess a belief in God or in a supreme being. The nearest the song comes to professing a religious belief is "the smallest pray'r will still be heard." "I Believe" was written by Ervin Drake, James Shirl, Irvin Graham, and Al Stillman.

Artie Glenn wrote the song "Crying in the Chapel" about a personal experience. According to the songwriter's son, Larry, the chapel referred to in the title was Loving Avenue Baptist Church in Fort Worth, Texas. His father, who was recuperating from spinal surgery, had gone there to pray. While Glenn was in the hospital, he had bargained with God. If God helped him get well, he would be a better person. As he prayed in the chapel that evening, the tears he shed were tears of joy. The song was first recorded in 1953 by the songwriter's seventeen-year-old son, Darrell. Country and western vocalist Rex Allen had success with it on both the country and pop charts, and the rhythm and blues group the Orioles, featuring Sonny Til, had good success with their version. However, June Valli's recording was the most successful version on the pre-rock pop charts.

Les Paul and Mary Ford's recording of "Vaya Con Dios" was one of the biggest hits of 1953. In late 1952, jazz singer Anita O'Day was in a recording session when her orchestra leader Larry Russell showed her a song he had cowritten with Inez James and Buddy Pepper named "Vaya Con Dios." O'Day cut the song and released it for the independent Clef label. She was scheduled to perform the song in early 1953 on television, but the evening before her appearance on *Juke Box Jury*, she was arrested on a heroin charge. By the time the drug charge was resolved, she had missed the chance to promote her recording of "Vaya Con Dios." Les Paul and Mary Ford had heard O'Day's recording on the radio and immediately recorded their own version. It became their biggest chart single. Their recording of the song was inducted into the Grammy Hall of Fame in 2005.

Singer and songwriter Stuart Hamblen discovered a dilapidated hunter's hut with a dead man inside while on a hunting trip in Texas. Moved by what he had seen, Hamblen wrote, published, and introduced "This Ole House." Hamblen's version of the song charted, but Rosemary Clooney's recording of it became a number-one hit in 1954. The singer tells the listener his house once was filled with the laughter of his family. In the chorus, we learn that he doesn't need the house anymore because he's "a-gettin' ready to meet the saints." Hamblen also wrote "It Is No Secret (What God Can Do)," which was popularized in 1951 by Jo Stafford.

Founded at Fairfield Missionary Baptist Church in Nashville as a young gospel group in the forties, the Fairfield Four became one of the best known and most influential African American a cappella gospel quartets. Their "Don't Let Nobody Turn You Around," which was named by RIAA and NEA as one of its *Songs of the Century*, represents postwar black gospel music at its best. The National Endowment for the Arts presented the group with the prestigious National Heritage Award in 1989.

Mahalia Jackson grew up singing black gospel music in church as a youngster in New Orleans. As a teenager, she moved to Chicago where she eventually went into the real estate business and other business ventures. She continued to sing the gospel music she loved, finally signing with Apollo Records in the thirties. In 1948, producer Art Freeman insisted Jackson record W. Herbert Brewster's "Move On Up a Little Higher." Her single became the best-selling gospel record of all time, selling in such great quantities that stores could not even meet the demand. Her recording of his song was named by RIAA and NEA as one of its *Songs of the Century*.

FOLK TREND

"Goodnight, Irene" became a two-million-selling record that launched the folk singing group The Weavers and brought American folk music to its widest audience ever in 1950. For this hit, famous folksinger John Lomax adapted a song Huddie "Leadbelly" Ledbetter had written in 1936 while he was serving time in the Louisiana State Prison.

The traditional definition of a folk song is a song that has passed down from one generation to another by oral tradition, not one that is written or composed by some living person. But famous folk singer Burl Ives described folk songs as "songs we sing, not songs that are sung to us." He claimed that any song taken up by the people of an area as a part of their singing and musical expression became a folk song. Other characteristics of folk songs are a limited vocal range so everyone can sing them, simple melody, and uncomplicated chord structure. "Goodnight, Irene" qualifies as a folk song under those characteristics.

"Goodnight, Irene" has a verse and chorus form (two-part strophic song form) that is very common in folk material, gospel songs, and of songs from the late seventies, like the "Jeremiah was a bullfrog" song, "Joy to the World." In addition to being simplistic, the lyrics are morose and almost senseless, like when the lyrics say sometimes the singer lives in the country, and sometimes he lives in town, and then sometimes the singer wants to jump into the river to drown. However simplistic or senseless the song may be, the public loved it.

The flip side of "Goodnight, Irene" was the recording of "Tzena, Tzena, Tzena," the first Hebrew folk song to become a popular song hit. "Tzena, Tzena, Tzena" went through a metamorphosis before it got to this recording. The song dates from the preindependence days of Israel. Written in 1941, it was rewritten by Julius Grossman in 1947 and arranged by Spencer Ross to lyrics by Gordon Jenkins. That version was forced off the market by legal action. The 1950 version had lyrics by Mitchell Parish and was recorded by the Weavers with Gordon Jenkins and his orchestra.

Another traditional folk song, "On Top of Old Smoky," became a hit for the Weavers in 1951. The song dates to at least the early 1800s, when American pioneers sang it as they headed west. Like many American folk songs, it probably originated overseas and was brought to the United States by the settlers of Appalachia. Children sometimes sing this song to the words "On Top of Spaghetti." The Weavers' recording of "On Top of Old Smoky" was named by RIAA and NEA as one of its *Songs of the Century*.

The Weavers also had chart hits with "The Roving Kind" (an adaptation of the English folk song "The Pirate Ship"), the famous New Orleans funeral march, "When the Saints Go Marching In," "Kisses Sweeter Than Wine," which became a hit for Jimmie Rodgers in 1957, and "Wimoweh," the South African Zulu song that became a number-one hit for the Tokens as "The Lion Sleeps Tonight" in 1961.

Folk artist Woody Guthrie wrote "This Land Is Your Land" in 1940 as a response to Irving Berlin's "God Bless America," which Guthrie considered unrealistic and complacent. So he came up with an alternative that he originally titled "God Blessed America for Me." The melody was essentially note-for-note from the hymn "When the World's on Fire." Some sources, however, claim the melody came from a Carter Family song titled "Little Darlin' Pal of Mine." Guthrie recorded his song in 1944, but it wasn't published until 1951, when "copyright 1945" was written on the cover.

In 2002, "This Land Is Your Land" was chosen by the Library of Congress to be added to the National Recording Registry, and RIAA and NEA named it one of its *Songs of the Century* for 1947.

ADAPTATIONS

In 1951, Frank Sinatra was under contract with Columbia Records, but according to Mitch Miller, A&R director for the company at the time, Sinatra's recordings weren't selling then. Miller racked his brain to come up with songs that would meet Sinatra's approval and that would also sell. But Sinatra, whose contract gave him veto power, balked at Miller's suggestions. On one occasion, Miller had set up a recording session for a couple of songs and had an orchestra and chorus waiting. When Sinatra refused to even consider the songs Miller had selected and walked out of the session, Miller called in Guy Mitchell, who recorded "My Heart Cries for You" and "The Roving Kind."

"My Heart Cries for You" was taken from a melody by France's eighteenth-century Queen Marie Antoinette, "Chanson de Marie Antoinette." In 1950, lyricist Carl Sigman and composer Percy Faith adapted it into the song "My Heart Cries for You."

"Come on-a My House" is an adaptation of an Armenian folk song that playwright William Saroyan and his cousin, Ross Bagdasarian, remembered from childhood. On a 1949 automobile trip through the western states, the two adapted the song, which Saroyan used in his 1949 off-Broadway play *Son*. Mitch Miller decided to have Rosemary Clooney record the song. He also had the idea of using an amplified harpsichord in the recording, adding an unusual effect.

The lyrics invite someone to come to the singer's house for fruits and other things to eat. However, the song is a bit risqué. The offer of sexual favors seems to be implied, especially in the line "I'm gonna give you everything."

"Come on-a My House" was Saroyan's only popular songwriting venture, and it was one of Bagdasarian's best-known works that was not connected to his most famous creation, the Chipmunks musical group.

"Sweet Violets" was a cleaned-up version by Cy Cohen and Charles Grean of the bawdy folk song "There Once Was a Farmer." Grean had also been responsible for "The Thing," another adaptation, in 1950. "Sweet Violets" was popularized by a Dinah Shore recording with Henri Rene's orchestra.

Once again, the song is at least slightly suggestive. It begins, "There once was a farmer who took a young miss in back of the barn where he gave her a ...," and the music pauses long enough for the listener's imagination to fill in the blank. There are several instances of clever word play in the song.

"A Guy Is a Guy" was a 1952 adaptation. Folk artist Oscar Brand wrote it by adapting two similar sources: an eighteenth-century ribald song called "I Went Down to the Alehouse (A Knave is a Knave)" and a song titled "A Gob is a Gob," a bawdy number that had been sung by GIs during World War II. Brand had learned the song while he was in the service. Several years later, he cleaned up the lyrics, added a bridge, and changed the title. It became a hit for Doris Day. Her recording accompanied by Paul Weston's orchestra was the only popular version that charted. "Like a good girl should" could very easily have been the title because of the number of times the phrase is repeated in the song. The singer—a girl—walks down the street "like a good girl should," and a guy follows, just like she expected him to do. Why did she expect that? "Because a guy is a guy." By the end of the song, she has agreed to marry this guy.

IMPORTED HITS

British songwriter and bandleader Billy Reid's "I'm Walking Behind You" was popularized by Eddie Fisher in a 1953 recording. The subtitle of the song is a line that precedes the title: "Look over your shoulder." The lyrics are about the singer watching the one he loves marry someone else. He wishes her well, but promises if things go wrong, he'll be there for her.

"Oh! My Pa-Pa" was a big hit in 1954 for Eddie Fisher. His recording with Hugo Winterhalter's orchestra and chorus was very popular in the United States, but English trumpeter Eddie Calvert's recording, using the title "O Mein Papa," was also popular. The original German version was written by Paul Burkhard in 1948. It was published in Switzerland and was used in the musical *Schwarze Hecht* in Zurich. The show was revived in Hamburg, Germany, as *Feuerwerke* (Fireworks) in 1953, when the song began to gain international attention. Britain's Geoffrey Parsons and Jimmy Phillips, using the pen name John Turner, wrote the English lyrics.

The tango became a mini-trend in American popular music with "I Get Ideas" (1951), "Jealousy (Jalousie)" (1951), "Kiss of Fire" (1952), and "Hernando's Hideaway" from *Pajama Game* (1954).

The tango is a dance and also a type of music. Originating in Spain or Morocco, it came to the New World with Spanish soldiers and settlers and became associated particularly with Argentina. In the lower class section of Buenos Aires, the tango, the dance with the stop "Baile con Cartas," became a sensuous dance that drew criticism for being immoral.

One story of this dance's origin attributes it to the Argentine gauchos. The gauchos walked with bent knees because their chaps had hardened from their horses' body sweat. Very often they hadn't cleaned up before they visited crowded nightclubs to dance with the girls. The gaucho's dance partner would dance in the crook of his right arm, holding her head back. Her right hand was held low on her partner's left hip, near the pocket where he kept his wallet, perhaps anticipating payment for dancing with him. The couple danced around and between the small round tables in the club.

The famous dance team of Vernon and Irene Castle helped popularize the tango in America just prior to World War I. Rudolph Valentino further popularized the dance in the early twenties.

A 1929 Argentine tango entitled "Adiós Muchachos," by composer Julio C. Sanders, was transformed into the popular song "I Get Ideas" in 1951. The singer gets ideas when he's dancing with his love. They were most likely dancing the tango. Tony Martin had the most popular recording of the song, but Louis Armstrong and Peggy Lee also released popular recordings of "I Get Ideas" in 1951.

An Argentine tango, "El Choclo," which means "an ear of corn," written by A. G. Villoldo in 1905, was adapted by Lester Allen and Robert Hill into the hit song "Kiss of Fire" in 1952. The song became a number-one hit on *Your Hit Parade*, *Billboard*, and *Cash Box*. Georgia Gibbs's sultry rendition of the lyrics burned up the airwaves and jukeboxes, but other chart recordings include those by Tony Martin, Toni Arden, Billy Eckstine, Louis Armstrong, and Guy Lombardo and his Royal Canadians. The ballroom tango was featured in several movies, including *Last Tango in Paris* (1972), *Scent of a Woman* (1992), *Evita* (1996), *Moulin Rouge* (2001), *Chicago* (2002), and *Shall We Dance* (2004).

The mambo was so popular in the United States by 1954 that the year was dubbed "The Year of the Mambo," and a number of mainstream singers started cashing in, most notably Perry Como with "Papa Loves Mambo," Rosemary Clooney with "Mambo Italiano," and even crooner Vaughn Monroe with "They Were Doin' The Mambo."

The mambo is a Cuban musical form and dance style. The word "mambo" comes from the Ñañigo dialect spoken in Cuba. It occurs in the phrase *abrecuto y guiri mambo* (open your eyes and listen) that was used to open Cuban song contests. In the Bantu language of West Africa, "mambo" means "conversation with the gods," and in nearby Haiti, a mambo was a voodoo priestess.

The mambo as we know it today is actually a rhythm whose tempo may be slow or fast, and almost any standard tune can be played as a mambo. Cuban bandleader Pérez Prado is generally credited with developing the mambo about 1943, and according to Prado, the mambo is "more musical and swingier than the rhumba. It has more beat." Prado and his music moved from Havana to Mexico, and then to New York City. In April 1951, *Newsweek* reported that the Cardinal of Lima, Peru, denied absolution to anyone who danced *al compás del mambo* ("to the beat of the mambo") because he felt the dance was responsible for the wild exuberance of its practitioners. Prado and his band's greatest recording successes in the United States came in 1955 with "Cherry Pink and Apple Blossom White," which was more of a "cha-cha-cha" number, and with "Patricia" in 1958. Over the years, mambo music became homogenized so it would appeal to the mainstream American audience.

INSTRUMENTAL HITS

Leroy Anderson wrote what might be termed "semi-classical" music, and he is noted for his works that feature unusual effects. Examples include "The Syncopated Clock," with its clock that tick-tocks with a slight jazz or syncopated beat, "Sandpaper Ballet," with sandpaper scraped together to sound like a dancer's feet, and "The Typewriter," with its typing effects. Anderson had the inspired idea of combining the tango and blues, Argentine and African American musical types, in writing "Blue Tango." The shuffling tango rhythm may be heard under the melody, while little blues figures decorate the theme. The result is a fresh and original work by a brilliant composer. "Blue Tango" became Anderson's biggest hit, as a composer and as an orchestra leader.

Frank Chacksfield was a popular orchestra conductor from Battle, East Sussex, England. He is remembered for his numerous albums and appearances on radio and television during the era following World War II. Starting as a child prodigy pianist, Chacksfield began conducting in his early twenties. During the war, he was assigned to the British Army entertainment unit, and after the war he became a regular performer on BBC. In the early fifties, he formed an orchestra called The Tunesmiths and signed a recording contract. After a couple of years, he expanded the group into an orchestra with strings and released a series of albums for London Records. His biggest hit, in both the United Kingdom and the United States, was "Ebb Tide" in 1953, which firmly established his reputation worldwide. Chacksfield's recording of "Ebb Tide" opened with a solo oboe against a background of recorded waves hitting the shore. The most famous recording of "Ebb Tide" for more modern audiences was the Righteous Brothers' 1966 version. During Chacksfield's recording career, he sold an estimated twenty million recordings.

JOHNNIE RAY CRIED HIMSELF TO FAME AND FORTUNE

Johnnie Ray cried himself to fame and fortune in the fifties. Ray set a style trend of agonized vocals, so much so that he became known as "The Cry Guy" and "The Prince of Wails." The previous trend had been a relaxed crooner-style vocalist like Perry Como and Bing Crosby. Johnnie Ray had been partially deaf since age twelve and had worn a hearing aid since age fourteen, but his deafness did not hinder him from becoming a major hit maker of the early fifties.

In 1951 he signed a recording contract with Okeh. His first effort was a song he had written himself titled "Whiskey and Gin," which became a minor hit. Later that year he recorded two songs that were produced by Mitch Miller: "Cry" and "The Little White Cloud That Cried," with the Four Lads as his background singers. "Cry" became a smash hit, while "The Little White Cloud That Cried," written by Ray, peaked at number two on the *Billboard* chart.

Churchill Kohlman, a Pittsburgh dry-cleaning plant watchman, entered "Cry" into an amateur songwriting contest at the Copa Night Club in Pittsburgh. It was eliminated in the first round, while another Kohlman song made it to the finals. "Cry" didn't make much of an impression until Johnnie Ray recorded it. His recording of the song was inducted into the Grammy Hall of Fame in 1998.

Ray's passionate, soulful vocal style made him a sensation, but it also became fodder for comedians and mimics. After his success in 1952, he was moved to Okeh's parent label, Columbia, where he recorded several discs, but he never achieved another monster success. When he signed a movie contract, his first film was the Irving Berlin musical *There's No Business Like Show Business* in 1954.

KITTY KALLEN'S BIGGEST HIT

Singer Kitty Kallen was particularly active in the forties and fifties. Her most famous big band jobs were with Jimmy Dorsey and Harry James. She did the vocals on Jimmy Dorsey's recordings of "Bésame Mucho" (1944) and "They're Either Too Young or Too Old" (1944), and on Harry James's recordings of "It's Been a Long, Long Time" (1945), "I'm Beginning to See the Light" (1945), and "I'll Buy That Dream" (1945).

When she left the bands to try a solo career, she signed with Mercury in the late forties but transferred to Decca after a vocal problem almost ruined her singing career.

Kitty Kallen's recording of "Little Things Mean a Lot" with Jack Pleis's orchestra was a number-one hit in 1954. A Richmond, Virginia, disc jockey, Carl Stutz, and the amusement editor for the Richmond *Times-Dispatch*, Edith Lindeman, wrote this song that reportedly became a million-seller for Kitty Kallen, her only number-one hit as a solo artist.

KAY STARR'S GRAMMY HALL OF FAME RECORDING

Kay Starr was born on an Indian reservation in Oklahoma to a father who was a full-blooded Iroquois and a mother who was of Native American and Irish descent. After her family moved to Memphis, she sang with jazz violinist Joe Venuti's band when she was in her mid-teens. She left Venuti to join Bob Crosby's band, which carried her to New York City. There she recorded with Glenn Miller, but she rejoined Venuti and spent two years with Charlie Barnet's band before embarking on a solo career. She signed a recording contract with Capitol in the late forties.

Starr's biggest hit recordings were "Wheel of Fortune," which topped the *Billboard* chart for ten weeks in 1952, and "Rock and Roll Waltz," the first *Billboard* number one to have the term "rock and roll" in the title, which topped the chart for six weeks in 1956. Her recording of "Wheel of Fortune" was inducted into the Grammy Hall of Fame in 1998.

PROTOTYPE OF GIRL GROUPS

The Chordettes were the prototype of many girl groups that became famous over the next several years. The group was organized in Sheboygan, Wisconsin, in 1946. The father of Virginia Cole (one of the original members, called Jinny) was tremendously involved in barbershop quartet singing. Jinny, listed with both Osborn and Lochard as her last name, organized the group that sang barbershop tunes. In 1949, they won a spot on Arthur Godfrey's radio program *Talent Scouts* and stayed four years as Godfrey regulars, sticking to traditional barbershop material. They also cut some records for Columbia. Godfrey's musical director, orchestra leader Archie Bleyer, convinced the girls they should broaden their repertoire beyond barbershop. When Bleyer, who was dating Janet Ertel (a member of the group), quit Godfrey's show to concentrate on his new record company, the Chordettes became one of his new company's first signings. The record company and the singers' bond strengthened further when Bleyer and Ertel wed. "Mister Sandman" was the group's second single release for Cadence and it became their only number-one hit in 1954. Their second biggest hit was "Lollipop" in 1958, which peaked at number two on *Billboard*.

The Chordettes' recording of "Mister Sandman" was inducted into the Grammy Hall of Fame in 2002. The group was inducted into the Vocal Group Hall of Fame in 2001, and their recording of this song was named by RIAA and NEA as one of its *Songs of the Century*.

SUGGESTIVE LYRICS

More suggestive song lyrics became evident in 1954, perhaps a precursor of some future rock 'n' roll lyrics. R&B lyrics had been more suggestive than those in the pop field for some time, but they were usually cleaned up before they were recorded for the mass market, especially a market aimed principally at teenagers.

The title of the song, "Make Love to Me," sounded too sexually suggestive for the relatively conservative early to mid-fifties. Its suggestiveness may be attributable to its jazz roots since sexual innuendo was more tolerable in that venue. But the song became very successful in the pop market and reportedly became a million-seller for Jo Stafford. It became a number one on all the charts except *Your Hit Parade*, which probably considered it too risqué. The song began in 1923 as "Tin Roof Blues," written by five players in the New Orleans Rhythm Kings plus Walter Melrose, a composer, author, and publisher during the twenties. Melrose wrote the original lyrics, but Bill Norvas and Allan Copeland contributed the milder version in 1953.

"Teach Me Tonight" was the first collaboration between composer Gene DePaul and lyricist Sammy Cahn. Cahn had to give Warner Brothers first chance at the song because he was under contract to them, but when they turned it down, Cahn got it published by a small company owned by several songwriters. According to Cahn, the first recording was made by "some girl." He claimed the recording sold three copies, one each bought by the girl, Cahn, and DePaul. In 1954, however, their song became a hit when the DeCastro Sisters recorded it. Dinah Washington's recording of the song was inducted into the Grammy Hall of Fame in 1999.

JAZZ CLASSICS FROM THE ERA

"Misty" (1954) was created and recorded by jazz pianist Errol Garner before the haunting lyric was added by Johnny Burke. The Errol Garner Trio charted with the instrumental version in 1954. Johnny Mathis had a popular recording of the song in 1959. Lloyd Price charted with his version in 1963, and Ray Stevens revived it again in 1975. The 1971 Clint Eastwood film, *Play Misty for Me*, prominently featured the song. "Misty" was named by RIAA and NEA as one of its *Songs of the Century*.

The Modern Jazz Quartet was established in 1952. The original members were pianist and musical director John Lewis, vibraphonist Milt Jackson, bassist Percy Heath, and drummer Kenny Clarke. Connie Kay replaced Clarke on drums in 1955. The group's repertoire consisted mainly of bop and swing-era standards. One of the group's original compositions was "Django," by John Lewis, which was a tribute to the Belgian jazz guitar player Django Reinhardt. "Django" was named by RIAA and NEA as one of its *Songs of the Century*.

SONGS MARKETED TOWARD YOUTH

Prior to World War II, young people in America had little freedom or influence. With the development of postwar affluence and the subsequent baby boom, young people began to gain buying power and, throughout the fifties, greatly influence popular music, television, and films.

Corporations took note and devised marketing strategies for this new demographic. Youth were more open to change, new technology was easier for them to grasp, and their fashions transformed quicker than those of adults. It may well have been the popularity of "Too Young" by Sylvia Dee and Sid Lippman that convinced recording company executives that young people now had enough buying power that this segment of the population should receive consideration. A direct result was the rock 'n' roll music phenomenon of the mid-fifties. Nat "King" Cole's recording of "Too Young" with Les Baxter's orchestra became one of the top hit singles of 1951. "Too Young" claimed a dozen weeks at the top of *Your Hit Parade*, the most weeks ever of any song on that chart.

CLASSIC BLUES

John Lee Hooker recorded "Boogie Chillun'" after moving from Mississippi to Detroit. In 1948, Hooker presented a demo of "Boogie Chillun'" to a Detroit record store owner named Bernard Besman. Besman provided the studio and produced Hooker's record. Hooker is the only person on the recording. The only sounds are his distorted electric guitar, his stomping feet, and his deep voice performing something like a rap, three decades or more before the term was used for musical performances. Hooker's "Boogie Chillun'" was named by RIAA and NEA as one of its *Songs of the Century*.

ROCK 'N' ROLL'S INCUBATION PERIOD

Most pop music historians debate the actual birth of rock 'n' roll. Louis Jordan is definitely one of the roots of the genre. Jordan and his Tympany Five's recordings that have definite vibes of pre-rock include "Caldonia (What Makes Your Big Head So Hard?)" (1945), and "Saturday Night Fish Fry" (1949). "Caldonia" has some vocalizations that are very much like those of Little Richard and, in addition to its tempo and rocking rhythm, the chorus of "Saturday Night Fish Fry" contains the words "It was rockin'!" to explain the party's atmosphere at the fish fry.

Jordan, "The Father of Rhythm and Blues," began his music career playing in Chick Webb's swing band in the thirties, where he played alto sax and performed in comedy routines. His own band, the Tympany Five, began recording in 1938. His first big hits were "GI Jive" and "Is You Is Or Is You Ain't Ma Baby?" in 1944. All of his famous recordings had the basic rhythm of "shuffle boogie," which was later adopted by many early rock 'n' rollers like B. B. King, Chuck Berry, and Bill Haley. As Jordan said, he "made the blues jump."

R&B singer and pianist Fats Domino said what became known as rock 'n' roll was what he had been playing in New Orleans for fifteen years. Some pop music historians, like Richard D. Barnet, Bruce Nemerov, and Mayo R. Taylor—the authors of *The Story Behind the Song*—claim that the first rock 'n' roll recording was "Rocket 88, a tribute to the Oldsmobile Rocket 88 automobile, recorded by Ike Turner's band with vocalist Jackie Brenston in 1951 for a small independent Chicago label. Brenston's vocal was the same "jump blues" vocal styling that Louis Jordan had popularized in the forties. Due to a busted amplifier, Willie Kizart's guitar playing on the disc created what became known as "fuzztone."

The Dominoes' rhythm and blues recording of "Sixty Minute Man" is a good example of R&B beginning to evolve into rock 'n' roll. The Dominoes were an African American vocal group comprised of Clyde McPhatter, Bill Brown, Charlie White, and Joe Lamont, led by their pianist, manager, and songwriter Billy Ward. Ward, a classically trained vocal coach, along with New York talent agent Rose Marks, decided to put together a smooth vocal group to rival the Ink Spots, the Orioles, and similar groups that were beginning to gain acceptance with white audiences. The Dominoes were signed to Federal Records in 1950 and released several singles prior to "Sixty Minute Man." When it was released in May 1951, it quickly ascended to the top of the R&B chart and stayed there for fourteen weeks. Their recording used Bill Brown's bass voice as the lead. It featured the singer boasting of his sexual prowess, of being able to satisfy his women within sixty minutes. Many radio stations refused to play "Sixty Minute Man" because its lyrics pushed the limits of what was deemed acceptable. In later years, however, the Dominoes' record became a contender for the title of "the first rock and roll record."

By 1953, R&B was still an outsider in the white-dominated music business. However, $15 million worth of R&B records were sold that year, equal to the industry's entire sales fifteen years earlier. Major and independent recording companies saturated the field with almost exact musical duplications of the real thing: cover versions.

At this point, most of the independent R&B labels were only marketing their recordings to the African American market. At some time prior to 1954, these companies began to realize that white high school and college kids were purchasing their records. The majority of the white audience was not totally ready to accept this new sound, however.

African Americans had been instrumental in the birth of the blues, ragtime, jazz, and swing. Now it was their R&B music that became one of the chief ingredients of rock 'n' roll.

Bill Haley and His Comets. (Courtesy of Photofest)

Another ingredient that is often ignored by pop music historians that contributed to the birth of rock 'n' roll is country music (or country and western). By the mid-fifties, Bill Haley and His Comets had combined elements of rhythm and blues with their country-and-western sound to produce a type of rock 'n' roll music that began to gain acceptance. Their first hit was "Shake, Rattle, and Roll," a cover of Joe Turner's original rhythm and blues version. "(We're Gonna) Rock Around the Clock," written in 1953, recorded by Haley and His Comets in 1954, and included in the 1955 film *The Blackboard Jungle*, gave rock 'n' roll the national publicity it needed to rally the teenagers of the nation behind this new musical trend. The American Film Institute (AFI) named "Rock Around the Clock" as the No. 50 greatest song from an American film in its television special *100 Years . . . 100 Songs* (2004), for its appearance in *Blackboard Jungle*.

Are cover versions legal? The initial recorded version of Harvey Brooks's "A Little Bird Told Me" was released in 1947 by African American singer Paula Watson on the Supreme label. Watson's version was covered by the white chanteuse Evelyn Knight in 1949. Knight's recording was so nearly like Watson's that Supreme Records sued, but lost in a verdict that declared musical arrangements were not copyrighted property and therefore were not subject to the law's protection. Any legal barrier to the practice of cover versions was removed by the decision in the "Little Bird Told Me" case.

Even though historians argue about what the first rock 'n' roll recording was, most will agree that The Crew Cuts' cover version of the Chords' "Sh-Boom" in 1954 was the first number-one rock 'n' roll hit, even though today it seems only mildly rock, if that. Its success further proved to record companies that cover versions of rhythm and blues tunes could be very profitable. Soon many white, mainstream singers or groups were recording covers of R&B songs.

"Sh-Boom" was written and originally recorded by the Chords for Cat Records. The Chords' version sold well among African Americans, so Mercury Records had the Crew Cuts—a white Canadian group with closely cropped hair—cover the song. Their version zoomed to the top of the charts. The Chords (James Keys, Claude and Carl Feaster, Floyd MacRae, and James Edwards) were supposedly trying to approximate the sound of an atom bomb explosion when they wrote "Sh-Boom." During the Cold War of the mid-fifties, everyone was concerned about an attack by Soviet Russia. However, their lyrics also included an optimistic message that everything would ultimately be fine, as the song's subtitle, "Life Could be a Dream," attests. The 2006 Pixar animation film *Cars* uses The Chords' recording of "Sh-Boom" on the soundtrack.

Joe Turner recorded the original rhythm and blues version of Charles Calhoun's "Shake, Rattle and Roll." His Atlantic recording was inducted into the Grammy Hall of Fame in 1998 and was named by RIAA and NEA as one of its *Songs of the Century*. "Shake, Rattle and Roll" has a twelve-bar blues form, the most typical format of authentic blues. The traditional blues text is a rhymed couplet in iambic pentameter in which the first line is repeated, so during the first four bars the first line is sung, followed by some instrumental improvisation, in the second four bars the same first line is repeated often with the exclamation "I said," and once again followed by more improvising, and finally, the second line of the couplet, which is the kicker, is performed.

In order for R&B songs to become national hit material, sexual references—such as the lines "you wear those dresses, the sun comes shining through" and "I can look at you 'n' tell you ain't no child no more"—had to be removed. The original R&B version of "Shake, Rattle and Roll" was intended primarily for African American adults, while the cleaned-up version was meant for mostly white teenagers.

Bill Haley and His Comets also recorded the song, cleaned up the lyrics a little, and had a much bigger hit with their cover version. Their disc's success further proved there was a market for cover versions of R&B material.

Critics of cover versions often paint the original R&B artists as victims. In fact, the white cover versions often brought the R&B artists newfound fame from totally new, and formally closed, audiences. In the case of "Shake, Rattle and Roll," many listeners of Haley's version eventually sought out Turner's original.

Rock 'n' roll, however, was still a fad. It needed something or someone to take it into the mainstream and solidify its popularity.

5

The Early Years of Rock 'n' Roll

ROCK'S ROOTS

At its base, rock 'n' roll consists of three basic chords (I, IV, and V); a strong, danceable beat; and catchy melodies. Early rock 'n' roll was tremendously influenced by rhythm and blues, along with its predecessors, the blues and jazz, and by country, especially honky tonk and rockabilly, but also Southern gospel, traditional pop, and folk. These influences combined to form a new kind of popular music called rock 'n' roll in the mid-fifties. The first wave of rock 'n' rollers included some former R&B performers like Fats Domino, Chuck Berry, Little Richard, Bo Diddley, and several who came from country and western via rockabilly, including Elvis Presley, Bill Haley, the Everly Brothers, Carl Perkins, Jerry Lee Lewis, and Buddy Holly. Over the next several decades, artists replicated the sound of the first rockers but usually added their individual stamp, expanding the genre and keeping it alive and fresh.

FORMER R&B PERFORMERS CUM ROCK AND ROLL HALL OF FAMERS

The following Rock and Roll Hall of Fame members are some of the primary performers who led rhythm and blues into rock 'n' roll. All of these former R&B performers have claimed to be the inventor of rock 'n' roll.

Singer and songwriter Fats Domino's boogie-woogie piano and R&B vocals definitely helped rhythm and blues evolve into rock 'n' roll. Domino sold sixty-five million records—more than any fifties-era rocker except Elvis Presley. His most famous songs include "Ain't That a Shame" in 1955, which was made even more popular in the cover version by Pat Boone in the same year; "I'm in Love Again" in 1956, a revival of the 1940 song "Blueberry Hill" in 1957; "I'm Walkin'" in 1957; "Blue Monday" in 1957; and "Walking to New Orleans" in 1960. Fats's most successful chart singles were "Blueberry Hill," which peaked at number two, and "I'm in Love Again," which rose to number three on the *Billboard* chart. The Library of Congress National Recording Registry added Domino's "Blueberry Hill" in 2005.

Little Richard claims to be "the architect of rock and roll." His flamboyant stage personality, his frantic piano pounding, and his shouting vocals were perfect for such early rock 'n' roll classics as "Tutti Frutti," "Long Tall Sally," and "Good Golly, Miss Molly." As famous as Richard is, his highest chart single on the *Billboard* chart, "Long Tall Sally," peaked at No. 6.

Chuck Berry is most famous for his guitar playing—especially his guitar solos built around his trademark double-string licks—and for his stage antics while he played. His songs often had lyrics about cars and girls and include such classics as "Maybellene," "Johnny B. Goode," "Sweet Little Sixteen," "Rock and Roll Music," "School Day," and "Roll Over Beethoven," which was named by the Library of Congress to the National Recording Registry. Berry's highest ranked singles are "Sweet Little Sixteen" and "School Day," except for "My Ding-a-Ling" in 1972, which rose to number one on the *Billboard* chart.

WHITE COMMERCIAL ROCK

Two white Philadelphia songwriters, Max Freedman and James DeKnight (the former being the coauthor of the 1945 pseudo-hillbilly hit "Sioux City Sue"), persuaded a small rhythm and blues recording company to cut their song "(We're Gonna) Rock Around the Clock" with performer Sunny Dae, in 1953. A couple of years later, the song made quite an impact in the film *Blackboard Jungle* and through Bill Haley's recording. As we look back from the perspective of years, we credit Haley's recording of the song with launching rock 'n' roll nationally. Of course, there were evidences of it earlier, but the song's appearance in a major motion picture brought this new musical fad to national prominence.

One of the first examples of commercial white rock 'n' roll was Bill Haley and His Comets' "Shake, Rattle and Roll." Haley and His Comets' sound combined the drive of Louis Jordan and his Tympani Five and the sound of country and western. That sound soon became known as "rockabilly" and quickly became big money. This fusion of rock, country, and R&B brought Bill Haley and Elvis Presley to the fore. Next came Buddy Knox, the Crickets, and the Everly Brothers.

Buddy Knox wrote the song "Party Doll" in 1948, which made him one of the first singer and songwriters of the rock era. Ten years later, a Plainview, Texas, farmer pressed 1,500 copies of Knox's recording of "Party Doll." When the song became a local hit, a New York City label heard about it and signed Knox and his group. Their disc with Roulette Records reached number one on *Billboard* and *Cash Box* for one week each. The Knox brand of rockabilly was a southwestern style known as "Tex-Mex."

Buddy Holly was impressed with Buddy Knox's success with "Party Doll," so he shopped his demo of "That'll Be the Day" to several recording companies before signing with a Decca subsidiary. In a strange business quirk, because the parent company, Decca, owned "That'll Be the Day" by Buddy Holly, the song had to be released on Brunswick as "That'll Be the Day" by the Crickets. The Crickets recorded for Brunswick, and Buddy Holly recorded for Coral. Either way it was Buddy Holly and the Crickets. "That'll Be the Day" was their only *Billboard* number-one hit. Holly's "Peggy Sue" and the Crickets' "Oh, Boy!" were also popular, but never made it to the top. Holly's recording of "That'll Be the Day" was added to the Library of Congress National Recording Registry in 2005.

Don and Phil Everly's harmonies influenced several future groups including Simon and Garfunkel, the Beach Boys, the Mamas and the Papas, and the Beatles. Born into a country music family, the brothers began performing on the family's radio show in Shenandoah, Iowa. The family later performed their show on a Knoxville, Tennessee, radio station, but as live radio work became scarce, the family act disbanded. Don and Phil moved to Nashville, hung around the Grand Ole Opry, and peddled some songs they had written. They auditioned for Archie Bleyer at Cadence, but he and other Nashville companies turned them down. Columbia signed them to record four sides, which never amounted to much. When their option was not picked up, legendary country publisher Fred Rose convinced Bleyer to give the brothers a second chance and he signed them to his Cadence label.

Bleyer had futilely tried to get thirty other artists to record Felice and Bou-dleaux Bryant's "Bye Bye Love," but he insisted it be the brothers' first single. It quickly climbed the charts, making it to number one on *Cash Box* and peaking at number two on *Billboard*. It became *Variety's* number seven hit of the 1957.

Fred Rose became the brothers' manager and worked closely with Archie Bleyer on furthering their career. Their next single was "Wake Up Little Susie," but Bleyer was worried the song might be too suggestive. Instead of innocently falling asleep, he thought the lyrics made it sound like Susie and her boyfriend had been sleeping together at the drive-in movie, and he wasn't the only one. Several radio stations banned the song. If the lyrics were (or are) really suggestive, it didn't seem to matter to the listening pub-lic. The song made it to number one on both *Billboard* and *Cash Box*, and was *Variety's* number nine hit of 1957.

While serving in the U.S. Air Force in Korea, Jimmie Rodgers learned to play the guitar and formed a band with some of his Air Force buddies. When he was transferred to Stewart Air Force Base in Nashville, he began performing in some area clubs. One evening he heard another performer sing "Honeycomb." He liked the song and rearranged it to fit his style. After his Air Force days ended, he returned home to Washington state, per-formed in clubs for a while, then flew to New York City to audition for *Arthur Godfrey's Talent Scouts* TV show and for Hugo Peretti and Luigi Crea-tore at Roulette Records. He won the *Talent Scouts* show, and after a small delay signed with Roulette. His first single was "Honeycomb," which became his only *Billboard* number-one hit.

Jerry Lee Lewis was an early pioneer of rock 'n' roll. He was inducted into the Rock and Roll Hall of Fame in 1986 and also into the Rockabilly Hall of Fame. Lewis's first recordings were made for Sun Records in Memphis. His 1957 recording of "Whole Lot of Shakin' Goin' On" propelled him to interna-tional fame. It was added to the Library of Congress National Recording Registry in 2005. "Great Balls of Fire" followed and became his biggest hit. Lewis's singing was greatly influenced by his fundamental religious back-ground, but he is also famous as a pioneer of piano rock. He would practically destroy the instrument—kicking the piano bench out of the way to pound on the keys while standing, or playing gigantic glissandos up and down the piano keyboard, or sometimes even sitting on the keys or playing with his heels. Lewis's career was racked with scandal: he married his second wife before his divorce from his first wife was final. After that marriage failed, he married his thirteen-year-old distant cousin, and later was heavily into drinking and drugs.

After his rock career faded, he tried country. In 1989, a major motion picture based on his early life in rock 'n' roll, *Great Balls of Fire*, brought him back into the public eye. The film starred Dennis Quaid as Lewis.

R&B CROSSES OVER

Rhythm and blues was appealing to young people in many ways, but several factors contributed to its expansion from a mainly black audience to the national, white, pop hit charts in 1955. One was the fantastic popularity of the motion picture *Blackboard Jungle*, which introduced "Rock Around the Clock" to the world's youth, practically establishing the song as "the teenager's national anthem." Another was the increased number of cover versions of R&B hits made with white talent, plus the presence of R&B's Barnum, Alan Freed, who had moved to the big time in New York City.

One of the great rhythm and blues songs of the fifties is "Earth Angel," cowritten by Curtis Williams, the lead singer of the Penguins, the quartet that popularized the song. Their smooth harmony, as they sing "Earth angel, will you be mine?" helped make this one of the classic rhythm and blues hits. The Penguins' recording was inducted into the Grammy Hall of Fame in 1998 and was named by RIAA and NEA as one of its *Songs of the Century* for 1954. It was also named by the Library of Congress to its National Recording Registry.

At first, Curtis Williams was credited with writing the song, but Jesse Belvin and Gaynel Hodge filed a lawsuit to prove they also had a hand in writing it. The song's subtitle, "Will You Be Mine," was lyrically and melodically copied from The Swallows' R&B song "Will You Be Mine" from 1951. "Earth Angel," like many doo-wop ballads, was structured on the chord changes of Rodgers & Hart's "Blue Moon." This chord progression (I, iv, IV, V, I) came to be known as "Blue Moon changes" or "ice cream changes" and formed the basis for many fifties' songs.

Sam Cooke was a crossover artist from the Black gospel field. He had sung with the famous gospel group, the Soul Stirrers, but they fired him when he began recording pop songs. Cooke's third release, "You Send Me," became his first chart single and his only number-one single.

The Coasters had a string of wisecracking hits in the late fifties. First named the Robins, Atlantic Records bought their contract from Spark Records and contracted Jerry Leiber and Mike Stoller to be their producers. They changed the group's name to the Coasters and began producing hits.

Their first real success came with "Searchin'" in 1957. Their next chart single was "Yakety Yak (Don't Talk Back)," which became the group's only *Billboard* number-one hit. The Coasters managed a few more chart singles, but never had another top-ten hit.

COVER VERSIONS

Many people feel that cover versions of R&B material by white performers is legitimized piracy. The federal courts had legitimized cover versions in the "A Little Bird Told Me" case of 1949. But, primarily due to the race issue, cover versions by white performers of R&B material, which was prominent in the early years of rock, were practically nonexistent by the end of the fifties.

New Orleans rhythm and blues pianist and singer Antoine "Fats" Domino is estimated to be one of the top dozen artists in recording history. By 1960, he had twenty-three Gold Records. He is considered one of the pioneers in the evolution of rhythm and blues to rock 'n' roll. Today, Fats' recording of "Ain't That a Shame" is considered one of the early classics of rock 'n' roll, but in 1955, it was Pat Boone's cover version that was the big hit. Fats's recording of "Ain't That a Shame" was inducted into the Grammy Hall of Fame in 2002. As with other rhythm and blues songs of the period, when Fats's version began to climb up the R&B charts, a record executive decided to have

Fats Domino in *Jamboree* (1957). (Courtesy of Photofest)

some mainline pop artist cover the song so that his company might collect a national hit and reap the monetary benefits (the record company, of course, still had to pay royalties to the song's writers, Domino and Dave Bartholomew). To many people, such a practice appears to be grossly unfair to the original artist, and those same people are absolutely convinced it is racist. Undeniably, the social climate of the nation during the fifties was racial, but other factors were also germane. It was usually a white singer covering a rhythm and blues song, so this takes on racial implications. A song recorded by an African American artist did not become a national hit, while the cover version by a white singer did was primarily because African Americans were recording for small independent record labels that did not have the budget to promote the record nationally. Pat Boone was signed to a recording contract by a small independent recording company, Dot Records of Gallatin, Tennessee. If the owner of the company, Randy Wood, told him to record Fats Domino's "Ain't That a Shame" or Little Richard's "Tutti Frutti," which he did, Boone was not in a position to refuse. Boone admitted later that he was not thrilled when he had to record such numbers, but he did what the boss said. Domino's recording of "Ain't That a Shame" is full of soul, while Boone's version sounds pretty "soul-less." But in 1955, while Fats's version peaked at number ten on *Billboard*, Pat Boone's climbed to number one on *Billboard*.

Georgia Gibbs's "Tweedle Dee" was a cover version of a rhythm and blues song written by Winfield Scott and originally recorded by LaVern Baker. Rather surprisingly, the song's highest ranking was on *Your Hit Parade*. "Tweedle Dee" was a favorite teen dance number because of its catchy lyrics and peppy tempo.

In 1954, singer and songwriter Hank Ballard had success with a song he had cowritten with Johnny Otis titled "Work With Me, Annie," but the lyrics were so suggestive that many radio stations refused to play it. Then Etta James recorded the tune as "Roll With Me, Henry," but her version was still too raunchy for most listeners during the mid-fifties. Georgia Gibbs's cover version altered the suggestive lyrics and was marketed as "Wallflower," with the subtitle, "Dance With Me, Henry." Her disc became a number-one hit on *Billboard* but didn't fare as well on the other charts. The primary lyrical differences between Hank Ballard's "Work With Me, Annie," Etta James's "Roll With Me, Henry," and Georgia Gibbs's "Dance With Me, Henry" seem hardly worth the effort to modern ears, but "work with me" and "roll with me" sounded much more sexually suggestive to mid-fifties' ears than "dance with me." And, it wasn't only the lyrics, it was also the voices of

Ballard and James that seemed much more sexually suggestive than that of sweet little Miss Georgia Gibbs.

First popularized in late 1954 by Otis Williams and the Charms—a rhythm and blues quintet—"Hearts of Stone" was covered in 1955 by the Fontane Sisters. The Charms' R&B version peaked at number fifteen on *Billboard*, but the Fontane Sisters' cover version ascended to the top of the *Billboard* chart. The Fontane Sisters' disc is just another example of a cover version doing much better on the charts than the original R&B version. Actually, the Charms' recording was also a cover of an obscure West Coast group called the Jewels, who had been the first to record "Hearts of Stone." The song was written by Eddy Ray and Ruby Jackson.

In 1943, sixteen-year-old African American Johnny Bragg was sentenced to six consecutive life terms in the Tennessee State Prison for raping his girlfriend. He joined the prison's gospel group, the Prisonaires. In 1953, Frank Clement, then governor of Tennessee, heard the Prisonaires and was so impressed with their talent that he thought these were men who deserved rehabilitation. Over the next several years, Clement showcased the Prisonaires at state events, including some at the governor's mansion. Eventually, producer Sam Phillips signed the Prisonaires to a Sun Records deal. Bragg's claim to fame, however, lies in his authorship of the hit song "Just Walkin' in the Rain," which was popularized in 1956 by Johnnie Ray.

The Diamonds were a Canadian white vocal group who covered several R&B songs. They covered Frankie Lymon and the Teenagers' "Why Do Fools Fall in Love" for their first chart single in 1956. One of their most famous covers was of the Gladiola's "Little Darlin'" in 1957, which peaked at No. 2 on *Billboard*. By 1958, cover versions were passé. Teenagers had discovered the originals and generally refused to accept imitations. As a result, the Diamonds began to seek original song material to record. They found Clyde Otis and Nancy Lee's "The Stroll," based on a dance of the same name. The Diamonds performed the song several times on *American Bandstand*, and the repeated airings propelled the song to number one on *Cash Box* for one week. "The Stroll" was the group's last Top Ten hit.

ROCK 'N' ROLL DAMNED AND PRAISED

The impact of rock 'n' roll was considerable. Never before had such a drastic change in the style of popular music happened so quickly. At first, rock was damned and panned by clerics and fretters about "the future of our youth." It was called licentious, primitive, and depraved. It was accused of inciting riots and contributing to juvenile delinquency, but its proponents lauded and applauded the new beat and championed its vitality.

Parents objected strongly to what they deemed the sloppy dressing that young America adopted as a result of rock songs and rock performers. The motorcycle jackets, oily ducktail haircuts, long sideburns, sloppy long-sleeved shirts, tight sweaters, the sack dress, baggy sweaters, bikinis, Bermuda shorts, and the black stockings and uncombed hair influenced by the Beat Generation were just a few of the fashions exhibited by the youth of the period. Parents also objected to what they considered unacceptable lyrics ("leer-ics") in many rhythm and blues and rock 'n' roll songs. They equated the trend toward questionable lyrics with teenage misbehavior.

The alleged affinity between rock 'n' roll and juvenile delinquency found proponents who contended that the music's appeal to teenagers was good clean fun and didn't differ much from the Charleston of the twenties or Swing Era dances, like the jitterbug, of the mid-thirties.

Rock 'n' roll proponents countered by pointing out the questionable wording in some of the best known Cole Porter songs, including "Love for Sale" and "All of You." Porter's "Love for Sale" could only be broadcast without its lyrics. His "All of You," from the Broadway production *Silk Stockings*, was only acceptable on the networks once Porter agreed to change "I'd like to take a tour of you" to "the sweet of you, the pure of you." The objectors then countered with the idea that the lyrics for a "sophisticated" theater audience were not intended for mass consumption, while rock 'n' roll lyrics were aimed directly at impressionable young people. Neither side was willing to give in to the other's argument.

In 1958, Columbia Artist and Repertoire Director Mitch Miller advised parents to tell their children they liked rock 'n' roll so the teenagers would drop it at once.

GROUPS TO THE FORE

In the past, singing groups became known by performing with the big bands. A few of those groups, like the Pied Pipers and the Modernaires, broke away and became well-known recording artists. There were also the Ink Spots, the Merry Macs, the Four Aces, the Four Lads, the Gaylords, the Hilltoppers, the Weavers, the Crew Cuts, the Chordettes plus several brothers or sisters acts like the Mills Brothers, the Ames Brothers, the Andrews

Sisters, the Fontane Sisters, the Dinning Sisters, and the Decastro Sisters. Some particularly noteworthy groups of the early rock years were the Browns, the Fleetwoods, Danny and the Juniors, and the Kingston Trio.

When Jim Ed Brown was in high school in Pine Bluff, Arkansas, his school choir performed an arrangement of "The Three Bells." He never forgot the song, which was originally a French song, "Les Trois Cloches," written by Jean Villard in 1945. After high school, Brown formed a trio with his sisters Maxine and Bonnie, becoming the Browns. They became regulars on *The Louisiana Hayride* show in Shreveport, Louisiana, a show similar to Nashville's *Grand Ole Opry*, and signed a recording contract in 1956. By 1959, they were ready to break up the trio, but they decided to record one more time. For their "swan song," they chose "The Three Bells," which they had wanted to record since high school. Country legendary guitarist Chet Atkins, their record producer, and Anita Kerr, whose Anita Kerr Singers became important recording artists, helped the trio pare down the original lengthy piece to the three-minute requirement for a single. The Browns' retirement plans had to be postponed when the single was released and became a number-one hit on *Billboard, Cash Box,* and *Variety.* The recording became their only number-one hit on the pop charts, but their revival of "The Old Lamplighter" (1936) made the top five in 1960. The trio stayed together until 1967, when Maxine and Bonnie retired. Jim Ed began a successful solo career as a country artist.

Barbara Ellis and Gretchen Christopher were childhood friends in Olympia, Washington. They were junior high cheerleaders and occasionally sang together. They tried to find the right girl to form a trio, but gave up and remained a duo, calling themselves the Saturns. Gary Troxel tried unsuccessfully to play blues trumpet for them on an arrangement of "Stormy Weather," but a friendship developed and one day, while he and Gretchen were waiting for her mother to pick them up, he began to sing "dum dum, dum-bee-doo-wah"-type words. Gretchen knew that he was singing the same chord progression as the one in a song she had been writing titled "Come Softly." They put the two ideas together and sang it for Barbara. The result was favorable, and Gary joined the group to make it a trio called Two Girls and a Guy. They performed the song for several high school functions and got record producer Bob Reisdorff to listen to a tape of their performance of the song. Reisdorff was starting his own label in Seattle and signed the trio. They started recording as soon as they graduated from high school. Reisdorff was worried that the title was too suggestive, so he extended it to "Come Softly to Me," even though those words never appear in the lyrics. He also changed the trio's name. All three had the same telephone exchange—Fleetwood, so they became the Fleetwoods. Just as the song was reaching number one in mid-April, the trio performed "Come Softly to Me" on *The Dick Clark Saturday Night Beechwood Show*. Before the year was over, the Fleetwoods had another number-one hit with Dewayne Blackwell's "Mr. Blue." Blackwell had written the song with the Platters in mind. The trio couldn't capitalize on their recording success because Gary Troxel was in the Naval Reserves and was stationed in San Diego and could not travel with the trio or help promote their recordings.

Four Philadelphia teenagers—Dave White, Joseph Terranova, Frank Maffei, and Danny Rapp—formed a doo-wop group called the Juvenairs. They performed at local school dances, private parties, and clubs. Johnny Madera heard them at a record hop and suggested Artie Singer, owner of Singular Records, listen to them. When the group auditioned for Singer, after they sang a few arrangements of standards, they pulled out White's song called "Do the Bop." Singer liked it and cut a demo of the song to test it on local disc jockeys. One of the first people Singer sent the demo to was Dick Clark of *American Bandstand* fame. Clark was impressed, but made a couple of suggestions: change the group's name to Danny and the Juniors and, since the dance called "the bop" was on the way out, he recommended changing "bop" to "hop." The group went back into the studio and recut the song as "At the Hop." When Little Anthony and the Imperials canceled an appearance on *American Bandstand*, Clark brought in the group to replace them. Of course they sang "At the Hop," and the exposure on *American Bandstand* helped the record sell 7,000 copies in one week in Philadelphia alone. Singular Records couldn't handle the demand and leased the record to ABC-Paramount, which distributed it nationally.

The Kingston Trio started a folk revival with their hit single "Tom Dooley." They emerged from San Francisco's North Beach club scene to bring the rich tradition of American folk music into the popular music mainstream. During the late fifties and early sixties, the trio enjoyed considerable success and became world famous. Their first, and only, *Billboard* number-one single, "Tom Dooley," was an old Blue Ridge Mountains folk song originally titled "Tom Dula." The title character was a mountaineer who was hanged for murdering Laura Foster in January 1868. The trio— Dave Guard, Bob Shane, and Nick Reynolds—recorded the song on their first Capitol LP, *The Kingston Trio*. As radio disc jockeys around the country began playing the song, Capitol released the track as a single. The Kingston Trio won the Grammy for Best Country and Western Performance for their single, but it is folk material, not country and western. The Grammy awards wanted to honor the group and its recording, but didn't have a category that really fit. According to *The Songs of Doc Watson*, Tom Dooley was not the murderer. Instead of the triangle mentioned in the Kingston Trio version, it might actually have been a quadrangle. There were two men and two women involved. The sheriff, Mr. Grayson, and Tom Dooley had both courted Laura Foster and Annie Melton. It was Annie who murdered Laura, but Tom, with Annie there watching, buried her, making himself an accomplice.

PERFORMER/SONGWRITERS

In the decade leading up to the birth of rock 'n' roll, there were only a few songwriters who were also recording stars. Most recording stars did not write their own material. Johnny Mercer is the most prominent example of a songwriter cum performer. Hoagy Carmichael and Harold Arlen were primarily songwriters who also recorded occasionally. On the other side of the coin were singers who occasionally wrote a song that became popular, such as Mel Torme's "The Christmas Song," Tex Williams' "Smoke! Smoke! Smoke! (That Cigarette)," and Peggy Lee's "Mañana." In the early fifties, Johnnie Ray wrote and popularized "The Little White Cloud That Cried," Pee Wee King cowrote and popularized "Slow Poke," and a few other country stars like Hank Williams wrote and popularized their own songs on the country chart before the song crossed over into the pop field, but the song was usually popularized by a mainstream pop artist. There were also a few instrumentalists who popularized their own material, such as Leroy Anderson and his "Blue Tango."

However, during the pre-rock era, the performer and the songwriter, singular or plural, were most often two distinct professions.

As rock 'n' roll began, Elvis Presley was credited with being cowriter of "Heartbreak Hotel," "Don't Be Cruel," "Love Me Tender," and "All Shook Up," but his agent, Col. Tom Parker, had simply demanded his client be included as cowriter so he would share in the songs' royalties.

The singer/songwriter trend continued and increased in the sixties, especially with groups like the Beatles and the Rolling Stones. But even today, most listeners would be surprised if they noticed that many of the most famous recording artists do not write their own material, or at least do not write all the songs they record.

MORE CHRISTMAS CLASSICS

As rock 'n' roll began, a few more Christmas favorites were recorded, including Perry Como's "Home for the Holidays" in 1955, Barry Gordon's mischievous "Nuttin' for Christmas" in 1955, Harry Belafonte's recording of "Mary's Little Boy Child" in 1956, Bobby Helms's "Jingle Bell Rock" in 1957, "The Chipmunk Song" by David Seville and the Chipmunks in 1958, and "The Little Drummer Boy" in 1958.

"Home for the Holidays" has become almost as much of a nostalgic Christmas classic as "I'll Be Home for Christmas." The holiday season is simply a time when people become sentimental about home—the home of their childhood, their present home, or both. These two songs express the longing to be at home celebrating with family and loved ones.

Barry Gordon was a child actor in the fifties and sixties. He performed in many TV and stage roles, including the Broadway production and 1965 movie *A Thousand Clowns.* Gordon's "Nuttin' for Christmas" is about a little boy who expects nothing for Christmas because he is always doing mischievous things, like hiding a frog in his sister's bed and filling the sugar bowl with ants.

Harry Belafonte's calypso-flavored recording of Jester Hairston's "Mary's Little Boy Child" has since been covered by many artists, including All-4-One and Harry Connick, Jr.

As rock 'n' roll began casting its new rhythmic vitality over everything, including Christmas, Bobby Helms's recording of "Jingle Bell Rock" hit the stores in 1957. An advertising business songwriter from Texas, Jim Boothe, collaborated with Joe Beal, a New England-born public relations man, to create this fun Christmas ditty that charted on *Billboard* three of the next four years, becoming the rock era's biggest Christmas hit song.

The Chipmunks—a group of singing chipmunks—were created by Ross Bagdasarian in 1958. The three characters were Alvin, Simon, and Theodore. The trio's human "father" was David Seville, in reality Ross Bagdasarian. The voices were all performed by Bagdasarian, who sped up the playback to create the high-pitched, squeaky voices for the Chipmunks. He had used the recording process for a novelty song project, "The Witch Doctor," earlier in the same year. For the 1958 Christmas season, Seville and the Chipmunks released a recording of "The Chipmunk Song" or "Christmas Don't Be Late."

It was such a hit, it reached number one on *Billboard* and remained there for four weeks. It charted again during the '61 and '62 Christmas seasons. After their recording success made Seville and the characters nationally known, they were given life in animated cartoons and motion pictures.

Written by Harry Simeone (once Fred Waring's assistant), Katherine Davis, and Henry Onorati, "The Little Drummer Boy" has become a Christmas classic since its premier in 1958. The Harry Simeone Chorale's recording charted on *Billboard* during the next five Christmas seasons. A 1968 Rankin/Bass animated version of the song, about a drummer boy who follows the three wise men to Bethlehem to honor the Christ child, is rerun on television annually.

FOREIGN FLAVORS

The global influence in popular music increased as more and more French, Italian, Spanish, and German tunes, treatments, artists, and recordings found their way to the American public.

The French popular song "Les Feuilles Mortes" was written by Joseph Kosma in 1947. Poet Jacques Prévert wrote the French lyrics and Juliette Greco sang it in the French film *Les Portes de la Nuit*. Johnny Mercer penned the English lyrics. However, it was not the lyric version that became most popular in 1955. It was, instead, pianist Roger Williams's recording of "Autumn Leaves"—as the title was translated—that reportedly sold more than two million copies globally. Williams's instrumental version was number one on *Billboard* and *Cash Box*, while the song was a number-one hit on *Your Hit Parade*. His disc was *Variety's* number three hit of the year.

Very few foreign songs in the original language have become major hits in the United States. There have been several songs that use foreign words or phrases, but even in those instances most of the lyrics are in English. Domenico Modugno's "Nel Blu, Dipinto di Blu" is an Italian song that caught the attention of American popular music fans even though it was sung in the original language. Modugno was a four-time winner of Italy's prestigious San Remo Festival of Music, which annually selected the best new song of the year. In 1958, Modugno and lyricist Franci Migliacci won their first San Remo award with "Nel Blu, Dipinto di Blu." Migliacci's hard-to-understand lyric describes a dream in which a man paints his hands in blue and is flying through the "blue painted in blue." After becoming a million-seller in Italy, it came to America. The English lyric version, "Volare," was written by Mitchell Parish. "Volare," which means "to fly" was a part of Migliacci's original Italian lyric. Dean Martin's was the most popular Eng-lish version, but surprisingly, it was Modugno's Italian version that was the most popular in the United States. He also captured two of the most prestigious Grammy awards at the first awards show: Song of the Year and Record of the Year in 1988.

ADAPTATIONS

Adapting classical melodies into popular material is certainly nothing new. In the mid- to late fifties, "Melody of Love," "Fascination," "Don't You Know?" "Hot Diggity," and "Little Star" are examples of the practice. Adaptations were also involved in both "The Battle of New Orleans" and "Stagger Lee."

"Melody of Love" was adapted by songwriter Tom Glazer from "Melodie d'Amour," which had been written by H. Engelmann in 1903. The song sounds exactly like the turn-of-the-century, slow-tempo waltz it is. It must have been a nostalgia hit, causing adults to remember a more serene era. "Melody of Love" was orchestra leader Billy Vaughn's first big hit recording. Vaughn was musical director for Dot Records, so he was the arranger and conductor for most of Pat Boone's recordings. Vaughn's recording of "Melody of Love" topped the *Cash Box* chart, and the song reached number one on *Your Hit Parade*.

"Fascination" was an adaptation of 1932's "Valse tzigane" by F. D. Mar-chetti. In 1957, the song was revived in the film *Love in the Afternoon*, which starred Gary Cooper and Audrey Hepburn. Dick Manning was the lyricist. The song became a number-one hit on *Your Hit Parade*.

Another adaptation that year was "Don't You Know," which was popular-ized by Della Reese. Bobby Worth adapted "Musetta's Waltz" from Puccini's *La Boheme* for this hit song. Reese's recording topped the *Cash Box* chart for two weeks in 1959. "Don't You Know" was her biggest single and the only one that charted in the top ten.

"Hot Diggity (Dog Ziggity Boom)" was the big novelty hit of 1956 in an unlikely recording by Perry Como. The song was also an adaptation of a classi-cal melody. Al Hoffman and Dick Manning took the basic melody from the first theme of Alexis Chabrier's "España, Rhapsody for Orchestra" and added the catchy novelty lyrics to produce a silly song that describes "what'cha do to me."

The winner of the Grammy awards in 1959 for Song of the Year and Best Country and Western Recording was "The Battle of New Orleans." Presumably, the Song of the Year was given to a song written in the year in which the award was presented. In some ways "The Battle of New Orleans" qualified. In others, perhaps not. Originally an old square-dance tune called "The Eighth of January," it told the story of how Andrew Jackson defeated the army of British commander Pakenham in the last battle of the War of 1812. The battle actually took place on January 8, 1815, after the war was over, since neither side had received word that the Treaty of Ghent had been signed December 24, 1814. In 1955, Jimmy Driftwood was a teacher in Snowball, Arkansas, and he wrote new lyrics for the old square-dance tune to help his students learn about the War of 1812. Four years later, country artist Johnny Horton recorded Driftwood's song, and it became a number-one hit on *Billboard*, *Cash Box*, and the year's No. 2 hit on *Variety*. The folk-song character of "The Battle of New Orleans" fit perfectly into the folk trend that the Kingston Trio had begun the year before with their single "Tom Dooley" and their albums "The Kingston Trio at Large" and "Here We Go Again." "The Battle of New Orleans" was Johnny Horton's only number one on the pop charts, but he did chart highly with "Sink the Bismarck" and "North to Alaska" in 1960.

An old folk song, variously known as "Stagolee," "Stack-o-Lee," or "Stack-a-Lee," was a blues folk song about an African American murderer. Lloyd Price and Harold Logan adapted the original and wrote new lyrics because Dick Clark wouldn't allow the original tale of murder to be performed on *American Bandstand*. They changed the subject from gambling to fighting over a woman. The original blues lyrics, the first 1959 version, and the final version after Clark's objection can be read at http://en.wikipedia. org/wiki/Stagger_Lee. "Price's record was hard rock, driven by a wailing sax, and in retrospect his manic enthusiasm seems to be what many earlier versions lacked," wrote music journalist Greil Marcus (http://www.rockhall. com/hof/). Price's recording was *Variety*'s number nine hit of the year and was a number-one hit for four weeks on *Billboard*, and for three weeks on *Cash Box*. Price also had success in 1959 with "Personality," the song that gave him his nickname, "Mr. Personality." It peaked at No. 2 on *Billboard*. Price was inducted into the Rock and Roll Hall of Fame in 2006.

CALYPSO TREND

A commercial variant of calypso became a worldwide craze in the mid-fifties, although teenagers generally ignored the fad. Harry Belafonte particularly helped spread the calypso craze with "Jamaica Farewell," "Island in the Sun," and "Banana Boat Song (Day-O)" in 1956 and 1957. During the 1956 Christmas season, Belafonte popularized Jester Hairston's calypso

Christmas song "Mary's Little Boy Child." The calypso trend was aided by folk music groups such as The Kingston Trio, The Tarriers (with Vince Martin), and Terry Gilkyson and the Easy Riders.

"Banana Boat Song (Day-O)" was the collaboration of Erik Darling, Bob Carey, and Alan Arkin. The style of the song is more like that of a West Indian folk song than true calypso. Encyclopedia Britannica defines calypso as "a type of folk song primarily from Trinidad. The subject of a calypso text, usually witty and satiric, and the tone is one of allusion, mockery, and double entendre." "Banana Boat Song" is a song about working on a banana boat and wishing for quitting time, so the lyric doesn't fit the definition. It is neither witty nor satirical. And the song's tone is not one of allusion, mockery, or double entendre. However, "Banana Boat Song" was popularized by the Tarriers and Harry Belafonte in 1957. The song was the number-one hit on *Your Hit Parade* for one week.

Terry Gilkyson and the Easy Riders continued the trend with "Marianne" in 1957. It resulted in the biggest chart success of their career. *Your Hit Parade* seemed to appreciate the calypso songs more than the other charts. "Marianne" collected three weeks at number one on their hit survey.

GRAMMY AWARDS

The Grammy Awards were originally called the Gramophone Awards. They are presented by the National Academy of Recording Arts and Sciences (NARAS)—an association of professionals in the recorded music industry—for outstanding achievements in the recording industry. The Grammys are considered the approximate equivalent to the film industry's Oscars. The awards are named for the trophy that the winner receives—a small gilded statuette of a gramophone.

There are currently 108 categories within 30 genres of music such as pop, gospel, and rap. The awards are voted upon by peers rather than being based upon popularity or sales like some other award shows.

The organization also has a Grammy Hall of Fame.

The first Grammy Awards were presented in 1958. The most prominent winners were:

- Record and Song of the Year: "Nel Blu, Dipinto Di Blu (Volare)"
- Album of the Year and Best Arrangement: Henry Mancini's "The Music From Peter Gunn" (TV series)
- Best Vocal Performance, Female: "Ella Fitzgerald Sings the Irving Berlin Song Book"

- Best Jazz Performance, Individual: "Ella Fitzgerald Sings the Duke Ellington Song Book"
- Best Vocal Performance, Male: Perry Como, "Catch a Falling Star"
- Best Jazz Performance, Group: Count Basie, "Basie"
- Best Performance by a Vocal Group or Chorus: Louis Prima and Keely Smith's "That Old Black Magic"
- Best Comedy Performance and Best Recording for Children: Ross Bagdasarian, "The Chipmunk Song"
- Best Country and Western Performance: The Kingston Trio, "Tom Dooley"
- Best Rhythm and Blues Performance: The Champs, "Tequila"

At the second awards in 1959, some of the most prominent winners were:

- Record of the Year and Best New Artist: Bobby Darin, "Mack the Knife"
- Song of the Year: Jimmy Driftwood, "The Battle of New Orleans"
- Best Country and Western Performance: Johnny Horton, "The Battle of New Orleans"
- Album of the Year and Best Vocal Performance, Male: Frank Sinatra, "Come Dance With Me" LP (Billy May won the Best Arrangement award for his work on the same Sinatra LP)
- Best Vocal Performance, Female: Ella Fitzgerald, "But Not For Me"
- Best Jazz Performance, Soloist: Ella Fitzgerald, "Ella Swings Lightly"
- Best Rhythm and Blues Performance: Dinah Washington, "What a Dif'rence a Day Makes"

FIRST CERTIFIED GOLD RECORD

On March 14, 1958, the Record Industry Association of America (RIAA) awarded the very first certified Gold Record to Perry Como for his hit single, "Catch A Falling Star," written by Paul J. Vance and Lee Pockriss. In *Your Hit Parade*'s last year of operation, "Catch a Falling Star" achieved more weeks at number one (four) than any other song.

MAJOR INSTRUMENTAL HITS

For information on "Cherry Pink and Apple Blossom White" see **Number One Hits from Hollywood Films** in the "Hollywood's Biggest Hit Songs and Movie Musicals of the Postwar Years" chapter.

"Lisbon Antigua" had been written in 1937 by three Portuguese writers as "Lisboa Antigua," which literally means "Old Lisbon." In 1956, supreme arranger Nelson Riddle used it as the theme song of the motion picture titled *Lisbon*, which starred Ray Milland and Maureen O'Hara.

Les Baxter and his orchestra's recording of "Poor People of Paris" followed Nelson Riddle's "Lisbon Antigua" into the number-one spot on *Billboard* in 1956. That is the only time that instrumentals have been number one back-to-back. "Poor People of Paris" was actually a misnomer. The song had been popularized in France by Edith Piaf as "La Boulante du Pauvre Jean," which should have been translated as "The Ballad of Poor John." The poor John in the French title was the kind of man who always seems to meet the wrong kind of women. When the Paris office of Capitol cabled the title to the Hollywood office, "Jean" came out "gens," which translates "people." The error was never corrected.

For more on "Moonglow and Theme from *Picnic*," see **Number One Hits from Hollywood Films** in the "Hollywood's Biggest Hit Songs and Movie Musicals of the Postwar Years" chapter.

"Canadian Sunset" was popularized in 1956 in an instrumental recording by Hugo Winterhalter and his orchestra with the composer, jazz pianist Eddie Heywood, at the piano. Andy Williams also recorded a vocal version that used Norman Gimbel's lyrics.

Cozy Cole was a drummer who played with many of the greats in jazz, like Louis Armstrong, Benny Carter, Cab Calloway, and Lionel Hampton. During the fifties, he also led The Cozy Cole Combo, which recorded an instrumental featuring Cole's drumming, called "Topsy." The instrumental was put out on a 78-rpm disc with "Topsy, Part I" on one side and "Topsy, Part II" on the flip side. It was "Part II" that was most popular, making it to number one on *Cash Box* for one week.

"The Happy Organ" was Dave "Baby" Cortez playing the electric organ, an instrument not usually associated with R&B or rock 'n' roll. He and Ken Wood wrote the song originally titled "The Dog and the Cat." *Billboard*'s review of the single thought it sounded like it had been based on the old song "Shortnin' Bread." Cortez's recording collected two weeks at No. 1 on *Cash Box* and one week at the top of the *Billboard* chart.

A guitar duo—two brothers from Brooklyn named Santo and Johnny Farina—recorded the instrumental "Sleep Walk." The brothers and their sister, Ann, had written the song. Even though he was from Brooklyn, Santo had fallen in love with the steel guitar when he listened to a country radio show. Johnny played electric guitar. "Sleep Walk" collected two weeks at number one on the *Billboard* chart.

In 1957, Gene Autry signed Californian singer and songwriter Dave Burgess to his label, and he became its A&R director. Burgess hired saxophonist and pianist Danny Flores for an instrumental session, primarily to record an excellent Burgess composition, "Train to Nowhere." Burgess played rhythm guitar and Cliff Hils filled in on bass. Needing a "B" side, they chose a tune Flores had written while on vacation in Tijuana. The musicians for that session were Flores, drummer Gene Alden, guitarist Buddy Bruce, and bass guitarist Cliff Hils. The song was based on a vamp figure and was recorded quickly since it was to be the "B" side. During the session, Burgess suggested Flores, who used the stage name Chuck Rio, shout "tequila" during some of the instrumental breaks. Therefore, "Tequila," which became an instrumental classic, was created almost as an afterthought. A group name was needed to release the single. Someone suggested they name themselves after Gene Autry's horse, Champion. They became The Champs. "Train to Nowhere" didn't get much attention, but when DJs began to play the flip side of the record, "Tequila" caught on. In addition to becoming the group's first, and only, number-one hit single, it also won the Grammy for "Best R&B Performance." Although the Champs were never able to duplicate the success of "Tequila," the group is famous for some of its later members—Glen Campbell, Jim Seals, and Dash Crofts.

TEEN IDOLS

A teen idol is a person who receives great adulation from teenagers, particularly young females. Several popular music teen idols arose with the advent of such television programs as *American Bandstand*. In the early years of rock 'n' roll, Ricky Nelson and Frankie Avalon fit the mold.

Ricky Nelson grew up on television. His mother and father's radio show *The Adventures of Ozzie and Harriet* had premiered in 1944. When it transferred to ABC-TV in 1952, Ozzie, Harriet, and their sons, David and Ricky, were all regulars on the show. Ricky was twelve at the time. While he was in high school, trying to impress a date, he announced he was going to make a record. His first recording was a cover of Fats Domino's "I'm Walking," mainly because the song consisted of two chords that Ricky could play on his guitar. He performed the song on the April 10, 1957, episode of the family show. The flip side, "A Teenager's Romance," actually did better on the charts, peaking at number two on *Billboard*. Imperial Records became interested in Ricky and found out that he had never signed a contract with Verve, so they immediately signed him. His seventh chart single for Imperial, "Poor Little Fool" became his first *Billboard* number-one hit. Ricky knew what he wanted the recording to sound like, so he was his own record producer.

Frankie Avalon was a child prodigy trumpet player. He appeared on the *TV Teen Club*, hosted by Paul Whiteman, who suggested the name change from Avallone to Avalon. When Bob Marcucci was starting Chancelor Records, he asked Avalon if he knew any singers. He suggested Marcucci come listen to the two singers in his band. They sang, but Avalon did also, and Marcucci offered him and the whole band a contract, despite Avalon's protests that he was an instrumentalist. After a few unsuccessful releases, Avalon cut a song written by Peter DeAngelis and Marcucci, "Dede Dinah," which became his first chart single in 1958. After a couple of other chart singles, Marcucci and DeAngelis had Avalon record "Venus," a song written by Ed Marshall. This song was completely different from the songs he had been recording. The combo was replaced by an orchestra, female vocals, bells, and chimes over a soft cha-cha and calypso beat. Soon after the recording session, Frankie mentioned the song on a live telephone interview with Dick Clark on *American Bandstand*. The single was released the following week, and within a month or so, it was a number-one hit. Late in 1959, Avalon scored again with "Why"—the shortest title of any number-one *Billboard* hit. Once again, Marcucci and De Angelis were the songwriters and record producers. "Why" became Avalon's only other number-one hit, and his last Top Ten hit. He then turned to an acting career, starring in *The Alamo*, *Voyage to the Bottom of the Sea*, *The Carpetbaggers*, and numerous beach-party movies with Annette Funicello. He also appeared in a fantasy sequence in *Grease* (1978), where he sang "Beauty School Dropout."

ONE HIT WONDERS

The Elegants had their one and only chart single "Little Star" make it to the top of the *Billboard* chart. Vito Picone and Carmen Romano were in a Staten Island, New York, group called the Crescents in 1956. When that group folded, they recruited Artie Venosa, Frankie Fardogno, and Jimmy Moschella to form the Elegants. They took their name from a Schenley's Whiskey advertisement as "the liquor of elegance." Picone and Venosa took Mozart's "Twinkle, Twinkle, Little Star" and adapted it into "Little Star."

Songwriter Jenny Lou Carson originally wrote "Let Me Go, Lover" in 1953 under the title "Let Me Go, Devil" as a song concerning alcohol addiction. Mitch Miller, Columbia's A&R chief, suggested the lyrics be revised. Al Hill got cowriting credit for the revised version. Eighteen-year-old Joan Weber recorded the new version and gained her only major hit. It was number one on *Billboard*, *Cash Box*, and *Your Hit Parade*. Her recording was number ten for the year on *Variety*.

In 1961, Phil Spector started his own label, Phillies Records, and became famous for his "wall of sound" productions for several of the famous girl groups of the sixties, including the Crystals and the Ronettes. He was also the Righteous Brothers' producer. After producing the Beatles' *Let It Be* album and solo albums for George Harrison and John Lennon, Spector went into seclusion and worked only sporadically. However, long before his production career, Spector had a number-one record in a group called The Teddy Bears. After Spector graduated from high school in 1958, he organized the group with Marshall Leib and Harvey Goldstein. They soon added fifteen-year-old Annette Kleinbard, who later changed her name to Carol Connors and became a songwriter of such hits as "Gonna Fly Now (Theme from *Rocky*)" and "With You I'm Born Again." Before they released a record, Goldstein left the group and they continued as a trio. Spector was inspired to write "To Know Him Is to Love Him" by an inscription on his father's tombstone. At the recording session, Spector also served as producer, which later became his chief profession.

Bill Justis was older than most teenage music fans and had little interest in rock 'n' roll. Unlike many other rock artists, he was well educated, from a well-to-do family, and had formal musical training. However, when he heard there was a lot of money to be made in rock, he switched from trumpet to saxophone and bought several rock 'n' roll records to study the style. His switch paid off with the 1957 recording of "Raunchy," a number-one hit on *Cash Box* for two weeks. The song, originally titled "Backwards," was changed to "Raunchy" when Justis heard a teenager describe the song as "raunchy," which meant "dirty" in fifties' teenage slang. The tune was a little Southern melody that Justis recalled from his childhood in Birmingham, Alabama. Justis and Sid Manker reworked the original. Their recording consisted of Manker playing a short guitar riff over and over, alternating with Justis on tenor sax accompanied by Sam Phillips's Sun Records house band. Manker's guitar riff was later picked up by Duane Eddy. "Raunchy" was Justis's biggest hit single. Shortly after recording it, he became music director for Sun Records, arranging hits for Johnny Cash, Jerry Lee Lewis, and other

Sun artists. After leaving Sun, he produced for his own label and later moved to Nashville, where he continued arranging and producing. Justis also wrote the score for the Burt Reynolds film *Smokey and the Bandit* and later produced recordings for Bobby Vinton.

The Silhouettes were one of the classic Philadelphia doo-wop groups of the late fifties. They began as a gospel quartet in the mid-fifties with Billy Horton, Richard Lewis, Raymond Edwards, and Earl Beal as the original members. When they branched out into R&B songs, they changed their name to the Thunderbirds and later to the Silhouettes. One of the members, Richard Lewis, collaborated with the group's arranger, Howard Biggs, to write their only hit, "Get A Job," which went to number one on both the pop and R&B charts. Sha Na Na, a popular rock 'n' roll revival group in the late sixties, took its name from the lyrics of "Get A Job."

One of the last number-one hits on *Your Hit Parade* was "Chanson d'Amour (Song of Love)" in 1958. The song was popularized by the husband-and-wife duo of Art and Dotty Todd. They were another of the one-hit wonders of the era.

A religious song became a number-one hit in 1958. The spiritual "He's Got the Whole World in His Hands" was adapted by Geoff Love into a rousing number popularized by thirteen-year-old British singer Laurie London. His recording climbed to the top of *Billboard* and stayed there for four weeks and topped the *Cash Box* chart for two weeks. The song was number one on *Your Hit Parade* for three weeks, just before the show ended in June. However, the song was London's only chart single.

PERFORMERS WITH ONLY ONE CHART TOPPER

What is the only number-one hit written by a U.S. vice president? The answer needs some explanation. In 1912 Charles Gates Dawes, Calvin Coolidge's vice president in 1925, wrote a piece titled "Melody in A Major." Carl Sigman added lyrics to Dawes's melody in 1951, making it "It's All in the Game." Several recording artists, including Tommy Edwards, recorded the song in 1951, but none were especially successful. In 1958, Edwards rerecorded "It's All in the Game," but instead of using the original 1951 arrangement, he updated it with more of a rock 'n' roll feel. This time the single quickly rose to the top position on the charts. This was Edwards's only number-one single and his only recording that reached the Top 10.

Gogi Grant's first chart hit was "Suddenly There's a Valley" in 1955. During a recording session, the label owner, Herb Newman, pulled out a yellowed manuscript of a song he and Stan Lebousky had written when they were college students at UCLA. The song, "The Wayward Wind," was written for a male singer, so Gogi changed some of the lyrics to give it a female perspective, and with only fifteen minutes left in the recording session, recorded "The Wayward Wind," which became her only other chart hit and her only chart topper.

As a teenager, Conway Twitty—whose real name was Harold Lloyd Jenkins—considered a career in the ministry, but when he graduated from high school with a .450 batting average, he was offered a contract with the Philadelphia Phillies. Before he signed with the Phillies, his Army draft notice arrived. Serving in Japan, he formed a band and played in clubs in the Far East. After his discharge, the Phillies were still interested, but by then he was convinced he could be the next Elvis. One of his band buddies had recommended he contact manager Don Seat, who suggested he change his name. His stage name came from the names of two southern towns: Conway, Arkansas, and Twitty, Texas. One night at a gig with his new band, he and Jack Nance wrote "It's Only Make Believe" during an intermission. His first single, recorded with Elvis's background group, the Jordanaires, was "It's Only Make Believe." His recording sounded so much like Elvis that many fans were convinced it was "the King." It became Twitty's only number-one hit on the pop charts. However, when he became a country artist, he collected thirty-five number-one singles as a solo artist and five more with Loretta Lynn.

TV SERIES THEME

"The Ballad of Davy Crockett" was introduced on a "Frontierland" segment of Disney's mid-fifties TV series. Popular recordings of the song were released by Bill Hayes, Tennessee Ernie Ford, and by the series' star, Fess Parker. The song became a number-one hit on *Your Hit Parade*, *Billboard*, and the *Cash Box* chart, and it was *Variety's* number seven hit of 1955. A ballad typically tells a story, and indeed, this ballad chronicles some of the exploits of the legendary Crockett, who was "king of the wild frontier." "Davy Crocket" caps became the rage among little boys as a result of the popularity of the television programs.

CIVIL WAR SONG POPULARIZED

"The Yellow Rose of Texas" experienced incredible success in 1955, especially for a song written approximately 102 years earlier. The song most likely originated on the Northern minstrel show circuit before it became a favorite of Civil War soldiers. Its composer is anonymous, known only as "J. K."

Composer-arranger Don George took this old campfire song, eliminated some of its racial overtones, and set it to a marching beat. Mitch Miller discovered George's arrangement on an album of Civil War songs and gave it a new arrangement, adding an exciting snare drum part. If Miller had not been the all-powerful A&R director at Columbia, the record might have never been released, but his uncanny choice of material was vindicated when it topped the *Billboard, Cash Box,* and *Your Hit Parade* charts. Singer Johnny Desmond also had a recording of "The Yellow Rose of Texas" that made the *Billboard* chart. Stan Freberg's comic treatment also charted in 1955.

A 1944 Roy Rogers film bore the same title. Elvis Presley performed the song as part of a medley in his 1964 film *Viva Las Vegas.*

REVIVALS

There were some reworkings of such standards as "Tonight You Belong to Me," "Love Letters in the Sand," "I'm Gonna Sit Right Down and Write Myself a Letter," "Blueberry Hill," and "So Rare" that shared limelight with the rock 'n' roll beat.

Billy Rose—entertainer Fanny Brice's second husband—wrote the lyrics for "Tonight You Belong to Me," and Lee David contributed the music in 1926. It was originally popularized by Gene Austin in 1927, but the song also became a hit in 1956 for Patience and Prudence. They were the eleven-year-old and fourteen-year-old daughters of orchestra leader Mack McIntyre. Their father brought his daughters' audition tape to Liberty Records in the summer of 1956. One of the songs on the tape was their cover version of "Tonight You Belong to Me."

Pat Boone had a major hit in 1957 with a revival of an oldie, "Love Letters in the Sand," from 1931. One of the key ingredients connected with the sound of the early years of rock is present in Boone's recording of this song. The song is in four-four time (quadruple meter), but the accompaniment, especially the piano, is playing triplets, repeating the chord three times in each beat, which sounds like twelve-eight rhythm.

Billy Williams revived "I'm Gonna Sit Right Down and Write Myself a Letter," a song that Fats Waller had popularized in the mid-thirties.

Fats Domino's most successful chart single was 1940's "Blueberry Hill" in 1957. The Library of Congress National Recording Registry added

Domino's "Blueberry Hill" in 2005, and it was number eighty-one on *Rolling Stone*'s "500 Greatest Songs of All Time" list.

Big band leader and saxophonist Jimmy Dorsey resurrected the 1937 song "So Rare" in a 1957 recording with much more of a rock backbeat than the original. Jimmy died of cancer shortly after "So Rare" became a number two hit on *Billboard*.

SLOW ROMANTIC BALLADS

Even though the rock 'n' roll era had arrived, not every song was rock oriented. There were also substantial numbers of romantic songs in a slow tempo, like Debbie Reynolds's "Tammy," Johnny Mathis's "Chances Are" and "It's Not For Me to Say," Pat Boone's "April Love," and Frank Sinatra's "All the Way," among others.

Actress Debbie Reynolds starred in *Tammy and the Bachelor* in 1957. She performed the film's title song, "Tammy," on the soundtrack, and when the song was nominated for an Oscar, she performed it at the awards ceremony. Her Coral recording of the song hit number one on all the charts. Her disc was the only single by a female artist to top the *Billboard* chart between July 28, 1956, and December 1, 1958. Debbie Reynolds's soundtrack version was recorded to piano accompaniment only. Henry Mancini added other instruments to the track later.

"Chances Are"—written by composer Robert Allen and lyricist Al Stillman in 1952—became Johnny Mathis's first and only number-one *Billboard* hit. Mathis, who was an excellent athlete in high school and college, began his recording career in 1957 with "Wonderful! Wonderful!" and "It's Not For Me to Say."

MULTIPLE VERSIONS OF HITS

Prior to the rock era, it was quite common for multiple artists to record the same song and fight for the public's approval through airplay and sales of recordings. Of course, the more artists who recorded a song meant more potential revenue for the song's publisher. In the rock era, however, multiple artists competing with each other for high chart positions were very rare. Heated battles for number one on the *Billboard* chart occurred in 1957 with competing versions of "Young Love" by Tab Hunter and Sonny James, and of "Butterfly" by Andy Williams and Charlie Gracie.

"Young Love" had first been recorded by Ric Cartey, cowriter of the song with Carole Joyner. When his version sputtered, he got country singer Sonny James to record it. Dot Record president, Randy Wood, figured James's disc would do well on the country chart, but doubted its crossover potential, so he decided to release a pop version. He contacted actor Tab Hunter—who had never been known as a singer—for the job. Within ten days, Wood had the song available in stores. Hunter's film studio, Warner Brothers, was furious that Hunter had recorded for Dot. As a result, they started their own label in 1958. Hunter's recording topped the *Billboard* chart for six weeks, while James's version managed one week at the top of that chart. *Cash Box* lumped both recordings together, and they collected six weeks at the top. "Young Love" was tops on *Your Hit Parade* for five weeks. It was *Variety*'s number six hit of the year.

Charlie Gracie's first recording for Cameo Records was "Butterfly," which became his biggest recording, reaching number one on *Billboard* for two weeks. His was not the most popular version of the song, however. Andy Williams's recording of "Butterfly" made it to number one on *Billboard* for three weeks. Williams had sung with his three brothers since the late thirties. He left the family act in 1952 to pursue a solo career. After a few unsuccessful recordings, "Butterfly" became his first, and only, number-one *Billboard* single. Williams became one of the most popular vocalists in the country and was signed to what was at that time the biggest recording contract in history. His greatest success was as an album artist. By 1973 he had collected seventeen Gold Album awards from RIAA. Williams also had a highly successful television show in the sixties.

NOVELTY HITS

There were several novelty hits in 1958: "The Purple People Eater," "Witch Doctor," and "The Chipmunk Song."

The following riddle was making the rounds among school children: "What has one eye, flies, has a horn, and eats people?" The answer was, "A one-eyed, one-horned, flying people eater." When a friend repeated the riddle to Sheb Wooley, he immediately saw the makings of a song, "The Purple People Eater." At a meeting with the president of MGM Records, Wooley sang almost everything in his repertoire, but was asked if he had anything else. Rather reluctantly he pulled out "The Purple People Eater," which turned out to be his only number-one hit. Wooley was also an actor.

He played a cattle drive scout for several years in Clint Eastwood's *Rawhide* television series. He also appeared in numerous films and TV series. In recording the song, Wooley recorded the voice of the people eater and his saxophone at a slower speed and played them back at a faster speed, a technique used successfully by Ross Bagdasarian for "Witch Doctor" and "The Chipmunk Song."

Ross Bagdasarian's first musical success was "Come on-a My House," which he cowrote with his cousin, William Saroyan. In 1956, he had a minor novelty recording under the name Alfi and Harry. But when he became David Seville, his fortunes improved. He had been stationed near Seville, Spain, and took the city's name and added David for his alter ego. He got the idea for "Witch Doctor" from a book title, *Duel with the Witch Doctor.* Like Sheb Wooley in "The Purple People Eater," he came up with the idea of playing back the music and vocals at different speeds. After several months of experimentation, he recorded the voice of the witch doc- tor at half-speed and played it back at normal speed, creating a voice twice as high as the original, which gave it a squeaky comical sound. He used the same technique again later in the year for "The Chipmunk Song." One day while he was driving through Yosemite, a stubborn chipmunk refused to get out of the road. That incident became Bagdasarian's inspiration for The Chipmunks. He named the rodents after some Liberty Records executives and modeled the mischievous Alvin after his youngest son, Adam, who was always asking if it was Christmas yet. "The Chipmunk Song (Christmas Don't Be Late)" eventually sold twelve million copies. A prime time ani- mated series, *The Alvin Show,* ran for a year on CBS-TV in 1961. It was repeated on CBS's Saturday morning schedule for the next three years. After Bagdasarian died in 1972, the Chipmunk legacy was carried on by his son, Ross Bagdasarian, Jr.

GRUESOME HIT

The biggest hit of 1959 was the gruesome old Broadway musical excerpt "Mack the Knife." German expatriate Kurt Weill and Berthold Brecht had written *Die Dreigroschenoper (The Threepenny Opera)* in 1928 while they were still in Germany. It was an adaptation of the eighteenth-century English bal- lad opera *The Beggar's Opera,* by John Gay, and was a socialist critique of capitalistic society. The musical has been presented on Broadway several times, but in 1954 Marc Blitzstein's translation had been presented in an Off Broadway production. The song, "Mack the Knife," began to catch on and was recorded by several artists.

Bobby Darin's 1959 jazzy version was by far the most popular of the dozens that were released. Considering the song's subject matter, it is astounding that it was popular at all, much less the top song of the year. The original title was "Moritat," which in German means "murder deed." In Blitzstein's revised version it was "The Ballad of Mack the Knife (Die Moritat von Mackie Messer)." It was the song that introduced the character Macheath, "a thief, murderer, arsonist, and rapist." Blitzstein's adaptation cleaned up the lyrics from the original, dropping the last two stanzas, which had been about arson and rape. Still, there are lyrics about a shark bite that causes "scarlet billows" of blood, and about Macheath who is so skillful with his jackknife that when he stabs someone, there's "nevah a trace of red." In another instance, the lyrics sing gleefully about putting a dead body in a cement bag and throwing it in the river.

Bobby Darin's disc is definitely a swinging arrangement of the song and, unless listeners pay close attention to the lyrics, it is a delightful, big-band, jazz-type recording. Not only was it the top hit of the year on *Billboard* and *Variety* (number two for the year on *Cash Box*) in 1959, it also won two Grammy awards for Best New Artist and Best Vocal Performance by a Male.

Bobby Darin had suffered from rheumatic fever as a child and had heart problems as an adult. He had driven himself to achieve fame by age twenty-five, because he was convinced he wouldn't be alive by age thirty. Actually, he made it to thirty-seven, when he died of heart failure. Not only was he successful as a recording artist, but he was successful in movies, for which he received an Oscar nomination for Best Supporting Actor for his role in *Captain Newman, M.D.* (1963); in television, in which he starred in his own NBC prime-time variety series (1972–73); and in personal appearances. In 2004, Kevin Spacey starred in the film *Beyond the Sea*, a biopic about Bobby Darin.

THE DAY THE MUSIC DIED

In "American Pie," Don McLean described February 3, 1959, as the day the music died. Buddy Holly, Ritchie Valens, and the Big Bopper were killed in a plane crash on that date. For more on this tragic incident, please visit http://www.fiftiesweb.com/crash.htm.

ROCK 'N' ROLL IS HERE TO STAY!

No half decade in history revolutionized the music scene as quickly and as thoroughly as the early years of rock 'n' roll. Rock seemed to burst upon the nation's attention. Prior to 1955, nobody knew what rock 'n' roll was. Although it had been evolving from rhythm and blues, it seemed to materialize overnight. The youth culture of the mid-fifties became almost completely dominant. No performer from the year-end top twenty in 1954 made it into the top twenty in 1959.

Rock 'n' roll is here to stay!

6

Hollywood's Biggest Hit Songs and Movie Musicals of the Postwar Years

The fiftieth anniversary of motion pictures was observed in 1944, and with a booming post-World War II economy, movies became more popular than ever. Some of the era's most popular songs were introduced in the movies.

The public loved the songs from Hollywood films, and the film studios hired some of the most talented composer and lyricists to write songs for their extremely talented performers.

NUMBER-ONE HITS FROM HOLLYWOOD FILMS

There were fifty songs from Hollywood films that topped one or more of the charting services during the postwar years. Several of the songs became Academy Award winners for Best Song. Others claimed nominations for that award.

Bing Crosby introduced "Ac-Cent-Tchu-Ate the Positive" in the movie musical *Here Come the Waves* (1944). Crosby played a singing idol, a parody of crooners like himself. His recording of the song with the Andrews Sisters was very popular but not as popular as Johnny Mercer and the Pied Pipers' recording, which was number one on *Billboard*. The song was a number-one hit on *Your Hit Parade* in 1945. The Grammy Hall of Fame inducted Mercer and the Pied Pipers' recording in 1998. The song crystallized one day when Mercer reminded composer Harold Arlen of a spiritual-sounding tune he had been humming lately. When Arlen began singing the tune without a lot of gusto, Mercer remarked, "You've got to accentuate the positive." Arlen began trying to fit the line into his melodic idea. By the time they arrived at the studio, the song was practically written. The sermon style of the song was a chance for Crosby to clown around with a fake minstrel-show dialect as he "preached" the lyrics of the song. The music suggests a slow and "sermon-like" tempo. Arlen and Mercer's collaboration received an Academy Award nomination for Best Song.

The war had brought about a multitude of changes, even changes in attitudes about dreams and love. During the war, a lot of the songs were about the prospect of reuniting with a loved one, of living happily ever after once the catastrophic war ended. When the end finally came, "I'll Buy That Dream" was the song that expressed the idea of many of the GIs. They all wanted their piece of the American dream. In the film *Sing Your Way Home*, Anne Jeffreys introduced "I'll Buy That Dream," which collected an Oscar nomination as Best Song. The most popular recording of the song was a duet by Helen Forrest and Dick Haymes. The song managed two weeks at the top of *Your Hit Parade*.

Marion Hutton introduced "My Dreams Are Getting Better All the Time" in the Bud Abbott and Lou Costello film *In Society* (1944). Les Brown and His Orchestra's recording of "My Dreams Are Getting Better All the Time," with his vocalist Doris Day, was a number-one hit on *Variety*, *Billboard*, and *Your Hit Parade* in 1945.

Randy Newman, who narrated an American Movie Classics special titled *The Hollywood Soundtrack Story*, said "the most famous song to emerge from a movie was 'Laura' from the classic 1944 murder mystery of the same name." It wasn't originally written as a song. "David Raskin wrote it as the haunting main theme for the film, and if ever a theme haunted a movie this one surely does," said Newman. Lyrics were added by Johnny Mercer a few months after the film's release. Woody Herman's band had the most successful recording of the song, which managed to top the *Your Hit Parade* chart.

Dick Haymes introduced composer Harry Warren and lyricist Mack Gordon's "The More I See You" in the movie musical *Billy Rose's Diamond Horseshoe* (1945). The song became a *Your Hit Parade* number-one hit.

Richard Rodgers and Oscar Hammerstein II had already been successful with *Oklahoma!* (1943) and *Carousel* (1945) on Broadway. Now, they tried a Hollywood movie musical with *State Fair* in 1945. The film was a musical remake of a 1933 nonmusical. The song "It Might As Well Be Spring" was introduced in the movie by Jeanne Crain, whose vocals were dubbed by Louanne Hogan. "It Might As Well Be Spring" won the Academy Award for Best Song in 1945. Composer Richard Rodgers had originally written the music for this song at a bright, medium tempo, but the studio's musical director considered it a slow ballad. Rodgers argued with him until the director promised to reshoot the song if it was not received well by the preview audience. When Rodgers finally saw the film, he admitted the song was better at a slower tempo. Lyricist Oscar Hammerstein II wanted the singer to show all the symptoms of spring fever even though the state fair was in the fall. In Rodgers's autobiography, *Musical Stages*, he explains how he came to write the melody for this song: it "is a good example of the way a tune can amplify the meaning of its lyric. The first lines are: 'I'm as restless as a willow in a wind storm, / I'm as jumpy as a puppet on a string.' Taking its cue directly from these words, the music itself is appropriately restless and jumpy. Moreover, since the song is sung by a young girl who can't quite understand why she feels the way she does, I deliberately ended the phrase on the uncertain sound of the F natural (on the word 'string') rather than on the more positive F sharp." The song became a number-one hit on *Your Hit Parade*, and Dick Haymes's recording of it reached number three on *Billboard*. The 1962 Twentieth Century Fox version of *State Fair* starred Pat Boone, Bobby Darin, Ann-Margret, and Pamela Tiffin (Anita Gordon dubbed Tiffin's singing).

Betty Grable introduced "I Can't Begin to Tell You" in the movie musical *The Dolly Sisters* (1945). It was reprised in the final scene by Grable and John Payne. The song was an Academy Award nominee in 1946. The real Dolly Sisters were Hungarian twins who emigrated to the United States in 1905. They became a famous dancing act in beer halls, on the vaudeville circuits, and eventually in the *Ziegfeld Follies*. Bing Crosby's 1945 recording of "I Can't Begin to Tell You," with pianist Carmen Cavallaro, became a *Billboard* and *Your Hit Parade* top hit.

"Doctor, Lawyer, Indian Chief" was introduced by Betty Hutton in the movie musical *Stork Club*. Hutton's frantic singing style fit the song perfectly as she tried to explain that no one could love her boyfriend more than she did. Her recording of "Doctor, Lawyer, Indian Chief" was very popular, topping *Billboard*'s chart in 1946. The song only managed to reach number four on *Your Hit Parade*.

It had been six years since Hoagy Carmichael created a big hit, but in 1946 he and Jack Brooks collaborated to produce the Academy Award nominee "Ole Buttermilk Sky." Carmichael introduced the song in the film *Canyon Passage*. Kay Kyser and his orchestra, with Michael Douglas as vocalist, had the most successful recording of the song. Their version topped the *Billboard* chart and also was a number-one hit on *Your Hit Parade*.

"Linda" was introduced in the 1945 film *The Story of G.I. Joe*, about famous war correspondent Ernie Pyle, who joined Company C, 18th Infantry, in North Africa and Italy during World War II, reporting many human interest stories to his readers back home. Buddy Clark with Ray Noble and his orchestra had a 1947 hit recording of "Linda" that topped *Billboard*'s chart and was number seven for the year on *Variety*. The song also was a number-one hit on *Your Hit Parade* and was nominated for the Best Song Oscar.

"Mam'selle" was introduced in a French cafe scene in the 1946 film of Somerset Maugham's novel *The Razor's Edge*, which was set during World War I. Both Art Lund and Frank Sinatra popularized the song with successful recordings that topped the *Billboard* chart. The song was also a number-one hit on *Your Hit Parade* in 1948. British movie director Edmund Goulding and American lyricist Mack Gordon collaborated on "Mam'selle."

"On the Atchison, Topeka and the Santa Fe" was written by composer Harry Warren and lyricist Johnny Mercer for the movie musical *The Harvey Girls*. The song captured the Oscar for Best Song in 1946. The Harvey girls were actually a group of refined waitresses taken to the Wild West by restaurateur Fred Harvey. In the film, the song was performed by Judy Garland, Ray Bolger, and a train full of Harvey girls. Most popular songs are love songs, but this is a song about anticipating the arrival of a train. The train does carry a valuable cargo: women, beautiful, young women—something the men out West desperately craved. Johnny Mercer and the Pied Pipers were primarily responsible for popularizing the song. Their recording was a number-one hit on *Billboard* and the number-three hit in *Variety*'s Top Ten for 1945.

Jerome Kern and Oscar Hammerstein II wrote "All Through the Day" for the movie musical *Centennial Summer* (1946). Larry Stevens, Cornel Wilde, and Louanne Hogan, who dubbed the singing for film star Jeanne Crain, introduced the song. The song was nominated for the 1946 Academy Award for Best Song. "All Through the Day" is not as operatic as many of Kern's earlier songs. Even such a master as Kern had difficulty spanning the gap between the operettas, which had been fashionable, and the popular music that was now in vogue. Kern died shortly after completing the score for the film. "All Through the Day" was a number-one hit on *Your Hit*

Parade. Frank Sinatra's version was the most popular recording, but Perry Como and Margaret Whiting's versions also charted.

The success of *The Jolson Story*, and the even greater success of its soundtrack album, enabled Al Jolson to achieve the most remarkable comeback in popular music history. The film was a sentimentalized biography of the performer called "The World's Greatest Entertainer." In many ways, Jolson's story is similar to the character he played in *The Jazz Singer* (1927). A Jewish boy, against his father's will, goes into show business, becomes a star, and marries a dancer who is not Jewish. Larry Parks portrayed Jolson, but Jolson recorded all the songs on the soundtrack, which contained more than a dozen of his many hits. Jolson's recording of "Anniversary Song" was the number-nine hit in *Variety*'s Top Ten for 1947 and a chart topper on *Billboard* and *Your Hit Parade*. The song was Saul Chaplin's adaptation of the melody of Ivanovici's "Danube Waves," with lyrics by Chaplin and Al Jolson. Jolson's recording from the film's soundtrack reportedly sold more than a million copies.

"A Gal in Calico" was written by Leo Robin and Arthur Schwartz for the 1946 movie musical *The Time, the Place and the Girl*. An Academy Award nominee, this decidedly western-flavored song was introduced by Jack Carson, Dennis Morgan, and Martha Vickers in the film. Johnny Mercer had the most popular recording of the song, which managed to top the *Your Hit Parade* survey of hits in early 1947.

The Jimmy Van Heusen–Johnny Burke song "Personality" was introduced by Dorothy Lamour in a performance in a saloon in the movie musical *Road to Utopia* (1946), another "road film" with Bing Crosby, Bob Hope, and Dorothy Lamour. *Road to Utopia* was one of the zaniest and most successful of the series. Songwriter and recording artist Johnny Mercer made "Personality" popular in a recording with the Pied Pipers. Mercer's disc was *Variety*'s number-nine hit of the year and a chart topper on *Billboard*.

The Perils of Pauline was first a 1914 silent movie serial, then a 1934 talkie movie serial, a 1947 movie musical, and a 1967 feature film. In the 1947 version, Betty Hutton starred in a fictionalized account of silent film star Pearl White's rise to fame. Frank Loesser's "I Wish I Didn't Love You So" was introduced by "The Blonde Bombshell," Betty Hutton. The song was an Academy Award nominee for Best Song. Both Dinah Shore and Vaughn Monroe had very popular recordings of the song. Both peaked at number two on *Billboard*. However, it topped the *Your Hit Parade* survey of hits for two weeks.

"I Wonder Who's Kissing Her Now" had been introduced in the 1909 musical *The Prince of Tonight*. In 1947, a film biography was made of one of the song's writers, Joe E. Howard, called *I Wonder Who's Kissing Her Now*. The movie's release helped the song become popular again. The most popular 1947 recording was by Ted Weems and his orchestra, with Perry Como as vocalist. His recording was a number-one hit on *Billboard* and *Your Hit Parade*.

Mother Wore Tights was a movie musical that chronicled the life of a turn-of-the-century vaudeville family. Many nostalgic musical numbers were interspersed, but "You Do," an Academy Award nominee, was introduced in the movie musical. The song was popularized in a successful recording by Dinah Shore and was a number-one hit on *Your Hit Parade*.

In *The Paleface*, Bob Hope and Jane Russell introduced "Buttons and Bows," the Academy Award–winning song of 1948. Dinah Shore's recording was a number-one hit on *Billboard* and *Your Hit Parade*. It was also *Variety*'s number-one hit of the year. "Buttons and Bows" has a distinct western flavor in lyrics and melody. The lyrics make several allusions to Hope's comic character in the film, an eastern dude dentist. He isn't fond of people who "tote a gun," and his bones ache from riding the bouncing buckboards. The song appeared again with new lyrics in the sequel, *Son of Paleface* (1952).

The screwball cartoon character Woody Woodpecker first appeared on the screen in *Knock Knock* in 1940. After 1946, with a change of directors, Woody calmed down slightly. In 1947, the character got his own theme song when George Tibbles and Ramey Idriess wrote "The Woody Woodpecker Song," making ample use of the character's famous laugh. The song first appeared in the 1948 short *Wet Blanket Policy*. Kay Kyser and His Orchestra's recording of the song reportedly sold a million copies and was a number-one hit on *Billboard* and *Your Hit Parade*. It was number ten for the year on *Variety*. Gloria Wood was the vocalist on Kyser's recording. The song was also nominated for the Academy Award for the year's Best Song from film for 1948.

Marlene Dietrich introduced "Golden Earrings" in the 1946 film of the same name, but the song didn't become popular until 1948 in a recording by Peggy Lee. The song was a number-one hit on *Your Hit Parade* and peaked at number two on *Billboard*.

Romance on the High Seas was Doris Day's first film. She introduced "It's Magic" in the film, and it became a number-one hit on *Your Hit Parade*. The song was an Academy Award nominee for Best Song.

Movie songs among the biggest hits of 1949 included "Again," a Latin-flavored ballad that was introduced by Ida Lupino in the motion picture *Road House* (1948). The song climbed to number one on the *Your Hit Parade* chart and was tied as number ten on *Variety*'s hits of 1949. The most popular recorded versions were by Gordon Jenkins and his orchestra, with Joe Graydon as vocalist, and the one by Doris Day.

"Mona Lisa" was introduced in the 1949 film *Captain Carey, U.S.A.* Even though it was heard only in fragments that were sung in Italian on the soundtrack, it won the Oscar for the Best Song from a film in 1950. Nat "King" Cole agreed to record the song only after the writers twisted his arm. His recording topped the *Billboard, Cash Box*, and *Your Hit Parade* charts. His disc was number three on *Variety* for the year. Cole's recording was inducted into the Grammy Hall of Fame in 1992, and RIAA and NEA named it one of their *Songs of the Century*.

Anton Karas, a zither player from Vienna, was hired to furnish the soundtrack music for Orson Welles's *The Third Man*, which needed music appropriate to postwar Vienna. *"The Third Man* Theme" was a number-one hit on *Billboard, Cash Box*, and *Variety*. Two recordings—one by the composer and one by Guy Lombardo and his Royal Canadians—made it one of the biggest hits of 1950.

Written by lyricist Ned Washington and composer Victor Young, "My Foolish Heart" was the title song of a 1949 film. Susan Hayward sang the title song on the soundtrack, which was an Academy Award nominee. Gordon Jenkins and his orchestra, with vocalist Sandy Evans, had the most popular recording of the song. Their version topped the *Cash Box* chart and the song became a number-one hit on *Your Hit Parade*.

"Nevertheless" was written by lyricist Harry Ruby and composer Bert Kalmar in 1931. When Ruby and Kalmar's screen biography, *Three Little Words*, was released in 1950, "Nevertheless (I'm in Love With You)" found new life. It was performed in the film by Fred Astaire and Vera-Ellen (whose voice was dubbed by Anita Ellis). The song climbed to the top of *Your Hit Parade* for one week in December 1950. The most popular recording of the song was by Paul Weston and his orchestra, with the Norman Luboff Choir.

"Be My Love" was introduced by Mario Lanza and Kathryn Grayson in the 1950 movie musical *Toast of New Orleans*. The song was nominated for the Academy Award for Best Song and topped the *Billboard, Variety*, and *Cash Box* charts in 1951. One of the most phenomenal vocal talents of the early fifties was Mario Lanza, a former piano mover who had signed with

RCA Victor in the late forties. Lanza straddled the classical and pop fields with his recordings. His was the only operatic voice to break into the pop field since Enrico Caruso in the early years of the twentieth century. His recording of "Be My Love" sold over one-and-a-half million copies—the only RCA Victor classical recording to be included on jukeboxes.

"Because of You," a song written by lyricist Arthur Hammerstein—uncle of famed lyricist Oscar Hammerstein II—and composer Dudley Wilkinson in 1940, became popular in 1951 when it was featured in the film *I Was an American Spy*. It was also used as incidental music in the 1951 Claudette Colbert film *Let's Make It Legal*. Tony Bennett had his first million-selling recording with "Because of You," which became the top hit of 1951 and stayed on top of *Your Hit Parade* for eleven weeks that year (the second longest stay at number one on *Your Hit Parade*). Bennett's disc was also a number-one hit on both *Billboard* and *Cash Box*, and the top hit of the year on *Variety*.

"The Song from *Moulin Rouge* (Where Is My Heart?)" came from the screen biography of Toulouse-Lautrec in 1953, performed on the film's soundtrack by Muriel Smith singing for actress Zsa Zsa Gabor. The tune was by composer Georges Auric. The original French title was "Le Long de la Seine" with French words by Jacques Larue. The song became the top hit of the year, topping *Cash Box*, *Billboard*, *Variety*, and *Your Hit Parade*. Surprisingly, the song was ignored by the Academy when nominations for the Oscar were announced. Percy Faith and His Orchestra's recording was the most popular version. Their disc was basically an instrumental, although Felicia Sanders does sing the English lyrics toward the end. The 2001 film of the same name was a musical and had a completely different plot.

"That's Amore" was a Jack Brooks (lyrics) and Harry Warren (music) Academy Award nominee for 1953 that was introduced in *The Caddy*, which starred Dean Martin and Jerry Lewis. Martin's recording of the song was *Variety*'s number-nine hit of 1954. It was Martin's first million-seller, selling more than four million copies over the next decade.

The Academy Award–winning song for 1953 was "Secret Love" from *Calamity Jane*. Doris Day's recording of the song became one of the top hits of 1954, topping all the charts. Her recording was inducted into the Grammy Hall of Fame in 1999. Doris Day starred as Calamity Jane, while Howard Keel portrayed Wild Bill Hickock.

Lyricist Sammy Cahn and composer Jule Styne's "Three Coins in the Fountain"—from the film of the same name—was the Academy Award winner for Best Song in 1954. Frank Sinatra sang the song on the soundtrack, but it was the Four Aces' recording that made it to number one on *Cash Box*, *Billboard*, and *Your Hit Parade*. The inspiration for the song came from the legend that whoever throws a coin into the water of the Trevi Fountain in Rome will return to that Eternal City. The film's three couples were Dorothy McGuire and Clifton Webb, Jean Peters and Louis Jourdan, Maggie McNamara and Rossano Brazzi.

"Young at Heart" originated as the melody for a 1939 song called "Moonbeam" by Johnny Richards. Carolyn Leigh added new lyrics in 1953. The song was then used as the title and theme song for a 1954 film, which was a remake of the 1938 film *Four Daughters*. Frank Sinatra's recording of "Young at Heart" helped popularize the song to the number-one spot on *Your Hit Parade* for two weeks in the spring of 1954. Sinatra's recording peaked at number two on both *Billboard* and *Cash Box*.

"Rock Around the Clock" was written by Max C. Freedman and Jimmy DeKnight in 1953 and recorded by Sunny Dae the same year, and by Bill Haley and His Comets in 1954. The song was included in the 1955 film *The Blackboard Jungle*. The film would probably be forgotten by now had it not showcased the song, which was heard during the opening credits. The film starred Glenn Ford as a young teacher and an even younger Sidney Poitier as one of his rebellious students. Haley's recording of the song was rereleased when the film began to cause a sensation, and it zoomed up the charts. It became a number-one hit on *Billboard*, *Cash Box*, and *Variety*. The song even managed two weeks at No. 1 on the conservative *Your Hit Parade* hit survey. Haley's recording was inducted into the Grammy Hall of Fame in 1982. The American Film Institute's *100 Years ... 100 Songs* (2004) named "Rock Around the Clock" as the number fifty greatest song from an American film.

"Cherry Pink and Apple Blossom White" had been written by Louiguy and Jacques Larue and published in Paris in 1950 as "Cerisier Rose et Pommer Blanc." In 1951, Mack David wrote the English lyrics. Mambo King Pérez Prado and his orchestra had recorded the song in 1951, but when it was selected for inclusion in the 1955 film *Underwater*, Prado cut a new version for the film. Prado's recording of this mambo was number one for the year on *Billboard* and *Variety*, and was *Cash Box*'s number-three hit of the year. The song also collected one week at the top of the *Your Hit Parade* survey.

Lyricist Paul Francis Webster and composer Sammy Fain's "Love Is a Many-Splendored Thing" was the Academy Award–winning song for 1955. It was the theme song from the motion picture of the same name. Based on the autobiography of Han Suyin, *Love Is a Many-Splendored Thing* was a romantic film about a Eurasian female physician who fell in love with an American journalist in Hong Kong at the time of the Korean War. Most artists and record producers felt the song was too heavy for wide popularity, but The Four Aces disagreed. Their judgment was vindicated when their recording became a number-one hit on *Billboard*, *Cash Box*, and *Variety*. The song also collected two weeks at number one on *Your Hit Parade*.

"Unchained Melody" by lyricist Hy Zaret and composer Alex North was the theme for the film *Unchained*. Two versions made *Billboard*'s year-end charts: Les Baxter and his orchestra's recording and Al Hibbler's vocal version. Hibbler's disc was *Cash Box*'s number-eight hit of the year, and Baxter's was *Variety*'s number nine. The song also topped the *Your Hit Parade* survey. The most famous recording of the song is the 1965 Righteous Brothers' version, which found new life in 1990 when it was included in the soundtrack of the movie *Ghost*. Their recording of the song was inducted into the Grammy Hall of Fame in 2000.

"Something's Gotta Give" was introduced by Fred Astaire in the movie musical *Daddy Long Legs* (1955). He sang it on a hotel balcony and then danced it with his costar Leslie Caron. The song won a nomination for the Oscar for Best Song in 1955. Jean Webster had written the novel *Daddy Long Legs* in 1912, and it had been filmed twice: once in 1919 and again 1931. Since Astaire was much older than Leslie Caron, the script writers had to resolve the problem over what to do about an older man and a much younger woman being in love with each other. The problem was solved by Johnny Mercer's song "Something's Gotta Give." When the "irresistible force," Caron, met the "immovable object," Astaire, something had to give! The most popular recording of the song was by the McGuire Sisters. The song managed one week at number one on *Your Hit Parade*.

Elvis Presley exploded into the nation's consciousness in 1956. The title song from his first film, *Love Me Tender*, was a number-one hit on all the charts. In 1957, he scored again with the title song from *Jailhouse Rock* and "(Let Me Be Your) Teddy Bear" from *Loving You*, and again in 1958 with "Hard Headed Woman" from *King Creole*. Please read more about Elvis and his songs in "The Top Recording Artists of the Postwar Years" chapter.

"Moonglow and Theme from *Picnic*" was an excerpt from the film *Picnic* (1956). "Moonglow" was a 1934 song written by Will Hudson, Eddie DeLange, and Irving Mills. The song had been popularized by Benny Goodman and His Orchestra, Duke Ellington and His Orchestra, Cab Calloway and His Orchestra, and by Glen Gray and the Casa Loma Orchestra. It found new fame in the mid-fifties when it was played as the backdrop to a sultry scene from *Picnic*, when Kim Novak and William Holden danced at a town picnic. As the band played "Moonglow," it was joined by the studio soundtrack orchestra playing the film's theme song. Morris Stoloff and George Cates and their orchestras were principally responsible for popularizing this clever contrapuntal mixing of the two songs. The song was a number-one hit on *Billboard*, *Cash Box*, and *Your Hit Parade*. The McGuire Sisters had a popular vocal version of the *Picnic* theme.

"Whatever Will Be (Que Sera, Sera)" (sometimes the title is reversed) was written by Jay Livingston and Ray Evans for the 1956 Alfred Hitchcock film *The Man Who Knew Too Much*, which starred Doris Day and James Stewart. The song captured the Academy Award for Best Song of 1956. It was Livingston and Evans's third Oscar. Doris Day's recording of the song was a number-one hit on *Your Hit Parade* and became the theme song for Day's 1968–1973 TV show.

"Tammy"—from *Tammy and the Bachelor*—became a number-one hit on *Billboard*, *Cash Box*, *Variety*, and *Your Hit Parade*. Jay Livingston and Ray Evans wrote the song. The film's star, Debbie Reynolds, had the most popular recording of the song on the charts.

The Joker Is Wild starred Frank Sinatra as Joe E. Lewis, a prohibition nightclub singer. When Lewis tried to leave one speakeasy for another, the mob boss had his thugs rough him up, slashing his vocal cords. After several lean years as an alcoholic gambler, he began a comeback as a comedian. Sinatra introduced Sammy Cahn and Jimmy Van Heusen's "All the Way" in the film. The song won the Oscar for Best Song of 1957, and Sinatra's recording of the song rose to number two on the *Billboard* chart in 1958, while the song rose to the top of *Your Hit Parade*.

Pat Boone scored in 1957 with the title song for *April Love*, which was written by the Academy Award–winning team of Sammy Fain and Paul Francis Webster. Boone's recording of the song became a number-one hit on *Billboard*, and the song also topped the *Your Hit Parade* chart. "April Love" was also nominated for the Best Song Oscar.

Around the World in 80 Days was an adaptation of Jules Verne's novel about a Victorian Englishman, Phileas Fogg, who wagered his entire fortune to prove it was possible to travel around the world in that amount of time. The film's title song became a number-one hit on *Your Hit Parade*. Popular instrumental recordings were issued by Mantovani and by the song's composer, Victor Young, while Bing Crosby released a popular vocal version. The song's lyrics were written by Harold Adamson.

ACADEMY AWARD WINNERS OF THE POSTWAR YEARS

The Academy Award–winning songs that became number-one hits were "It Might As Well Be Spring" (1945), "On the Atchison, Topeka and the Santa Fe" (1946), "Buttons and Bows" (1948), "Mona Lisa" (1950), "Secret Love" (1953), "Three Coins in a Fountain" (1954), "Love Is a Many Splendored Thing" (1955), "Whatever Will Be, Will Be (Que Sera, Sera)" (1956), and "All the Way" (1957). The 1958 winner, "Gigi," is discussed under **Original Musicals for Film** below.

Other Oscar-winning Best Songs include:

"Zip-a-Dee-Doo-Dah" from *Song of the South* (1946) was chosen by RIAA and NEA for their list of *Songs of the Century*. AFI's *100 Years . . . 100 Songs* (2004) named the song as the number forty-seven greatest song ever from an American film and it was the Academy Award winner for Best Song of 1947. Uncle Remus (James Baskett) tells his tales of Brer Rabbit's Laughing Place, The Briar Patch, and the Tar Baby to help little Johnny (Bobby Driscoll) deal with his parents' separation as well as his new life on the plantation. "Zip-a-Dee-Doo-Dah" was sung in the film by Uncle Remus. The song was popularized on the pop charts in recordings by Johnny Mercer and the Pied Pipers, by Sammy Kaye and his orchestra, and by the Modernaires with Paula Kelly. It's absolutely remarkable how the lyricist, Ray Gilbert, came up with such a unique phrase as "zip-a-dee-doo-dah" that expresses so precisely the jollity and carefree spirit of the scene in the film. Composer Allie Wrubel's bright, bouncy melody also allowed the lyrics to project the idea of a wonderful, sunshiny day when "ev'rything is 'satisfactch'll.'"

Frank Loesser wrote "Baby, It's Cold Outside" to perform at parties, never thinking it would become a hit. However, in 1948, he decided to allow it to be used in the Esther Williams film *Neptune's Daughter*. It was first sung by Esther Williams and Ricardo Montalban, then reprised comically by Red Skelton and Betty Garrett. "Baby, It's Cold Outside" was the Academy Award winner for Best Song of 1949. Several recordings charted, but Johnny Mercer and Margaret Whiting's version, and Dinah Shore and Buddy Clark's version, were the most popular ones. Other versions that charted include a duet by Ella Fitzgerald and Louis Jordan, Sammy Kaye and his orchestra's rendition, and a comical country parody by Homer and Jethro with June Carter.

Johnny Mercer and Hoagy Carmichael's "In the Cool, Cool, Cool of the Evening" won the Academy Award for Best Song of 1951. The song was introduced by Bing Crosby in a duet with Jane Wyman in the movie musical *Here Comes the Groom*. The song is also known by the title "Tell 'Em I'll Be There" because the phrase is heard often in the lyrics. Crosby and Wyman's duet from the soundtrack of the film was the most popular recording of the song, but Frankie Laine and Jo Stafford's version was also successful.

Ned Washington and Dimitri Tiomkin's "High Noon (Do Not Forsake Me)" won the Oscar for Best Song in 1952. The song was sung on the soundtrack by cowboy movie star and singer Tex Ritter, the father of actor John Ritter. At preview viewings, neither the film nor its music found favor. Tiomkin asked for and received publication rights to the song, and since Ritter initially refused to record the theme song, Tiomkin talked Frankie Laine into it. The recording was released four months before the film and became such a hit that interest was heightened in the film. Once the Laine disc became successful, Tex Ritter reconsidered and recorded the song. The film, *High Noon*, turned out to be profitable and achieved classic status among westerns perhaps because of its theme song, which is subtitled "Do Not Forsake Me." AFI's *100 Years ... 100 Songs* (2004) listed "High Noon" as the No. 25 greatest song ever from an American film.

The Academy Award–winning song for 1959 was Sammy Cahn and Jimmy Van Heusen's "High Hopes" from *A Hole in the Head*. Frank Sinatra starred as Tony Manetta, an unsuccessful Miami hotel owner and an impractical widower. Eddie Hodges played his young son, Ally. Cahn and Van Heusen wrote the song as a last-minute decision when the producers wanted a song for a particularly emotional father-and-son scene in the film. Tony certainly had his flaws, but when he and his son sing "High Hopes," the audience learns of his genuine affection for Ally.

FILM VERSIONS OF BROADWAY MUSICALS FROM THE PAST

Several movie musicals were made of Broadway musicals of the postwar years. The film versions of those musicals are discussed in connection with the original Broadway production. However, there were many other film versions of Broadway musicals from earlier eras that were released during the postwar years:

Good News (1947) was based on the twenties' collegiate musical by Ray Henderson, B. G. DeSylva, and Lew Brown from 1927. The most famous songs from the musical include "Varsity Drag" and "The Best Things in Life Are Free." One new song in the movie, "Pass the Peace Pipe"—by Roger Edens, Ralph Blane, and Hugh Martin—won a nomination for the Oscar for Best Song. The film's costars were June Allyson and Peter Lawford.

The Arthur Freed 1951 film version of Jerome Kern and Oscar Hammerstein II's 1927 musical *Show Boat* was a beautiful Technicolor rendering starring Kathryn Grayson and Howard Keel. Some of the musical's most famous songs include "Make Believe," "Can't Help Lovin' Dat Man," "Ol' Man River," "You Are Love," "Bill," and "Why Do I Love You?"

The Student Prince (1954) was the film version of Sigmund Romberg's 1924 operetta *The Student Prince of Heidelberg*. Actress Ann Blyth portrayed Kathie, the barmaid, while Edmund Purdom starred as the Prince (Mario Lanza dubbed his vocals). In addition to Romberg's original songs, three new ones were added by Nicholas Brodszky and Paul Francis Webster. Particularly noteworthy was the addition of "I'll Walk With God."

Pal Joey (1957) starring Frank Sinatra and Rita Hayworth (her singing was dubbed by Jo Ann Greer) was the film version of Richard Rodgers and Larry Hart's 1940 musical. The original 1940 *Pal Joey*, based on stories by John O'Hara, was not particularly well received because of its subject matter: A wealthy woman puts up the money for Joey's nightclub, and he becomes her gigolo. The 1957 film version was sanitized, the locale was changed from Chicago to San Francisco, and the score was drawn from several Rodgers and Hart shows. Famous songs include "There's a Small Hotel," "I Could Write a Book," "The Lady Is a Tramp," "Bewitched, (Bothered, and Bewildered)," and "My Funny Valentine."

It took twenty-four years for George Gershwin's American folk opera *Porgy and Bess*, to reach movie theaters. The 1959 film version starred Sidney Poitier as the crippled Porgy who loves the sultry Bess, played by Dorothy Dandridge. Poitier's singing was dubbed by Robert McFerrin and Dandridge's vocals were dubbed by Adele Addison. Other famous performers in the film include Brock Peters, Sammy Davis, Jr., Pearl Bailey, and Diahann Carrol. Famous songs include "Summertime," "I Got Plenty o' Nuttin'," "Bess, You Is My Woman Now," "I Loves You, Porgy," and "It Ain't Necessarily So."

ORIGINAL FILM MUSICALS

In at least two exceptional cases, Hollywood produced original musicals that rivaled those produced on New York City stages.

Alan Jay Lerner and Frederick Loewe's *Gigi* became a blockbuster MGM musical that captured nine Oscars, including Best Picture and the Best Song award for the title song in 1958. The film starred Leslie Caron as Gigi, the young girl who was being groomed by her grandmother to be the mistress of Gaston (Louis Jourdan). Maurice Chevalier, as Gaston's bon vivant uncle Honore, served as the film's narrator and performed several delightful songs, including "Thank Heaven for Little Girls." Leslie Caron's singing was dubbed by Betty Wand. Louis Jourdan introduced the film's most famous song, "Gigi."

Seven Brides for Seven Brothers (1954) was a movie musical based on a story by Stephen Vincent Benet titled *The Sobbin' Women*. The film had a strong story line and a delightful original musical score by Gene DePaul and Johnny Mercer. One of the film's chief delights was the exuberant dances choreographed by Michael Kidd. Howard Keel and Jane Powell starred, but the brides and brothers were also integral characters.

BIOGRAPHICAL MOVIE MUSICALS

There was a plethora of biographical movie musicals during the postwar years. Many of them were about famous composers or lyricists, but a few also dealt with the lives of popular performing artists. Hollywood tends toward exaggeration, so most of the biographies were not exactly accurate depictions of the subject's life story. Some of the most famous ones were:

A Song to Remember (1945) was purportedly the life story of the great Polish composer Frédéric Chopin starring Cornel Wilde, but the film's chief draw was Chopin's music. José Iturbi's pianistic skills were highlighted on the soundtrack, and his recording of Chopin's *Polonaise in A-flat* charted on *Billboard*. "Till the End of Time," the top hit of 1945, was inspired by this film and used Chopin's melody from *Polonaise in A-flat* as the song's tune.

Rhapsody in Blue (1945) was a fictionalized biography of composer George Gershwin, which starred newcomer Robert Alda. Pianist Oscar Levant recorded most of the piano playing in the movie. The film featured many of Gershwin's most famous popular songs.

American Broadway pioneer Jerome Kern's film biography, *Till the Clouds Roll By*, had been filmed in 1944, prior to Kern's death in 1945. However, its release had been delayed by copyright legalities until 1946. Like other movie biographies, this film tells Kern's story built around his numerous hit songs from his Broadway musical successes. The film featured a fifteen-minute condensation of *Show Boat*, presented three songs from Kern's Princess

Theater musicals performed by June Allyson and Ray McDonald, and two Judy Garland sequences portraying Broadway star Marilyn Miller. With all that and a total of fourteen songs performed by contemporary artists, there wasn't much time left for plot.

Night and Day (1946) was Warner Brothers' idealized film biography of Cole Porter, portrayed by Cary Grant. The movie's chief purpose was to highlight more than twenty of Porter's famous songs. Audiences loved it. What plot there was in between songs took Porter from his days at Yale in the 1910s through the height of his success in the 1940s. Cary Grant even sang a few songs, but most of the famous Porter compositions were performed by guest artists. All the songs were Porter oldies, but some charted again in 1946 due to the film's popularity.

Words and Music (1948) was the Hollywood biography of the famous songwriting team of Richard Rodgers and Lorenz "Larry" Hart. The film takes the team from their first meeting, covers some of their Broadway successes, and ends with Hart's unfortunate death at age forty-eight. The soundtrack was filled with guest stars performing Rodgers and Hart songs. Tom Drake portrayed Rodgers, while Mickey Rooney played Hart.

I'll See You in My Dreams (1952) was the screen biography of lyricist Gus Kahn, starring Danny Thomas and Doris Day. The film chronicles Kahn's success and decline, with his wife supporting him through good times and bad. Although there were a few non-Kahn songs, the vast majority were his most famous lyrics to popular songs he collaborated in writing.

Stars and Stripes Forever (1952) was the screen biography of John Philip Sousa, the famous bandleader and composer of immortal marches. The film follows Sousa from the 1890s as he leaves the U.S. Marine Corps Band and forms his own band, which became incredibly successful. The primary element of the film, however, was Sousa's wondrous music.

The Fabulous Dorseys (1947) was the screen biography of the Dorsey Brothers, Tommy and Jimmy. The film was primarily an excuse to highlight their music. The brothers even played themselves, and the film featured many of the artists from their respective bands.

Jolson Sings Again (1949) began where *The Jolson Story* ended (1946; see "Anniversary Song" above) and continued the story through World War II. Larry Parks once again starred as Jolson, but all the songs were dubbed by Jolson himself. The film became the highest-grossing film of 1949.

The Great Caruso (1951) was Mario Lanza's follow-up to *The Toast of New Orleans*. It became the most successful classical music entertainment in

Hollywood history. Most of the songs were opera excerpts. "The Loveliest Night of the Year" was a hit song for Lanza in 1951.

With a Song in My Heart (1952) was the screen biography of Jane Froman, whose singing career was interrupted when she was seriously injured in a Lisbon airplane crash in 1943. The accident left her crippled and in a wheelchair, but she valiantly entertained the Allied troops during World War II. Susan Hayward starred as Ms. Froman.

The Glenn Miller Story (1954) was the screen biography of the famous big band leader starring James Stewart and June Allyson. The film follows Miller's career from its beginning to his death over the English Channel in December 1944. Many of his most famous hits were the prime ingredients of the film.

Love Me or Leave Me (1955) was the screen version of nightclub singer and *Ziegfeld Follies* star Ruth Etting's often turbulent life, starring Doris Day. In addition to Etting's famous songs, a couple of new songs were specially written for the film. The most noteworthy was "I'll Never Stop Loving You," introduced by Day.

The Benny Goodman Story (1956) was an attempt to match the success of *The Glenn Miller Story* from 1954. Although the film isn't completely historically accurate, it chronicles Goodman's life from age ten to his Carnegie Hall concert in 1938. Of course, most of Goodman's biggest hits are included on the soundtrack, and many famous musicians appear as guest stars. Steve Allen starred as Goodman, while Donna Reed played his wife.

Hans Christian Andersen (1952) was the delightful but completely fabricated biography of the famous Danish fairy tale writer, portrayed by Danny Kaye. The movie featured several of Andersen's stories and a seventeen-minute ballet performance of "The Little Mermaid." Frank Loesser's "Thumbelina" was nominated for the Oscar for Best Song.

DISNEY ANIMATED MOVIE MUSICALS

Walt Disney began his full-length animated films with *Snow White and the Seven Dwarfs* in 1938. After the phenomenal success of that film, he continued with *Pinocchio* (1940), *Fantasia* (1940), *Dumbo* (1941), and *Bambi* (1942).

In the postwar years, he continued with the following especially memorable animated movie musicals:

Based on the famous Charles Perrault fairy tale, Walt Disney's *Cinderella* (1950) was a delightful and faithful retelling of the treasured tale. The film was greatly enhanced by a marvelous musical score by Mack David, Jerry Livingston, and Al Hoffman. Among the most remembered songs were "A Dream Is a Wish Your Heart Makes" and "Bibbidi-Bobbidi-Boo," which was nominated for the Best Song Oscar.

Alice in Wonderland (1952) was Disney's version of Lewis Carroll's classic, with some additions from the book's sequel, *Alice Through the Looking Glass*. Bob Hilliard and Sammy Fain furnished the songs, including the title song and the White Rabbit's "I'm Late."

Disney's *Peter Pan* (1953) was a pleasurable retelling of J. M. Barrie's original tale of the boy who refused to grow up and his adventures with Wendy and Captain Hook. The music was an important part of the fun, with songs like Sammy Cahn and Sammy Fain's "You Can Fly," and Frank Churchill and Jack Lawrence's "Never Smile at a Crocodile." Bobby Driscoll voiced Peter. Kathryn Beaumont's voice was used for Wendy, and Hans Conried voiced Captain Hook.

Lady and the Tramp (1955) was Walt Disney's first full-length animated cartoon in CinemaScope. Lady, a cocker spaniel, meets up with a mongrel dog who calls himself the Tramp. The most remembered songs, written by Sonny Burke and Peggy Lee, include "He's a Tramp," "Siamese Cat Song," and "Bella Notte." Peggy Lee voiced Darling and the three Siamese cats. Barbara Lundy voiced Lady. Larry Roberts was the Tramp, and George Givot was Tony, the cook who sang "Bella Notte."

OTHER FAMOUS MOVIE MUSICALS OF THE POSTWAR YEARS

Fred Astaire made forty-one films. Many of them are considered classic film musicals. His movie musical heyday was in the thirties, but he still produced several gems during the immediate postwar years.

Blue Skies (1946) was a variation of *Holiday Inn* (1942) and paired Fred Astaire and Bing Crosby again as former song-and-dance partners who were competing for the same girl. All the film's songs were Irving Berlin standards, except for "You Keep Coming Back Like a Song." The title song reentered the charts in 1946. Berlin's "White Christmas," also in the film, was a number-one hit again in 1946.

Easter Parade (1948) starred Judy Garland and Fred Astaire and a cornucopia of Irving Berlin songs. One of the film's highlights was Astaire's performance of "Steppin' Out With My Baby," which innovatively combined Astaire dancing in slow motion with the rest of the dancers performing in normal motion. Another memorable number was Astaire and Garland as a couple of tramps performing "A Couple of Swells."

The Barkleys of Broadway (1949) was Fred Astaire and Ginger Rogers's first film together in a decade. They played Josh and Dinah Barkley, an argumentative, but successful, husband-and-wife dance team. The musical highlights include "They Can't Take That Away From Me," which Astaire and Rogers had performed in *Shall We Dance* (1937), and the "Shoes With Wings On" number, in which Astaire, as a shoe repairman, puts on a pair of white dance shoes after they miraculously begin to dance on their own.

Three Little Words (1950) was the screen biography of songwriters Bert Kalmar (Astaire) and Harry Ruby (Red Skelton). Many of the songwriting team's biggest hit songs were featured in the film. Please read more about this film under "Nevertheless" above.

Poster of *Royal Wedding*. (Courtesy of Photofest)

In *Royal Wedding* (1951), Fred Astaire and Jane Powell—playing a brother-and-sister dance act—perform in London at the time of Princess Elizabeth's wedding to Philip Mountbatten. One of the film's wonderfully witty numbers was Astaire dancing with a hat rack and gym equipment, but the most famous number was his dancing on the walls and ceiling of his hotel room. One of the film's best known songs was the duet sung by Powell and Astaire, "How Could You Believe Me When I Said I Love You When You Know I've Been a Liar All My Life?" The song from the film that received the nomination for the Oscar for Best Song was "Too Late Now."

The Band Wagon (1953) had been a 1931 Broadway revue. Betty Comden and Adolph Green wrote a screenplay around the songs. Among the new songs for the film version was "That's Entertainment." Producer Arthur Freed asked composer Arthur Schwartz and lyricist Howard Dietz for a new "There's No Business Like Show Business"-type number. They wrote "That's Entertainment" in half-an-hour! Another clever number from the film was "Triplets," performed by Fred Astaire, Nanette Fabray, and Jack Buchanan as children.

Funny Face (1957) starred Fred Astaire and Audrey Hepburn. Astaire plays a fashion photographer who is charmed by a hippie intellectual (Hepburn). She accompanies him to Paris to pose for a magazine layout. In Paris, romance blossoms. Gershwin music and Givenchy fashion are also stars of the film.

Gene Kelly was known for his energetic and athletic dancing style. In 1951, he was awarded a special Academy Award "in appreciation of his versatility as an actor, singer, director and dancer, and specifically for his brilliant achievements in the art of choreography on film." In 1999, the AFI named Kelly the number fifteen Greatest Male Stars of All Time.

Kelly teamed up with Frank Sinatra for three movie musicals: *Anchors Aweigh, Take Me Out to the Ball Game,* and *On the Town.*

Anchors Aweigh (1945) was a movie about two sailors on leave in Los Angeles. Gene Kelly played the girl-chasing Joe, and Frank Sinatra played the girl-shy Clarence. The film is particularly noteworthy for Gene Kelly's innovative dance with the animated Jerry the Mouse. The song "I Fall in Love Too Easily" was an Academy Award nominee for Best Song. Kelly was also the film's choreographer and received his only Oscar nomination as Best Actor for this film.

Take Me Out to the Ball Game (1949) starred Esther Williams as the manager of a baseball team she inherited, and Kelly and Sinatra as two baseball-player vaudevillians. The songs were all oldies, like the 1908 song that gave the movie its title.

On the Town (1949) began as a ballet titled *Fancy Free*, then progressed to Broadway in 1944 as a musical by composer Leonard Bernstein, with book and lyrics by Betty Comden and Adolph Green. Jerome Robbins, who had choreographed *Fancy Free*, was also the musical's choreographer. For the film version, much of Bernstein's music was dropped in favor of new songs by the MGM's Roger Edens. Gene Kelly not only starred in the film, but also choreographed and codirected with Stanley Donen. As a result of Kelly's insistence, some of the scenes were actually shot on location in New York City. In addition to Kelly, the film starred Vera-Ellen, Frank Sinatra, Betty Garrett, Ann Miller, and Jules Munshin. The most famous song, "New York, New York," came from the original Broadway musical.

In his first Hollywood film in 1942, Gene Kelly had successfully teamed with Judy Garland in *For Me and My Gal*. Again starring Kelly and Garland, *The Pirate* (1948) featured Cole Porter songs. The most famous song from the film was "Be a Clown," Porter's boisterous celebration of the joys of playing the fool. Kelly was also the film's choreographer.

Garland and Kelly starred opposite each once more in *Summer Stock* (1950), Garland's last MGM film. One of the film's notable moments was Kelly's dancing with a squeaky floorboard and a newspaper, a routine that he devised and choreographed. Otherwise, Garland's "Get Happy" is a memorable number, which was refilmed three months after the movie's completion with a slimmed-down Garland. The result was one of her best and most remembered film sequences.

Kelly's two most honored movie musicals are *An American in Paris* and *Singin' in the Rain*.

In 1951, *An American in Paris* was awarded the Best Picture Oscar. Kelly starred as a struggling American painter in Paris who falls for Leslie Caron, a young French girl. The music was George Gershwin standards. The ballet finale of the film is now considered a cinematic treasure.

Singin' in the Rain (1952) has become the most acclaimed and popular movie musical ever. *Time* magazine named it one of the All-Time 100 Movies. According to Clive Hirschhorn in *The Hollywood Musical*, it "remains an undoubted masterpiece and the finest, most durable musical ever to have come out of Hollywood." The musical score is delightful, the comedy is cute and funny, and the choreography and dancing are spectacular. Almost all of the songs were Arthur Freed and Nacio Herb Brown golden oldies,

Gene Kelly as Don Lockwood in *Singin' in the Rain*. (Courtesy of
Photofest)

but they were never better. Just a few of the film's highlights include Gene
Kelly's unforgettable romp in the rain singing the title song; Kelly, Donald
O'Connor, and Debbie Reynolds's energetic singing and dancing of "Good
Mornin';" and O'Connor's incredible singing, dancing, and clowning
performance of "Make 'em Laugh," which was the No. 49 greatest song
from an American film according to the AFI's *100 Years . . . 100 Songs*
(2004).

Bing Crosby was movie magic. Put his name on the marquee and the
film generally made big bucks. He was a busy man during this era with his
recordings, business interests, and trips to the horse tracks and golf
courses. But he found time to film several noteworthy movie musicals.

Jimmy Van Heusen composed many of the songs for these Crosby movie
musicals to lyrics by either Johnny Burke or Sammy Cahn.

In *The Bells of St. Mary's* (1945), Crosby reprised the Father O'Malley role
he made so popular in *Going My Way* (1944). Ingrid Bergman costarred as

Sister Benedict. Crosby's performance earned him an Oscar nomination for Best Actor, the first time a person was nominated for playing the same character in two different films (he had been nominated for and won the Oscar for Best Actor in *Going My Way*). The film was also the first sequel to win a nomination for the Best Picture Oscar.

Road to Utopia (1946) is one of the classic Crosby, Bob Hope, and Dorothy Lamour "road" films. It spawned a number-one hit, "Personality." Please read more about this film and the song in the **Number One Hits from Hollywood Films** section, above. The fifth in the "road" series, *Road to Rio* (1948), was another typical Crosby, Hope, and Lamour romp. The most famous song from its score was "But Beautiful." *Road to Bali* (1953) had Crosby and Hope as a couple of vaudevillians on the run, this time ending up in the South Seas where they meet Lamour. Even though the same old gags were wearing thin, the film was still successful.

For more on *Here Comes the Groom* (1951) see "In the Cool, Cool, Cool of the Evening" in the **Academy Award Winners of the Postwar Years** section, above.

White Christmas became the top money-making film of 1954, with music by Irving Berlin and starring Bing Crosby, Danny Kaye, Rosemary Clooney, and Vera-Ellen. Two particularly noteworthy new songs from the musical score were "Count Your Blessings (Instead of Sheep)" and "Sisters." Crosby and Clooney performed "Count Your Blessings," while "Sisters" was first performed by Clooney and Vera-Ellen and then by Crosby and Kaye dressed in drag and miming a recording by the girls.

High Society (1956) was a musical remake of *The Philadelphia Story* (1940), with music by Cole Porter, starring Crosby, Grace Kelly, Frank Sinatra, and Celeste Holm. Another key character in the film was Louis Armstrong, who provided some humor and his delightful jazz. The song, "True Love," which was nominated for the Oscar for Best Song, was a duet sung by Crosby and Kelly as they reminisce about their time together. Their recording from the soundtrack became a million-seller.

7

The Best of Postwar Broadway

The 1930s are often called the heyday of musical theater, but the postwar years produced their share of hit musicals as well.

In Richard Rodgers's autobiography, *Musical Stages*, he said, there are "two kinds of music—one too popular to be good, the other too good to be popular. Why should we assume that goodness and popularity can't coexist?" Musicals were not the hit-making medium they had been in previous eras. There are, however, many wonderful songs from the era's stage musicals that have become well-known standards.

At its best, dramatic music fits into the context from which it came. In a Broadway musical, ideally, a song's music and lyrics should help set the mood, define the character of the performer, and advance the plot. The more a song fulfills those criteria, however, the less it can be removed from its dramatic context and achieve popularity as a "stand-alone song." There are, unfortunately, songs that could easily be omitted without affecting the story, but there are many wonderful songs that deserve attention that were essential to the plot and have not become well known to the general public.

The mid-forties on Broadway marked the transition from musical comedy to a more serious dramatic musical. That transition actually started in 1943 with Richard Rodgers and Oscar Hammerstein II's *Oklahoma!*

Rodgers had partnered with Lorenz "Larry" Hart for many years, but when Rodgers proposed this project, Hart wasn't interested. So, Rodgers teamed with Hammerstein for the first time, and the result was the block-buster musical *Oklahoma!*, which was based on Lynn Riggs's play *Green Grow the Lilacs*. *Oklahoma!* quickly became one of the most important productions in Broadway theater history: an intelligent, credible plot (although today it seems a bit superficial and innocent), enhanced by an impressive musical score that does not interrupt the action. It also used ballet to help develop the plot.

The major contribution of Broadway in 1945 was Richard Rodgers and Oscar Hammerstein II's transformation of Hungarian playwright Ferenc Molnar's play *Liliom* into the highly successful Broadway musical *Carousel*. Rodgers and Hammerstein changed the locale from Budapest to a New England fishing village in 1873. When asked what his favorite of all his musicals was, Richard Rodgers selected *Carousel*.

Carousel
Music: Richard Rodgers; Lyrics & Book: Oscar Hammerstein II
Premiered 1945; ran 890 performances

- Major Cast: John Raitt (Billy Bigelow), Jan Clayton (Julie Jordan), Christine Johnson (Nettie Fowler)
- Key Songs: "If I Loved You," "June Is Bustin' Out All Over," "You'll Never Walk Alone"

The musical's plot concerns a New England carnival barker, Billy, who falls in love with a factory girl, Julie. Once they marry, Billy proves to be an unreliable husband, but even though he is abusive, Julie stands by him. When he discovers she is pregnant, the unemployed Billy tries to provide for his unborn child by joining an unsavory pal in an attempted robbery. Billy dies when the scheme goes awry. Years later a kindly heavenly friend gives Billy a chance to redeem himself. He is allowed to return to earth for one day to help his wife and daughter get on with their lives.

One of the key songs was "If I Loved You," which comes soon after Julie and Billy meet. They are attracted to each other but have difficulty expressing their feelings. The dialogue sets the following song up perfectly:

> *Billy:* But you wouldn't marry a rough guy like me—that is—uh—
>   if you loved me?
> *Julie:* Yes, I would—if I loved you.

Their romance flourishes and soon Julie and Billy are married. "If I Loved You" was a number-one hit on *Your Hit Parade* in 1945. The most popular recording of the song was by Perry Como.

When Billy learns Julie is pregnant, he is overjoyed, but the prospect of a penniless future frightens him. He dies when he accidentally falls on his own knife during a failed robbery attempt. Overwhelmed with grief, Julie is comforted by her cousin, Nettie, with the song "You'll Never Walk Alone." In the musical's finale, the entire ensemble reprises "You'll Never Walk Alone" as Billy climbs a great stairway to heaven. Recordings by Frank Sinatra and by Judy Garland helped popularize "You'll Never Walk Alone" beyond the Broadway stage. Roy Hamilton charted with it in 1954.

Other memorable numbers from the score include "Soliloquy," when Julie tells Billy she is pregnant, he contemplates fatherhood, and "June Is Bustin' Out All Over," when the community is excited about the arrival of summer. The original Broadway cast album of *Carousel* was inducted into the Grammy Hall of Fame in 1998. The film version was released in 1956 starring Gordon MacRae and Shirley Jones.

Ethel Merman was a smash hit in Irving Berlin's *Annie Get Your Gun*, the Broadway musical about legendary sharpshooter Annie Oakley. Lyricist Dorothy Fields, who instigated the idea, intended to write the lyrics for this musical with composer Jerome Kern, but he died before the project began. The show's producers, Rodgers and Hammerstein (the only musical they produced that was not their own), signed Irving Berlin to write both words and music. The show became the second book musical to exceed the magical 1,000-performance figure on Broadway (*Oklahoma!* had been the first).

Irving Berlin's most recent Broadway project had been *This Is the Army*, the all-soldier revue in 1942. Most people probably thought he was past his prime. Not only was he alive and well, he wrote an exceptional score. Neither Berlin nor anyone else had ever written a Broadway musical score with more hit songs than *Annie Get Your Gun*.

Annie Get Your Gun
Music & Lyrics: Irving Berlin; Book: Herbert & Dorothy Fields
Premiered 1946; ran 1,147 performances

- Major Cast: Ethel Merman (Annie Oakley), Ray Middleton (Frank Butler)
- Key Songs: "Doin' What Comes Natur'lly," "The Girl That I Marry," "There's No Business Like Show Business," "They Say It's Wonderful," "I Got the Sun in the Morning," "Anything You Can Do"

Ethel Merman as Annie Oakley. (Courtesy of Photofest)

Annie Get Your Gun is about country hick Annie Oakley and her show-business career as a rifle sharpshooter. When she becomes enamored with Frank Butler, the star of Colonel Buffalo Bill's Wild West Show, she joins the show to be near him. Their rivalry keeps them apart until Annie finally realizes the only way to get her man is to let him win in a shooting contest.

When the unrefined, uneducated Annie is introduced, she explains that she thinks life should be natural. "Doin' What Comes Natur'lly" was popularized on the pop charts in recordings by Freddy Martin and His Orchestra, by Dinah Shore, and by Jimmy Dorsey and His Orchestra with vocalist Dee Parker.

When the audience meets the handsome Frank, in "The Girl That I Marry," he explains that he is only attracted to sweet and demure women, certainly not Annie's type. Frank Sinatra and singer Eddy Howard and His Orchestra had popular recordings of the song.

Buffalo Bill and Charlie convince Frank that a female partner would be good for business. They approach Annie with the idea and try to convince her how great show business is in "There's No Business Like Show Business." Since its introduction, "There's No Business Like Show Business" has become one of the unofficial anthems of the theater, but it was almost cut from the show. Berlin demonstrated several songs including "There's No Business Like Show Business" to the producers Rodgers and Hammerstein. In an early rehearsal, Rodgers noticed the song wasn't included. When he questioned Berlin about it, he told Rodgers he had dropped it. The reason for this is that when Berlin had demonstrated it earlier, he'd thought that the expression on Rodgers's face meant Rodgers didn't like it. Rodgers quickly assured Berlin that he loved the song and that he had only been concentrating on where it should go in the musical. So, thankfully, the song was reinstated. Bing Crosby, the Andrews Sisters, and Dick Haymes combined on a recording for a chart single of the song in 1947.

Frank asks Annie if she's ever loved anyone. Annie admits she hasn't, but she'd like to know if the things people have told her about love are true ("They Say It's Wonderful"). In 1946, the song climbed to number one on *Your Hit Parade*. Frank Sinatra's disc was the most popular recording, but Perry Como's recording, Andy Russell's disc, Bing Crosby's recording, and Ethel Merman and Ray Middleton's duet were also popular.

Later in the production, it becomes apparent that Pawnee Bill and Buffalo Bill's shows must merge to survive. Annie agrees to sell all her medals to pay for the merger. She explains she doesn't need the medals because she has "the sun in the morning and the moon at night." "I Got the Sun in the Morning" was popularized on the pop charts by Les Brown and His Orchestra, with vocalist Doris Day, and by Artie Shaw and His Orchestra, with vocalist Mel Torme.

Another feud between the two causes the merger to be called off and a shooting match is set to prove which one is the better shot. "Anything You Can Do" was the comic gem of a challenge song devised by Berlin for the culmination of their feud. Although it was not terrifically popular on the charts, the song has become a standard from the musical.

The original Broadway cast album of *Annie Get Your Gun* was inducted into the Grammy Hall of Fame in 1998.

The film version of the musical, MGM's top money-making musical of the year, was released in 1950, starring Betty Hutton and Howard Keel. The film adhered closely to the Broadway version except for the omission of two songs.

The idea for *Finian's Rainbow* came from lyricist E. Y. Harburg, who wanted to satirize the U.S. economic system that required the storage of gold reserves at Fort Knox. That spawned thoughts of leprechauns and their crock of gold that grants the finder three wishes. *Finian's Rainbow* also was the first musical to tackle the subject of racism, which was quite a risky thing to do in 1947.

Finian's Rainbow

Music: Burton Lane; Lyrics: E. Y. Harburg; Book: E. Y. Harburg & Fred Saidy

Premiered 1947; ran 725 performances

- Major Cast: Ella Logan (Sharon McLonergan), Albert Sharpe (Finian McLongergan), Donald Richards (Woody Mahoney), David Wayne (Og)
- Key Songs: "How Are Things in Glocca Morra?," "Old Devil Moon"

The plot concerns an Irish immigrant, Finian, who believes the United States became rich by planting gold at Fort Knox. He thinks he could get rich by stealing a crock of gold from the leprechauns and burying it there. Og, a leprechaun, follows Finian and his daughter, Sharon, to Rainbow Valley in the mythical state of Missitucky to retrieve the stolen crock of gold. Sharon falls for Woody, a union organizer, while Og falls for every woman he meets. In one of the three wishes granted by the crock, a bigoted Southern senator is turned black so he can learn firsthand about racial discrimination. Stanley Green, in *Encyclopedia of the Musical Theatre*, says, "the main philosophical point: people find riches not in gold but in trusting one another."

Shortly after Finian and Sharon arrive in the United States, the song of a bird, "the same skylark music we have back in Ireland," prompts Sharon's wistful reminiscence of her Irish home ("How Are Things in Glocca Morra?"). Chart recordings of the song were issued by Buddy Clark; by Martha Tilton; by Tommy Dorsey and His Orchestra, with vocalist Stuart Foster; and by Dick Haymes.

Sharon and Woody fall for each other and blame their mutual attraction on the "Old Devil Moon." The song was popularized on the pop charts in recordings by Margaret Whiting and by Gene Krupa and His Orchestra, with vocalist Carolyn Grey.

Other famous songs from the musical include "If This Isn't Love," sung by Sharon and Woody when they realize they are actually in love; "Look to the Rainbow," sung by Sharon as she tells Woody about a legend her father thought up; and "When I'm Not Near the Girl I Love (I Love the Girl I'm Near)," a hilarious song Og sings about his romantic fickleness.

The 1968 film version of the musical starred Fred Astaire as Finian, Petula Clark as Finian's daughter Sharon, and Tommy Steele as the leprechaun, Og. In the original, Finian did not sing or dance, but Astaire was given songs to sing and feature his dancing.

Brigadoon was Alan Jay Lerner and Frederick Loewe's third Broadway production, but their first hit musical. The production is a fantasy about an enchanted Scottish town. During the musical, the town's beloved schoolmaster explains how the enchantment occurred. He tells the two American hunters who stumble into the village that two hundred years ago the Highlands of Scotland were plagued with witches who were leading the folk away from God. The village's elderly minister feared for his flock's fate after his death, so he asked God to make the village and its people vanish into the Highland mist, to reappear for only one day every one hundred years, not long enough to be touched by the outside world. If any resident of Brigadoon should leave its borders, the enchantment would be broken and the town would vanish forever. A stranger may come to live there only if that person truly loves someone in Brigadoon.

Brigadoon
Music: Frederick Loewe; Lyrics & Book: Alan Jay Lerner
Premiered 1947; ran for 581 performances

- Major Cast: David Brooks (Tommy Albright), Marion Bell (Fiona MacLaren), George Keane (Jeff Douglas)
- Key Song: "Almost Like Being in Love"

The two lost New York hunters, Tommy and Jeff, discover Brigadoon when it materializes in the twentieth century. Tommy soon falls for one of the village girls, Fiona. In "Almost Like Being in Love," Tommy tells Jeff he has never felt better in his life. Popular recordings of the song by Frank Sinatra, by Mildred Bailey, and by Mary Martin helped popularize "Almost Like Being in Love" beyond the Broadway stage.

Jeff finally convinces Tommy to return home with him. Fiona and her village vanish into the mist for another hundred years. Months later, in a New

York City bar, Tommy calls off an impending marriage and heads back to Scotland. After a futile search for Brigadoon, just as they are leaving, they hear the strains of the title song in the distance. Suddenly, the sleepy old school-master appears in the mist saying, "Ye mus' really love her! Ye woke me up! Come, lad." He adds that when you love someone deeply, anything is possible, even miracles. As Tommy and the wise schoolmaster head for the village, Fiona comes to meet them and Brigadoon once again fades into the mist.

Other well-known songs from the musical's score include "Brigadoon," sung by distant voices as the eighteenth-century Scottish village appears out of the mist; "The Heather on the Hill," when Tommy accompanies Fiona to collect heather for her sister's wedding; "Come to Me, Bend to Me," with Charlie calling his bride, but she tells him it is bad luck for him to see her before the ceremony; and "There But For You Go I," when Tommy tells Fiona that after one short day, he feels he cannot live without her for fear of joining the other lonely men he sees in life.

The 1954 film version starred Gene Kelly, Van Johnson, and Cyd Charisse (her vocals were dubbed by Carole Richards).

Cole Porter's sophisticated lyrics and beautiful melodies were never better than those he wrote for *Kiss Me, Kate*. He mixed Elizabethan dialogue and American slang to create a unique and colorful production. The musical set Shakespeare's *Taming of the Shrew* to music. The show was inspired by the real-life acting partnership of husband and wife Alfred Lunt and Lynn Fontanne, who fought their way through a production of *Taming of the Shrew*. A play-within-a-play unfolds, where each of the main cast member's onstage performance is complicated by what is happening in their offstage life.

Kiss Me, Kate
Music & Lyrics: Cole Porter; Book: Bella & Sam Spewack
Premiered 1948; ran 1,070 performances

- Major Cast: Alfred Drake (Fred Graham), Patricia Morison (Lilli Vanessi), Harold Lang (Bill Calhoun), Lisa Kirk (Lois Lane), Annabelle Hill (Hattie)
- Key Songs: "Another Op'nin', Another Show," "So in Love," "Brush Up Your Shakespeare"

The musical's plot revolves around an egotistical actor, Fred, who is reunited with his ex-wife, Lilli, in the leading roles of Petruchio and Kate in

Taming of the Shrew. Throughout the production, they are mirror images of their onstage characters who bicker endlessly, but Fred and Lilli obviously still love each other. Meanwhile, due to mistaken identity, two gangsters harass Fred for an unpaid gambling debt. Also, two former cabaret performers cast in the play, Lois and Bill, attempt to keep their romance alive.

The musical opens as Hattie, the maid, introduces "Another Op'nin', Another Show." To seasoned performers, this particular performance was just another job that they hoped would make their future brighter. They had rehearsed for weeks and the show didn't seem to be coming together, but seemingly, abruptly, opening night had arrived. Excited again, the actors prepare for the curtain to rise. The song, along with Irving Berlin's "There's No Business Like Show Business," has become the best-known ode to show business and the theater.

When Lilli mistakenly receives flowers sent by Fred to Lois, her love for Fred is rekindled ("So in Love"). The song was popularized on the pop charts by Patti Page, by Gordon MacRae, and by Dinah Shore.

One of the era's best theater comedy songs was performed by the two gangsters who are hounding Fred about an IOU that was really Bill's gambling debt. Hanging around the theater, they have gotten caught up in the business and pay tribute to Shakespeare in "Brush Up Your Shakespeare."

Other familiar songs from the score include "Why Can't You Behave?" when Lois begs Bill to stop gambling; "Wunderbar," as Fred and Lilli reminisce nostalgically about their former performances together and their previous warm feelings for each other in the exaggerated sentiments of a Viennese waltz; "Too Darn Hot," during an intermission, as several of the cast relax outside the theater and complain about the hot weather; and "Always True to You in My Fashion," when Lois explains her different view of romantic fidelity to Bill.

Kiss Me, Kate won the first Tony Award for Best Musical. Cole Porter won the Tony for Best Composer, and Bella and Sam Spewack were honored as Best Librettist for *Kiss Me, Kate.*

The film version was released in 1953 starring Kathryn Grayson and Howard Keel. The movie was, according to Clive Hirschhorn, "a literate, witty, and thoroughly beguiling screen adaptation," except for the interpolation of Porter songs like "From This Moment On."

Several Porter songs were featured in the 2004 film *De-Lovely,* including "So in Love," which was performed on the soundtrack by Lara Fabian and Mario Frangoulis.

The Antoinette Perry Awards (the Tonys) for "distinguished achievement in the theater" began honoring musicals and performances of the year in 1949. The New York theater season runs from April 1 to March 31, so the award often comes in the year after a musical opened.

The next Rodgers and Hammerstein musical success, *South Pacific*, debuted in 1949 and ultimately ran even longer than *Oklahoma!* Hammerstein and Joshua Logan adapted two short stories from James A. Michener's Pulitzer prize–winning novel, *Tales of the South Pacific*, for the musical's plot: "Fo' Dolla," a short story that dealt with a South Seas native named Bloody Mary whose sixteen-year-old daughter, Liat, has a brief but intense affair with an American naval officer, and "Our Heroine," which dealt with the unlikely romance between a sophisticated, middle-aged French planter and a naive Navy nurse from Little Rock, Arkansas. The common element of both stories is the power of love to break down prejudice. The accepted "rules" of the musical theater maintained that if the main love story was serious, the secondary romance should provide comic relief. But in *South Pacific*, both were serious. The comic element was provided by an affable wheeler-dealer named Luther Billis.

An integral part of the musical was World War II, which was still very much in the minds of Americans.

South Pacific
Music: Richard Rodgers; Lyrics: Oscar Hammerstein II; Book: Hammerstein & Joshua Logan
Premiered 1949; ran 1,925 performances

- Major Cast: Mary Martin (Nellie Forbush), Ezio Pinza (Emile de Becque), William Tabbert (Lt. Joe Cable), Juanita Hall (Bloody Mary), Betta St. John (Liat)
- Key Songs: "Some Enchanted Evening," "Bali Ha'i," "A Wonderful Guy," "Younger Than Springtime," "You've Got to Be Carefully Taught"

On a South Pacific island during World War II, a middle-aged French plantation owner, Emile, falls in love with a U.S. Navy nurse. In "Some Enchanted Evening," Emile sings about the first time he saw Nellie and, for some inexplicable reason, decided to make her his wife. Perry Como's recording of the song was a number-one hit on *Billboard*, *Variety*, and *Your Hit Parade*. By September 1951, "Some Enchanted Evening" had sold over 2.5 million recordings.

When Lieutenant Cable arrives on the island, Bloody Mary immediately sees him as a prospective husband for her lovely daughter, Liat. Mary tries to stimulate Cable's interest in the forbidden island where the planters have taken their women ("Bali Ha'i"). The song was popularized on the pop charts in recordings by Perry Como, by Paul Weston and His Orchestra, by Bing Crosby, by Peggy Lee, and by Frank Sinatra.

Considering the differences in their age and background, Nellie decides that marrying Emile might be a mistake, but Emile convinces her that her fears are groundless. In "A Wonderful Guy," she celebrates her love for him. On the pop charts, the song was popularized in recordings by Margaret Whiting, by Fran Warren, and by Dinah Shore.

When Cable finally goes to Bali Ha'i, Bloody Mary introduces him to Liat. Though they speak different languages, they quickly fall in love. Cable sings "Younger than Springtime" to Liat. Gordon MacRae helped popularized this song beyond the Broadway stage with his recording.

The romances progress well until Nellie discovers that Emile has mixed-race children from an earlier relationship, and Cable refuses to marry Liat due to her race. Dejected and with nothing to lose, Emile and Cable agree to go on a dangerous mission, which Cable doesn't survive. Emile returns to the now understanding Nellie and his children.

Although not pop chart material, "You've Got to Be Carefully Taught" was a key song in the musical. Sung by Cable, the song crystallizes the musical's overall theme: people have to be taught to hate and fear others unlike themselves.

Other well-known songs from the score include "A Cockeyed Optimist," when Nellie introduces herself to Emile and the audience; "Bloody Mary," as American Seabees and Marines praise Bloody Mary, a Tonkinese con woman; "There Is Nothin' Like a Dame," about how the sailors think they have everything on the island they could possibly want except female companionship; "I'm Gonna Wash That Man Right Outta My Hair," when, considering the differences in their ages and backgrounds, Nellie decides that marrying Emile would be a mistake; and "This Nearly Was Mine," after Emile loses Nellie and he laments the loss of the love that was almost his.

At the 1950 Tony Awards, *South Pacific* won the award for Best Musical, Mary Martin for Best Actress in a Musical, Ezio Pinza for Best Actor in a Musical, Richard Rodgers for Best Composer, Oscar Hammerstein II for Best Librettist, and Joshua Logan was honored as Best Director. The musical also won a Pulitzer Prize for Drama, the third musical to be so honored.

The *South Pacific* original cast album, which reigned as the number-one LP for an astonishing sixty-nine weeks, was inducted into the Grammy Hall of Fame in 1987, and RIAA and NEA named it one of their *Songs of the Century.*

The 1958 screen version starred Rossano Brazzi and Mitzi Gaynor. Brazzi's vocals were dubbed by Giorgio Tozzi. The film's director, Joshua Logan, decided to use several newly developed colored filters in the filming, which caused the lush tropical settings to appear unnatural. The only original Broadway cast member in the film was Juanita Hall (Bloody Mary), but Richard Rodgers insisted Muriel Smith, who had played the role in London, dub her singing. "My Girl Back Home" was an added song for Lt. Cable in the film version.

Frank Loesser wrote both the music and lyrics for *Guys and Dolls*, a musical based on Damon Runyon's short story "The Idyll of Miss Sarah Brown." The musical also borrows characters and plot elements from other Runyon stories.

Guys and Dolls
Music & Lyrics: Frank Loesser; Book: Abe Burrows & Jo Swerling
Premiered 1950; ran 1,200 performances

- Major Cast: Robert Alda (Sky Masterson), Vivian Blaine (Miss Adelaide), Sam Levene (Nathan Detroit), Isabel Bigley (Miss Sarah Brown)
- Key Songs: "A Bushel and a Peck," "If I Were a Bell," "Luck Be a Lady"

The musical's plot revolves around the activities of several Times Square petty criminals and professional gamblers. Nathan runs "the oldest established crap game in New York," despite constant nagging from his fourteen-year-intended, Miss Adelaide, a nightclub singer. When several high rollers hit town, Nathan is pressured to find a place to hold his crap game, but he can't raise the $1,000 deposit required for the one place he finds.

At the Hot Box, Adelaide and the chorus girls perform a musical number, "A Bushel and a Peck." This song is not integral to the plot. Regardless, as recorded in a duet by Perry Como and Betty Hutton, it was a number-one hit in 1950 on *Your Hit Parade*.

Trying to raise the money, Nathan bets gambler Sky Masterson $1,000 if he can pick a "doll" who will go to Havana with him. When Sky accepts the bet, Nathan picks the Salvation Army "doll," Sarah Brown. Surprisingly, Sky manages to get Sarah to agree to the date, and over the course of their date in Cuba, he manages to break down Sarah's social inhibitions, and they begin to fall in love. When Sarah gets a bit tipsy on a drink she thinks is milk, she proclaims her love for Sky in a song that likens her feelings to a ringing bell, "If I Were a Bell." Frankie Laine's recording of the song charted in 1950.

Sky intends to make good on his promise to Sarah. At a crap game held in the sewer, Sky tries to talk the gamblers into attending the mission meeting, but no one listens. In desperation, he proposes another bet: if he loses, he will pay each gambler $1,000. If he wins, all the gamblers must show up at the mission at midnight. All the gamblers quickly accept the bet. As Sky prepares to throw the dice, he asks Lady Luck for help, and he wins the bet. "Luck Be a Lady" was named the number forty-two greatest song from an American film in AFI's *100 Years ... 100 Songs* (2004), even though it originated on Broadway.

Other important songs from the score include "Fugue for Tinhorns," when three gamblers read the daily horse race scratch sheet and trade tips about different horses; "The Oldest Established," about the frustration the gamblers feel by the potential loss of lots of money if the crap game can't continue; "I'll Know," with Sky accusing Sarah of hating all men, but she assures him she'll know when the right man comes along; "Adelaide's Lament," when Adelaide finds out Nathan is still running his crap game and she gets one of her chronic sneezing attacks, which are psychosomatic, caused by her frustration at being engaged for fourteen years; "Guys and Dolls," with a couple of the gamblers observing that both men and women have a weakness for the opposite sex; "I've Never Been in Love Before," after Sky and Sarah return from their Cuban trip and they discuss their newfound love; and "Sit Down, You're Rockin' the Boat," sung at a mission meeting, when Nicely-Nicely testifies about a dream he had about being on a boat to heaven.

Robert Alda won the Tony Award in 1951 for Best Actor in a Musical for his role as Sky Masterson. The film version of the musical was released in

1955. Marlon Brando was cast as Sky, Frank Sinatra as Nathan, Jean Simmons as Sarah Brown, and Vivian Blaine repeated her role as Adelaide from the original Broadway production. Frank Loesser wrote the song "Adelaide" especially for Sinatra to sing in the film version. "A Bushel and a Peck" and "I've Never Been in Love Before" were replaced by "Pet Me Poppa" and "A Woman in Love."

Once Broadway star Gertrude Lawrence read Margaret Landon's novel *Anna and the King of Siam* and saw the 1946 film version, which starred Irene Dunne and Rex Harrison, she was convinced it would make a wonderful musical. She first presented the idea to Cole Porter and then approached Richard Rodgers and Oscar Hammerstein II. Even though Rodgers and Hammerstein were familiar with Lawrence's vocal limitations (a narrow range and a tendency to sing flat), they agreed to write and produce the musical, giving it the title "The King and I."

Rodgers didn't try to create authentic Siamese music. He did not believe Western audiences would appreciate or relate to those sounds. His music was American music with Siamese influences.

The King and I
Music: Richard Rodgers; Lyrics & Book: Oscar Hammerstein II
Premiered 1951; ran 1,246 performances

- Major Cast: Gertrude Lawrence (Anna Leonowens), Yul Brynner (The King), Doretta Morrow (Tuptim), Larry Douglas (Lun Tha)
- Key Songs: "Getting to Know You," "Hello, Young Lovers," "We Kiss in a Shadow"

Set in the 1860s, the plot concerns a young English widow, Anna Leonowens, who travels to Siam (Thailand) to teach English to the royal children of a semibarbaric monarch, King Mongkut. She finds Siamese customs to be quite different from English ones, which places her often in conflict with the king. She soon falls in love with her students, and though Anna and the king disagree on many things, they eventually learn to trust and admire each other. After one particular disagreement, she prepares to leave Siam, but when she hears of the king's imminent death, she decides to remain to help his son rule.

Gertrude Lawrence suggested to Rodgers the need for a song within the first act that included the children. For the music, Rodgers resurrected the melody he had originally planned for Lt. Cable to sing to Liat in *South Pacific* but had discarded in favor of "Younger Than Springtime." Hammerstein penned a charming lyric about Anna's pleasure in learning things about the Siamese people, which he appropriately titled "Getting to Know You."

Just prior to the song "Hello, Young Lovers," Lady Thiang, the king's head wife, explains to Anna that Tuptim, the king's new Burmese wife, is in love with a young man from her own country, but they will never be able to see each other again. Anna feels deep sympathy toward them. "Hello, Young Lovers" was one of the most popular songs from the score on the charts. Perry Como's recording was the most liked version on the market.

Tuptim and her lover, Lun Tha, meet secretly in the darkness of a palace garden ("We Kiss in a Shadow"). Frank Sinatra's version of the song popularized it beyond the Broadway stage.

Many of the musical's songs fit into the plot perfectly and, although they might not be hit material, were wonderfully crafted songs that furthered the plot, including "I Whistle a Happy Tune," as Anna and her son arrive in Siam and she tries to allay her own fears and those of her son by whistling; "Something Wonderful," when the king's head wife tries to help Anna understand the king; "I Have Dreamed," with Tuptim and her lover, Lun Tha, making plans to run away together; "The Small House of Uncle Thomas," for some visitors from England who are entertained with a ball and a ballet based on Harriet Beecher Stowe's classic Uncle Tom's Cabin; and "Shall We Dance?" when Anna tries to teach the king European social dancing.

The King and I won the Tony Award for Best Musical in 1952. Gertrude Lawrence, who died in 1952 during the run of the show, was awarded the Tony for Best Actress in a Musical. Richard Rodgers claimed the prize for Best Composer, while Oscar Hammerstein II won for Best Librettist. RIAA and NEA named the original cast album one of their *Songs of the Century*.

The film version of *The King and I* was released in 1956 starring Deborah Kerr as Anna and Yul Brynner again as the king, with Rita Moreno playing Tuptim. Kerr's vocals were dubbed by Marni Nixon. Four numbers were excised for the movie version.

Pygmalion, the king of Cyprus in Greek mythology, thought womankind was so inferior he resolved to never marry. However, after sculpting the statue of Galatea, he fell in love with his creation. In 1913, Irish playwright George Bernard Shaw adapted that myth to modern-day England. The primary idea of Shaw's story was that class distinction would crumble if all Englishmen would learn to speak the language properly. That idea is as relevant today as ever. Right or wrong, colloquialisms and racial jargon define people and relegate them to specific social strata.

In 1956, Alan Jay Lerner and Frederick Loewe adapted Shaw's play *Pygmalion* into *My Fair Lady*, the most esteemed musical of the fifties and one of the most celebrated productions in Broadway's illustrious history. At the end of the opening night's performance, according to Julie M. Fenster in *The Hottest Tickets in Broadway History*, "in a night like no other, they jumped up as one at the final curtain, hollering all the while. Even that wasn't enough. They rushed into the aisles toward the stage, not wanting to leave *My Fair Lady* or ever let it get away" (http://www.americanheritage.com/entertainment/articles/).

My Fair Lady
Music: Frederick Loewe; Lyrics & Book: Alan Jay Lerner
Premiered 1956; ran 2,717 performances

- Major Cast: Rex Harrison (Henry Higgins), Julie Andrews (Eliza Doolittle), Stanley Holloway (Alfred P. Doolittle), Robert Coote (Colonel Pickering), Michael King (Freddy Eynsford-Hill)
- Key Songs: "I Could Have Danced All Night," "On the Street Where You Live"

My Fair Lady is about Professor Higgins, who bets his colleague, Col. Pickering, that he can transform an unrefined flower girl into an aristocratic Victorian lady by merely changing her speech. After they hear Eliza Doolittle's Cockney babblings outside London's Covent Garden, Higgins selects her for the experiment. With trepidation, Eliza eventually agrees to become his test case. After many grueling days of elocution lessons, Eliza learns to speak properly. Higgins decides to introduce her to his mother's snobbish guests at the Ascot Race. When the impeccably dressed Eliza is presented at the Ascot Race, her unladylike cheering and crass language soon reveal her unrefined origins. Regardless, a young aristocrat, Freddy Eynsford-Hill, finds Eliza irresistible and follows her home, where he sings "On the Street Where You Live." Rarely has such a beautiful song been introduced in a musical by such an insignificant character. "On the Street Where You Live" is the musical's only romantic ballad and the show's most popular song on the pop charts. Recordings by Vic Damone and by Eddie Fisher helped popularize it nationwide in 1956, while Andy Williams revived it successfully in 1964.

Just as Higgins and Pickering feel the experiment is failing, Eliza triumphantly succeeds by passing herself off as a lady at the Embassy Ball. After they celebrate their success, it is late at night, and the housekeeper urges Eliza to go to bed, but she is too exhilarated to sleep. She sings "I Could Have Danced All Night." It became one of the most popular songs beyond the musical. It was popularized on the pop charts in a recording by Sylvia Syms. After Eliza's success, Higgins takes all the credit and ignores her efforts. Eliza angrily leaves him. It is then that Higgins finally realizes he has become attached to her (he really doesn't admit love) and doesn't want to live without her.

Although many of the musical's songs were not pop chart material, they helped establish characters and fit perfectly into the plot. Other well-known songs from the score include "Wouldn't It Be Loverly?" which is Eliza's introductory song and aptly evidences her Cockney speech patterns that interest Higgins; "With a Little Bit of Luck," sung by Eliza's squalid father, Alfred Doolittle, to explain his slovenly philosophy of life; "The Rain in Spain," a song that begins as an elocution lesson for Eliza and ends with a celebration of her success; "Get Me to the Church on Time," which Eliza's father, now famous for his earthy philosophy, uses to announce his decision that it is time he married the woman he has been living with for years, though he still wants one last night on the town; and "I've Grown Accustomed to Her Face," with Higgins finally realizing he has grown so attached to Eliza, he would have a difficult time getting along without her.

Tony Awards for the musical include Best Musical, Rex Harrison for Best Actor in a Musical, Frederick Loewe for Best Composer, Alan Jay Lerner for Best Librettist, and Moss Hart for Best Director.

RIAA and NEA named the original cast recording in its *Songs of the Century*, even though the entire score isn't exactly "a song."

The Hollywood movie version was released in 1964, with Rex Harrison reprising his role as Higgins and with Audrey Hepburn as Eliza. Hepburn's vocals were dubbed by Marni Nixon. Producer Jack Warner insisted on a more proven box office star than Julie Andrews—whose vocals would not have needed to be dubbed—for the role of Eliza. However, Andrews got the last laugh when she won the Best Actress Oscar for her starring role in *Mary Poppins* the same year. Jeremy Brett portrayed Freddy Eynsford-Hill, but his vocals were dubbed by Bill Shirley. The film was rather faithful to the original Broadway production, primarily because Alan Jay Lerner adapted it for the movie version. *My Fair Lady* earned twelve Oscar nominations in 1964 and took home eight statuettes, including Best Director, Scoring, Costumes, Art/Set Direction, Color Cinematography, and Best Picture of the Year.

One of Broadway's most significant musicals is Leonard Bernstein's *West Side Story*. Based, at least in a broad sense, on Shakespeare's *Romeo and Juliet*, the musical's chief subject was the growing menace of gang warfare,

West Side Story Playbill, 1957. (Courtesy of Photofest)

which is still extremely relevant. Originally called *East Side Story*, the script was to have dealt with a Christian–Jewish romance, but by the time the project materialized six years later, a far more timely subject was racial tensions between whites and Puerto Rican immigrants.

West Side Story
Music: Leonard Bernstein; Lyrics: Stephen Sondheim; Book: Arthur Laurents
Premiered 1957; ran 732 performances

- Major Cast: Carol Lawrence (Maria), Larry Kert (Tony), Chita Rivera (Anita)
- Key Songs: "Maria," "Tonight," "America," "One Hand, One Heart," "I Feel Pretty," "Somewhere"

The plot of *West Side Story* revolves around two feuding street gangs on the mean streets of 1950s New York City. The Sharks, a Puerto Rican gang, are trying to assimilate into American society, while the Jets, a native-born white gang, resent these newcomers into their territory. At a dance in a neighborhood gym, Tony, a retired Jet, falls for Maria, the Sharks's leader's sister, who has recently arrived from Puerto Rico. At a rumble between the gangs, which Tony tries to stop, he ends up killing Maria's brother, Bernardo. Bitter over losing Maria's love to Tony, and to avenge the death of gang leader Bernardo, Maria's Puerto Rican suitor kills Tony.

Leonard Bernstein often used tritones in the music of *West Side Story*. A tritone is an augmented fourth or diminished fifth (three whole tones). They are featured as the opening melodic interval of "Maria" and "Cool," and are also prominent in "Gee Officer Krupke," "Something's Coming," and "Jet Song." Why? It is likely the tension caused by the unusual interval, melodically and harmonically, was ideal for the uneasiness the music needed to exhibit in this gang atmosphere.

By the late fifties, Broadway songs seldom, if ever, made the pop charts. Leonard Bernstein's excellent score is filled with memorable songs, many of which became even better known after the film version was released in 1961 and garnered the Best Picture Oscar. As a matter of fact, the film was more successful than the original Broadway stage version.

When Maria and Tony dance together at the gym and are obviously attracted to each other, Maria's brother, Bernardo, stops their dance and sends her home. In "Maria," Tony sings about his newfound love. As he sings, Maria appears on a fire escape above him. They pledge their love in the song "Tonight."

In "America," a playful argument develops between Bernardo's girlfriend, Anita, and some homesick Puerto Rican girls over the relative merits of life back home compared to their lives in Manhattan.

When Tony visits the bridal shop where Maria works, she begs him to stop the rumble between the gangs. He promises he will. In "One Hand, One Heart," they enact a touching mock marriage ceremony.

As the gangs meet to rumble, Tony arrives and begs them to stop, but things quickly get out of hand. In the ensuing action, Bernardo stabs one of the Jets, and Tony grabs the weapon and knifes Bernardo.

Unaware of what has transpired, Maria sings "I Feel Pretty" as she gaily prepares to meet Tony.

Chino, Maria's Puerto Rican suitor, tells her that Tony has killed her brother. He pledges to kill Tony. While Maria is praying, Tony enters, explains the killing, and Maria forgives him. Desperately clinging to each other, they envision a new world where they can live together and be free from all this violence ("Somewhere").

Other significant songs from the score include "Tonight Quintet," one of the musical's most musically thrilling numbers, in which Tony and Maria sing of their love, Anita makes plans for her date with Bernardo after the rumble, and the two gangs make their plans for the confrontation; "Gee, Officer Krupke!" when Officer Krupke questions the Jets about the murders, and they ridicule social workers, the police, psychiatrists, and judges who all fail to understand what motivates their behavior.

In addition to an amazing musical score, Jerome Robbins's choreography was outstanding. It was admittedly strange at first to see New York City gangs dancing down the street, but once accepted, the athletically masculine dances seem perfectly natural.

West Side Story has become a cultural icon of the Broadway stage, but it was honored by the Tony Awards only for Jerome Robbins's choreography. It won more honors for the 1961 film version starring Natalie Wood and Richard Beymer (their singing voices were dubbed by Marni Nixon and Jimmy Bryant, respectively). Rita Moreno sang "America" herself, but "A Boy Like That" was dubbed by Betty Wand. Marni Nixon voiced both Wood and Moreno's vocals in "Quintet." The film won ten Academy Awards, including Best Picture, Best Supporting Actor for George Chakaris, Best Supporting Actress for Rita Moreno, and Best Director. Only *Ben Hur* (1959) and *Titanic* (1997) captured more Oscars. RIAA and NEA named the original cast recording in its *Songs of the Century*.

Songwriter Meredith Willson was born in Mason City, Iowa, where he learned to play piccolo and flute in high school. For a couple of years in the early twenties, Willson toured the United States, Cuba, and Mexico as the flutist with John Phillip Sousa's Band, an experience that certainly aided him in his writing of *The Music Man*.

The Music Man
Music, Lyrics & Book: Meredith Willson
Premiered 1957; ran 1,375 performances

- Major Cast: Robert Preston (Harold Hill), Barbara Cook (Marian Paroo)
- Key Songs: "Seventy-Six Trombones," "Till There Was You"

Set in 1912 Iowa, *The Music Man* introduces con man "Professor" Harold Hill, who travels from town to town taking prepaid orders for musical instruments and uniforms, claiming that he will teach the youngsters to play and form a town band. Hill's scam runs into complications in River City, when he becomes attracted to Marian, the local librarian and piano teacher. Although she recognizes his scheme, Marian falls in love with him. Hill is finally exposed and apprehended, but he stays to face the consequences. The local youngsters miraculously perform as a band, and the parents are so proud and excited to hear their children play, they drop the charges against Hill. Harold decides to end his con man career and settle down with Marian.

In "Seventy-Six Trombones," the "Professor" charms the townspeople with a story of the time six of the greatest marching bands came to town on the very same day. The song is reprised near the end by the students.

Also near the end of the musical, Marian reveals to Hill that she knows he's not what he claims to be, but she doesn't care. In "Till There Was You," she tells him she loves him and realizes that the joy he has brought to the children of River City is worthwhile. The song was popularized in 1959 in a recording by Anita Bryant, and it was covered by the Beatles in 1963 on their second album, *With the Beatles*. It is the only showtune the Beatles ever recorded.

There are several other clever songs from the score that deserve mention, even though they weren't popular on the pop charts: "Ya Got Trouble," which Hill uses to whip the townspeople into a civic frenzy about the dangers of the new pool hall. He asks them how, with the pernicious influence of billiards around, will they keep the kids "moral after school." His answer: a town band. "Goodnight, My Someone" cleverly uses the same melody as "Seventy-Six Trombones," but as a slow waltz, when one of Marian's piano student confides to her that she worries she'll never find a sweetheart, and Marian consoles her with the song. "Pick-a-Little, Talk-a-Little/Goodnight Ladies," is used by Hill to quiz the Ladies Auxiliary about Marian, and they begin to gossip like a flock of hens pecking away. Then, when school-board members appear requesting his credentials, Hill distracts them into singing "Goodnight Ladies," while the town's women continue singing "Pick-a-Little . . .," which develops into a wonderful contrapuntal number. "Gary, Indiana," sung by Winthrop, in his cute lisping way after returning home from a fishing trip with Hill, shows his mother and sister what the "Professor" has taught him.

The Music Man won the 1958 Tony Award as Best Musical, Robert Preston received the Tony for Best Actor in a Musical, Meredith Willson won for Best Composer, and he and Franklin Lacey won the Best Librettist award. RIAA and NEA named the original cast recording in its *Songs of the Century.*

The film version was released in 1962 and starred Robert Preston again as Harold Hill and Shirley Jones as Marian the librarian. The Buffalo Bills barbershop quartet returned from the original stage production for the film. The film was nominated for six Academy Awards, including Best Picture, but won only for Best Music, Scoring of Music, Adaptation or Treatment.

Gypsy was based on the autobiography of stripper Gypsy Rose Lee, published in 1957. The emphasis of the plot is Gypsy's overly ambitious mother.

Gypsy

Music: Jule Styne; Lyrics: Stephen Sondheim; Book: Arthur Laurents
Premiered 1959; ran 702 performances

- Major Cast: Ethel Merman (Rose), Jack Klugman (Herbie), Sandra Church (Louise)
- Key Songs: "Let Me Entertain You," "Everything's Coming Up Roses"

Gypsy follows Rose and her two daughters, June and Louise, as they play the vaudeville circuit during the Great Depression. Rose is the prototypical stage mother who pushes her children to perform. The audience soon learns that Louise is meek and shy, while June is the talented daughter. Rose meets Herbie and persuades him to become their manager. When June tires of show business and her mother's obsessiveness, she runs away to marry one of the boys in the act. Rose then vows to make Louise a star.

As vaudeville begins to die, Louise and her act wind up at a burlesque house. Rose almost accepts Herbie's marriage proposal, but can't let go of her dream to see one of her daughters become a star. She volunteers Louise to do a striptease as a last-minute replacement. Reluctantly, Louise goes on stage singing a version of the silly song she and her sister had used in their act years earlier. She only removes her glove, but the audience goes wild. In the months that follow, she becomes more confident, always following Rose's advice to "Make 'em beg for more and then don't give it to them!" Ultimately, Louise becomes a major burlesque star. Now Rose feels unneeded and unwanted. Even Herbie walks out on her. Rose fantasizes about what it would have been like if she had been the star, and finally admits that she pushed her daughters for her own gratification. At the musical's end, mother and daughter tentatively step toward reconciliation.

In real life, June took the name June Havoc. Louise became Gypsy Rose Lee.

One song is heard in several different versions in the musical. As kids, "Baby June" and "Baby Louise" sing "May We Entertain You." As they age, their act transforms, and the song transforms with them. Finally, it becomes "Let Me Entertain You," which Louise uses in her burlesque act.

At the end of Act One, the indomitable Rose announces to a horrified Louise that she will make her a star. In "Everything's Coming Up Roses," Rose is so sure of herself, she can barely contain her excitement. She is determined to live her dream through her daughters at any cost, so the title has multiple meanings: everything's going to be better, everything's going to turn out just as Rose had planned from the start, or everything is going to turn in Rose's favor.

Other well-known songs from the score include "All I Need Is the Girl," sung by one of boys in the act, who is rehearsing a routine he demonstrates to Louise, who dreams of being that girl; "Together Wherever We Go," as Rose and Herbie try to reassure Louise, who rebels at the new act Rose devises for her, which is just a transparent reworking of previous acts.

Louise isn't talented and knows it. "You Gotta Have a Gimmick," used by some of the broken-down strippers to explain trade secrets to Louise; and "Rose's Turn," as a defiant Rose, alone on the darkened, empty stage, wishes she had had the chance to be a star.

The 1962 film version starred Rosalind Russell as Rose, Natalie Wood as Louise, Karl Malden as Herbie, and Morgan Brittany as June. The film was nominated for three Oscars. Most of Russell's songs were dubbed by Lisa Kirk. However, her voice can be heard in "Mr. Goldstone" and in parts of "Rose's Turn." "Together Wherever We Go" was cut from the film version.

The Sound of Music became the second longest running Broadway musical of the fifties. It was the last Rodgers and Hammerstein musical because the lyricist Hammerstein died of cancer just nine months after it opened. The plot was adapted from Maria von Trapp's autobiography, *The Trapp Family Singers*. Howard Lindsay—Mary Martin's husband—and Russel Crouse contributed the libretto.

The Sound of Music
Music: Richard Rodgers; Lyrics: Oscar Hammerstein II; Book: Howard Lindsay & Russel Crouse
Premiered 1959; ran 1,443 performances

- Major Cast: Mary Martin (Maria Rainer von Trapp), Theodore Bikel (Capt. Georg von Trapp), Patricia Neway (Mother Abbess), Lauri Peters (Liesl von Trapp)
- Key Songs: "The Sound of Music," "My Favorite Things," "Do-Re-Mi," "Climb Ev'ry Mountain"

The Sound of Music is set in Salzburg, Austria, where Maria is studying to become a nun. She is sent from her convent to be the governess to seven children of a widower naval commander, Captain von Trapp. Initially the children are hostile and mischievous, but eventually come to love Maria when she introduces them to the joys of music. Unwittingly, Maria falls in love with the captain, and he with her.

When the Nazis take over Austria, they attempt to force the captain into their service. Unwilling to serve the Reich, he insists he is part of the Von Trapp Family Singers and must remain with them during a performance at the Salzburg Music Festival. After a curtain call, the whole family flees and hikes over the mountains to safety in Switzerland.

In the musical's title song, Maria is out on the mountain, singing her tribute to nature and music.

In the original Broadway production, the Mother Abbess hears Maria singing and thinks she recognizes the song. After Maria sings a chorus of "My Favorite Things," the Mother Abbess sings some herself, and they end this catalogue of simple pleasures in a duet, whereas in the 1965 film version, it is sung to the children when they become afraid during a thunderstorm.

After his wife's death, the captain had become a taskmaster and the children little more than tiny soldiers in his regiment. However, when Maria teaches them the song "Do-Re-Mi," they learn to sing and enjoy life. Her music lesson solidifies her position with the children.

When Maria realizes that she has fallen in love with the captain, she returns to the abbey, where, in the song "Climb Ev'ry Mountain," the Mother Abbess advises her that the love of a man and a woman is holy and that she must reach out to meet life. At the musical's end, as the family makes their way to freedom over Maria's beloved mountains, the nuns wish them Godspeed by reprising the song.

Other familiar songs from the musical score include "Sixteen Going on Seventeen," when the oldest Von Trapp child, Liesl, is in the throes of first love and steals out to meet a village boy; "The Lonely Goatherd," helps Maria win Liesl's confidence, and that of all the other children, as she entertains them during a thunderstorm. In the film version, the song was used for a puppet show that was not in the original Broadway version. "So Long, Farewell," sung by the children at a party, as they say their good nights to the guests. The party is given by the captain with the encouragement of his fiancée, Elsa, who has returned from Vienna with him and a friend. The song is sung again at the end of the family's performance at the Salzburg Music Festival, which begins their escape. "Edelweiss," a folk-like expression of the captain's love for his homeland is also sung at the music festival.

The Sound of Music shared the Tony Award for Best Musical with *Fiorello!* for the year 1960. The Best Composer award was also a tie between Richard Rodgers for *The Sound of Music* and Jerry Bock for *Fiorello!*, as was the Best Librettist award for Howard Lindsay and Russel Crouse for *The Sound of Music* and Jerome Weidman and George Abbott for *Fiorello!* Mary Martin won for Best Actress in a Musical for her portrayal of Maria. Patricia Neway, who played the Mother Abbess, won the award for Best Featured Actress in a Musical.

In the film version, Christopher Plummer portrayed Captain Von Trapp, but his vocals were dubbed by Bill Lee. "I Have Confidence" and "Something Good" were specially written for the film version by Richard Rodgers. "An Ordinary Couple" was deleted from the original score.

It's interesting to note that although Julie Andrews had been deemed too much of an unknown to star in the film version of *My Fair Lady*, she won the Best Actress Oscar for *Mary Poppins* in 1964 and also was nominated for her protrayal of Maria in *The Sound of Music* in 1965.

Other noteworthy musicals include:

- *Where's Charley?* – Music & Lyrics: Frank Loesser; Book: George Abbott, based on Brandon Thomas's 1892 play *Charley's Aunt*; premiered 1948; ran 792 performances; starred Ray Bolger; most famous songs: "My Darling, My Darling," a number-one hit for Jo Stafford and Gordon MacRae in 1949, and "Once in Love With Amy." The 1952 film version also starred Ray Bolger and Allyn McLerie from the Broadway stage version.
- *Gentlemen Prefer Blondes* – Music: Jule Styne; Lyrics: Leo Robin; Book: Joseph Stein & Anita Loos; premiered 1949; ran 740 performances; starred Carol Channing; most famous song: "Diamonds Are a Girl's Best Friend." The 1953 screen version starred Jane Russell and Marilyn Monroe. Several new non-Styne/Robin songs were added, and several from the original score were deleted.
- *Call Me Madam* – Music & Lyrics: Irving Berlin; Book: Howard Lindsay & Russel Crouse; premiered 1950; ran 644 performances; most famous songs: "It's a Lovely Day Today" and "You're Just in Love;" Ethel Merman won the Tony Award for Best Actress in a Musical. The 1953 film version also starred Ethel Merman.
- *Paint Your Wagon* – Music: Frederick Loewe; Lyrics & Book: Alan Jay Lerner; premiered 1951; ran 289 performances; most famous song: "They Call the Wind Maria." The 1969 film starred Lee Marvin, Clint Eastwood, and Jean Seberg. Marvin and Eastwood sang, but Miss Seberg's vocals were dubbed by Anita Gordon. The plot was drastically different, some of the original songs were abandoned, and Alan Jay Lerner and André Previn added five new songs.
- *Wish You Were Here* – Music & Lyrics: Harold Rome; Book: Arthur Kober & Joshua Logan; premiered 1952; ran 598 performances; most famous song: "Wish You Were Here," a *Billboard* number-one hit for Eddie Fisher in 1952.
- *Kismet* – Music & Lyrics: Robert Wright and George Forrest, based on music by Aleksandr Borodin; Book: Charles Lederer & Luther Davis; premiered 1953; ran 583 performances; most famous song: "Stranger in Paradise," based on Polovetsian Dance number two from Aleksandr Borodin's *Prince Igor*, became a pop

hit for Tony Bennett in 1954. It was a number-one hit on *Cash Box* and *Your Hit Parade*.

- *Me and Juliet* – Music: Richard Rodgers; Lyrics & Book: Oscar Hammerstein II; premiered 1953; ran 358 performances; most famous song: "No Other Love," a number-one hit on *Billboard, Cash Box*, and *Your Hit Parade* in 1953 for Perry Como.

- *The Pajama Game* – Music & Lyrics: Richard Adler & Jerry Ross; Book: George Abbott & Richard Bissell; premiered 1954; ran 1,063 performances; most famous songs: "Hey There" was the top hit of 1954—a number-one hit on *Billboard, Variety, Cash Box*, and *Your Hit Parade*; Rosemary Clooney's recording was a blockbuster success; "Hernando's Hideaway," a number-one hit on *Your Hit Parade*, Archie Bleyer and His Orchestra's recording was the most popular version; and "Steam Heat" won Tony Awards for Best Musical, Composer, and Librettist.

- *Peter Pan* – Music: Mark Charlap & Jule Styne; Lyrics: Carolyn Leigh, Betty Comden & Adolph Green; premiered 1954; ran 152 performances; most famous songs: "I've Got to Crow," "I'm Flying," and "I Won't Grow Up;" Mary Martin won the Tony Award for Best Actress in a Musical for her portrayal of Peter. A very celebrated television version starring Mary Martin premiered in 1960.

- *Damn Yankees* – Music & Lyrics: Richard Adler & Jerry Ross; Book: George Abbott & Douglass Wallop; premiered 1955; ran 1,019 performances; most famous songs: "Heart," "Whatever Lola Wants (Lola Gets);" won Tony Awards for Best Musical in 1956, Gwen Verdon as the devil's temptress for Best Actress and Ray Walston as Mr. Applegate, the devil, for Best Actor; Adler and Ross won their second consecutive Tony for writing the musical, and George Abbott and Douglass Wallop won the award for Best Librettist. The film version was released in 1958 starring Tab Hunter as Joe, Gwen Verdon again as Lola, and Ray Walston again as Mr. Applegate.

- *Bells Are Ringing* – Music: Jule Styne; Lyrics & Book: Betty Comden & Adolph Green; premiered 1956; ran 924 performances; Judy Holliday won the Tony Award for Best Actress in a Musical; most famous songs: "Just in Time" and "The Party's Over." Judy Holliday also starred in the 1960 film version.

8

Country and Western Music of the Postwar Years

Country music is America's music because it subscribes to values Americans love: God, country, home and family (especially mother), good triumphing over evil, and right winning over wrong. The music is an amalgam of musical elements and styles, but the end result is distinctively American. It may have once been primarily rural and tagged as "hillbilly," but that has long since passed.

In *Sing Your Heart Out, Country Boy,* Dorothy Horstman denotes country music's qualities as:

- country music "tells it like it is"
- it is fundamentally Protestant
- it is lyric music, and most of the songs tell a good story
- it is reasonably simple music, in melody, chords, and form
- it is sad music, reflecting the hard, severe lives of its writers, performers, and listeners
- it is often financially motivated, created for financial gain

A song on the pop charts usually had a rather short life, but the great country songs were sung for years, both by their originator and by various other artists. Country has been far more song-driven than the pop field. Of course, a talented recording artist helps, but the song is the primary ingredient for success.

COUNTRY MUSIC'S RISE AND INFLUENCE

The barriers that once had existed between the "classy" music of Broadway and Hollywood and what had been scornfully defined as "hillbilly" were definitely broken by the beginning of the fifties. "Hillbilly" was now becoming known as "country and western," just as "race records" were becoming "rhythm and blues." The general public was lining up to buy recordings of country songs either by the original country artists or covered by mainline pop artists.

World War II was a particularly important event in the history of country music. Up until the early forties, "hillbilly" music was decidedly regional—Southern, to be specific. But as Southern troops came in contact with soldiers from other parts of the nation, they introduced their buddies to the country sound. The same thing happened in the business world when people from various geographic regions were employed in defense plants.

The first evidence of the emergence of the genre was a survey taken in occupied Germany by the Armed Forces Radio Network (AFRN) that polled GI's musical preferences. As a result, the AFRN broadcast of the *Hillbilly Jamboree* program from Munich. Further evidence came when one of the biggest hits of the war years was Elton Britt's "There's a Star-Spangled Banner Waving Somewhere" (1943). Primarily a country artist, his crossover hit reportedly sold four million copies. Britt was also invited by President Roosevelt to perform his song at the White House. As country music spread, a square-dancing fad emerged. The Venice Pier in California was converted to the Los Angeles Country Barn Dance, and in 1943 *Billboard* reported "the dominant music of the U.S. today is hillbilly." (Oermann) By the end of the decade, *Downbeat* magazine reported, "Hillbilly music is now such a vogue that it is just about pushing popular tunes, jazz, swing, bebop and everything else right out of the picture." (Oermann)

COUNTRY CROSSOVERS

One of the first country songs and artists to enter the pop mainstream was Tex Williams's western swing-and-talking-blues-influenced "Smoke! Smoke! Smoke! (That Cigarette)" (1947). Tex Williams and Merle Travis wrote this comic patter song, which Williams recorded with his band, the Western Caravan. Williams's disc became Capitol's first million-seller, reportedly selling more than 2.5 million copies. With all the antismoking campaigns in recent years, it's surprising this song hasn't been revived.

Before World War II, infidelity, although certainly not novel, was shameful behavior and not a public subject. But as many more women entered the work force and husbands and wives were separated by military service obligations, lonely women began to seek companionship in the nation's bars and honky-tonks. Although society viewed cheating as wrong and churches preached against it, country songwriters began to write songs about infidelity as a result of what they experienced and witnessed nightly.

Floyd Tillman wrote the classic cheating song, "Slipping Around," one of the first songs to tackle the subject of adultery. Tillman got the idea for his song when he stopped at a diner and overheard a woman in a phone booth say, "Now, Honey, you call me, and if a man answers, hang up." Tillman thought, "Poor girl, she's just like me ... slipping around" (Horstman). The popularity of Tillman's recording of the song on the country market convinced Capitol Records to record a pop version. They decided on a duet combining pop vocalist Margaret Whiting, and country-western singer and cowboy movie personality Jimmy Wakely. Their version topped both the pop and country-western charts in 1949.

One of the biggest country crossover discs of 1950 was Red Foley's recording of "Chattanoogie Shoe Shine Boy," the Country Music Hall of Famer's only number-one hit on the pop music charts. Foley's recording reportedly was an eventual million-seller. The song's tune is basically a boogie-woogie bass turned into a melody. "The Chattanoogie Shoe Shine Boy" pops his shoeshine rag to a boogie-woogie beat. Unfortunately, "boy" was a term White people used to refer to African American males, regardless of age. The term was also used in basically the same context in Mack Gordon's lyrics for "Chattanooga Choo Choo" (1941). A common job that black males could obtain in the early 1940s was shining shoes in barber shops, hotels, or on trains.

1951 was an extraordinary year for Les Paul and Mary Ford. The duo, with their multitrack technique, racked up six million in sales. The multitrack-recording technique produces a decidedly richer sound, like a choir of thirty singers has a deeper, richer sound than a choir half that number. Paul and Ford's recording of "Mockin' Bird Hill" was one of the first multitrack recordings. This waltz tune is a verse-and-chorus type of song (two-part form) that has a simple chord structure (only three chords). The song's lyrics have a folk song character that describes the pleasure of living on "Mockin' Bird Hill."

Pee Wee King and his Golden West Cowboys recorded "Slow Poke" with vocalist Redd Stewart. Their recording made it to number one on the country charts then crossed over and climbed to number one on the pop charts, also in 1952.

COUNTRY COVERS

> The primary avenue for country music's making inroads into the pop field was cover versions. If a song began to have success on the country and western chart, some mainline popular artist would rerecord the song in a pop version.
>
> Mainstream pop singers released "cover versions" of country songs just as they did of rhythm and blues songs prior to the birth of rock 'n' roll. Examples of covers of country material include:
>
> - "Room Full of Roses," by Sammy Kaye and his orchestra in 1949
> - "Bouquet of Roses," by Dick Haymes in 1949
> - "Tennessee Waltz," by Patti Page in 1950 and 1951
> - "Hey, Good Lookin'," by Frankie Laine and Jo Stafford in 1951
> - "Cold, Cold Heart," by Tony Bennett in 1951
> - "You Belong to Me," by Jo Stafford in 1952
> - "Half As Much," by Rosemary Clooney in 1952
> - "Any Time" and "Just a Little Lovin'," by Eddie Fisher in 1952
> - "Jambalaya," by Jo Stafford in 1952
> - "Don't Let the Stars Get in Your Eyes," by Perry Como in 1953
> - "Kaw-Liga," by Dolores Gray in 1953
> - "Seven Lonely Days," by Georgia Gibbs in 1953
> - "Your Cheatin' Heart," by Joni James in 1953
> - "This Ole House," by Rosemary Clooney in 1954
> - "Sixteen Tons," by Tennessee Ernie Ford in 1955
> - "Singing the Blues," by Guy Mitchell in 1956
> - "Why Baby Why," by Pat Boone in 1957
> - "Heartaches by the Number," by Guy Mitchell in 1959

Patti Page had extraordinary success with "The Tennessee Waltz," a duet with herself, thanks to the wonders of tape and overdubbing. The song became the biggest hit in fifty years, selling over six million records, over two million via Patti Page's version alone, and over two million copies of sheet music. Pee Wee King's RCA single of "The Tennessee Waltz" hit the country charts in early April 1948, which prompted Mercury to have Patti Page record it in 1950 (see chart information in 1951). Patti Page's recording of the song was inducted into the Grammy Hall of Fame in 1998 and was named by RIAA and NEA as one of its *Songs of the Century.*

Many songs have been created by a writer being inspired by listening to another song. Such was the case of "Tennessee Waltz." During a trip back to Nashville from a gig in Arkansas, Pee Wee King and his band's vocalist, Redd Stewart, heard bluegrass legend Bill Monroe's "Kentucky Waltz" on the radio. That prompted a discussion as to why there had never been a waltz written about the State of Tennessee. They resolved to write one before someone else did. They wrote the lyrics to fit a tune the band had used as a theme song, called "No Name Waltz." So, in 1946, Pee Wee and Redd wrote the lyrics to "The Tennessee Waltz." In 1965, the State of Tennessee chose "Tennessee Waltz" as one of its official songs (the state has five official state songs).

The biggest country influence of 1955 was country singer and songwriter Merle Travis's "Sixteen Tons." It became Tennessee Ernie Ford's biggest hit, reportedly sold more than one million copies in three weeks, and became the fastest-selling single to date. It became *Variety's* number three hit of the year, and was a number one on *Billboard, Cash Box,* and *Your Hit Parade.* Ford's recording of the song was inducted into the Grammy Hall of Fame in 1998. Travis, the son of a Kentucky tobacco farmer-turned-coal miner, wrote the song to include on his own "Folk Songs of the Hills" album, an eight-song collection themed around the plight of the coal mining community. In the late forties, the worker-sympathetic theme of these songs was viewed by some as Socialist propaganda. However, when "the little ole pea-picker," Tennessee Ernie Ford, recorded "Sixteen Tons" in the mid-fifties, the lyrics' homey cynicism struck a chord with the record-buying public. About the song's conception, Travis said, "There was an old saying around the coal mines in the Depression days. Somebody'd say, 'How you doing?' And he'd say, 'Well, all right, I guess. I can't afford to die, because I owe my soul to the company store.' I just wrote around that." In many instances, the company owned the town, the houses that it rented to the workers, and the stores that sold groceries, clothing, and whatever else was needed. The workers were practically obligated to buy from the company stores and often ran up quite a charge account there. Therefore, many of them owed the company store so much, it felt like they owed their soul. People empathized with not being able to get ahead despite working hard, getting older, and never getting out of debt.

Mitch Miller, Columbia's A&R director, changed Guy Mitchell's style to capitalize on the current Presley vogue, and his "Singing the Blues" became 1956's biggest hit. He also changed Mitchell's name from Al Cernick, which he deemed inappropriate for a performer. "Singing the Blues" was written by Melvin Endsley, a young songwriter from Arkansas who was confined to a wheelchair due to his having been a polio victim when he was three years old.

Guy Mitchell heard Marty Robbins's country version of "Heartaches by the Number" and asked Mitch Miller if he could record it. Songwriter Harlan Howard explained the origin of "Heartaches by the Number" as follows: "I was in the Army as a paratrooper for three years. Everything was done by the numbers. We even ran by the numbers and had to count cadence ... I had used several terms and expressions that are used almost exclusively in the service. I was really just fooling around with words and seeing if I could take this Army expression and put it into a love song. That's the game songwriters play. Sometimes it works and sometimes it don't. In this case it did" (Horstman). "Heartaches by the Number," which counts the myriad ways that love hurts, was a number-one hit by Guy Mitchell on *Billboard* and *Cash Box* in 1959. Ray Price had a successful country recording of the song prior to Mitchell's pop cover version.

Several Hank Williams songs were covered by mainstream pop artists. A couple of the more popular ones were "Cold, Cold Heart" in 1951 and "Jambalaya" in 1952. Hank Williams's wife, Audrey, explained how "Cold, Cold Heart" was written: "I was in the hospital for some minor ailment. We had had an argument. He and the children had come to visit me ... During the entire visit I spoke to the children, but I didn't speak to Hank. On his way home he told our housekeeper ... 'She's got the coldest heart I've ever seen.' That same night he wrote this song. Among the 100 songs Hank Williams wrote, this was his favorite" (Horstman). Tony Bennett's cover of the song was a number-one hit in 1951.

A Louisiana Cajun dish furnished the title for the Hank Williams song "Jambalaya," a song about bayou culture and the language of the Creoles. A very similar Cajun–French song, "Grand Texas," is also about life, parties, and Cajun cuisine. Country superstar Hank Williams was sometimes accused of buying his songs from lesser known writers, a practice that was fairly prevalent in the country-song market during the era, but there has never been any proof that he was not the writer of "Jambalaya." Jo Stafford's recording of "Jambalaya" was inducted into the Grammy Hall of Fame in 2002.

According to Curley Williams's wife, Louise, "Half as Much" came about like this: "My husband Curley just got up from the supper table one night and went down to the radio station where he was working in Anniston, AL. He stayed down there about thirty minutes, and when he came back, he said, 'Baby, I wrote us a good song tonight.' He played and sang it for me, and of course I thought it was good, but next he played it for the boys in his band, the Georgia Peach Pickers, and they all laughed at him. Then he recorded it and sent it to Acuff-Rose, and instead of writing back, like they usually did, Fred Rose called him and said, 'I just want you to know you've got a damned hit!' Curley had the first record on it at Columbia, but just as it started to go big ... the Columbia pressing plant went on strike for seven weeks, and when they came off, Christmas songs were in and that killed his version of it. Then Rosemary Clooney came out with it and made it popular in the pop field, and then Hank Williams picked it up" (Horstman). Rosemary Clooney's recording was a *Billboard* number-one hit in 1952. The chord structure of "Half as Much" is definitely simpler than most of music of the forties. Music was gravitating toward amateurism, a trend even more apparent in the later part of the decade and over the next several years.

Chilton Price, a broadcast-station record librarian from Louisville, Kentucky, became friends with country and western bandleader Pee Wee King. Price brought several song ideas to King, and in 1952, two of the ideas produced hit songs: "Slow Poke" and "You Belong to Me." Price wrote both songs, but gave cowriting credits to Pee Wee King and Redd Stewart in exchange for a few refinements, and for helping her get the songs published and recorded. Sue Thompson was the first to record "You Belong to Me" on Mercury's country label. It was soon covered by Patti Page with "I Went to Your Wedding" on the flip side. However, it was Jo Stafford's recording that became a number-one hit on all the charts (number two for the year on the combined charts).

THE GRAND OLE OPRY

Country music has spread around the nation and the world, but the "Mother Church" is the Ryman Auditorium in Nashville, the former home of the *Grand Ole Opry.*

The *Grand Ole Opry* is a weekly Saturday night country music radio program broadcast live on WSM radio in Nashville, Tennessee. It has become the longest-running radio program in the United States, having been broadcast since November 28, 1925.

The National Life and Accident Insurance Company began radio station WSM in 1925. The station's call letters stood for the company's motto: "We Shield Millions."

George Hay, the station's first program director, had started a barn dance program on Chicago's WLS, so soon after joining the station, he launched the *WSM Barn Dance*, which was renamed the *Grand Ole Opry* in 1927. The company built an auditorium for 500, but it quickly outgrew that space and moved several times before 1943, when it landed at the Ryman Auditorium, a former revival hall built in 1892 by a riverboat shipping executive, Captain Thomas Ryman, for evangelist Samuel Jones.

The *Opry* broadcasted from the Ryman for more than thirty years. In 2004, it moved to a new Grand Ole Opry House. However, the Ryman is

Grand Ole Opry from the Ryman, circa 1956. (Courtesy of Photofest)

still used for concerts and, at certain times of the year, some *Opry* shows originate from there.

The program's fame spread even more when the NBC radio network began carrying it in 1939. Country stars performed on the *Opry* on weekends and traveled around the nation during the week, spreading the music's appeal.

During World War II, country stars often performed for American soldiers at home and abroad. After the war, in 1949, the *Opry*'s first European tour featured Red Foley, Roy Acuff, Minnie Pearl, Rod Brasfield, Little Jimmie Dickens, and Hank Williams.

In the mid-fifties, as television became more important, the *Opry* began an hour-long, regional network TV program from the Ryman. It is still a significant honor for any country artist to become a member of the Opry family of performers.

For a vaudeville performer, the Palace Theater was the "big time." For a country music artist, it is the *Grand Ole Opry*, which averages 5,000 attendees per week at its weekend performances. Six million from all over North America and the world have attended the show since it first went on the air. The *Grand Ole Opry* has remained a vital part of country music. It is attended, listened to, or watched on TV by multitudes on a regular basis into the twenty-first century.

The various styles of country music that were popular during the postwar years include bluegrass, country gospel, singing cowboys, western swing, honky-tonk, the Nashville sound, and rockabilly.

BLUEGRASS

When immigrants from Ireland, Scotland, and England came to the United States, they brought the music of their homeland with them. Those ballads and dance music combined with some of the music they discovered in their new homeland to form the basis of bluegrass music. The banjo, which has African American origins, was an important addition, adopted once they settled mostly in the Appalachian regions of the Virginias and Carolinas, Tennessee, and Kentucky.

The Monroe Brothers—Charlie and Bill, from Kentucky—became one of the most popular duet teams of the twenties and thirties. Charlie played the guitar, Bill played the mandolin, and they sang duets in harmony. When the brothers split up in the late thirties, both formed their own bands. Bill Monroe and the Blue Grass Boys are credited with originating the style that was named bluegrass (from the band's name), and Bill Monroe has become known as the "Father of Bluegrass Music."

Monroe's band was different from other country music bands of the time because of its usually faster, harder, and more technically demanding instrumentals and distinctive vocal harmonies. The basic instrumentation consisted of mandolin, banjo, fiddle, guitar, and bass.

"Blue Moon of Kentucky" is a famous bluegrass song, written by Bill Monroe in 1947. Monroe's recording with the Blue Grass Boys has received many honors over the years. RIAA and NEA included it in their *Songs of the Century*, Country Music Television (CMT) named it number one on its *100 Greatest Songs in Country Music*. In addition, the song is the official bluegrass song of Kentucky, and the Library of Congress chose Monroe's recording of it as one of fifty recordings to be added to the National Recording Registry. Bill Monroe was inducted into the Country Music Hall of Fame in 1970.

Bluegrass songs, even more than any other country style, seem to stay around and remain popular. "Orange Blossom Special," written by Ervin T. and Gordon Rouse in 1938 (Chubby Wise claims writing credit also), is still a number sung or played by almost every bluegrass ensemble, but particularly by Bill Monroe's band. Fiddlers who perform "Orange Blossom Special" frequently employ special techniques to imitate the sound of the train, since that is the origin of the title. To hear an instrumental version of the song go to http://www.mamarocks.com/orange_blossom_special.htm.

The bluegrass style known today is a product of the postwar years. Most scholars believe the classic bluegrass sound jelled in 1945, shortly after banjo player Earl Scruggs and guitar player and singer Lester Flatt joined Monroe's band. Scruggs's innovative three-finger picking style on the banjo and Flatt's lead vocals with Monroe's tenor harmonies also became distinctive elements of the bluegrass sound.

When Flatt and Scruggs left Monroe to form their own group, The Foggy Mountain Boys, in the late forties, they added the sound of the Dobro (or Resophonic guitar) to their band. The Dobro was invented by the Dopyera Brothers ("Do" from Dopyera, "bro" from Brothers), immigrant musicians and inventors originally from the Slovak Republic. The Dobro's distinctive sound comes from its use of a slide placed on the guitar's neck to produce the appropriate notes.

Flatt and Scruggs became a major force in spreading bluegrass music across the nation. Scruggs wrote and recorded one of bluegrass music's most famous instrumentals, "Foggy Mountain Breakdown," which was used in the soundtrack for the film *Bonnie & Clyde* (1967). They also played for *The Beverly Hillbillies* TV series and appeared on the show from time to time. Flatt and Scruggs and their Foggy Mountain Boys were inducted into the Country Music Hall of Fame in 1985. "Foggy Mountain Breakdown," by Lester Flatt with Earl Scruggs and the Foggy Mountain Boys, was named to the Library of Congress National Recording Registry. Randy Scruggs, Earl's son, still performs and helps perpetuate the style.

Bluegrass songs were about issues important to everyday people. Religion was a prominent subject and gospel music figured heavily in the development of the bluegrass sound. Secular songs tended to focus on love, home, and family, sometimes exploring the darker side of these issues.

There are two major schools of bluegrass: the instrumental style, often compared to jazz, most frequently associated with Bill Monroe and the "high lonesome sound" vocal bluegrass, as exemplified by the Stanley Brothers.

Carter and Ralph Stanley formed their bluegrass band, the Clinch Mountain Boys, in 1946. Carter played guitar and sang lead while Ralph played banjo and sang with a strong, high tenor voice. Their harmonies were much admired and influenced many future country vocalists, including the Everly Brothers.

Bluegrass music was particularly important in the movie *Deliverance* (1972), which introduced "Dueling Banjos," played by Eric Weissberg on banjo and Steve Mandel on guitar.

Bluegrass also got a shot in the arm when the music was featured on the movie soundtracks of *O Brother, Where Art Thou?* (2001) and *Cold Mountain* (2003). Two of the Stanley Brothers' most famous songs, "I'm a Man of Constant Sorrows" and "Angel Band," were heard on the soundtrack of *O Brother, Where Art Thou?* "You Will Be My Ain True Love," performed by Alison Krauss and one of the song's cowriters, Sting, and "The Scarlet Tide," written by Elvis Costello and Sting, and also performed by Alison Krauss on the *Cold Mountain* soundtrack, were nominated for the Best Song Oscar.

Fiddler and vocalist Roy Acuff became the first living artist to be elected into the Country Music Hall of Fame in 1962. His 1947 recording of "Wabash Cannonball" was named to the Library of Congress National Recording Registry in 2005.

COUNTRY GOSPEL

Country gospel is one of the oldest styles in country music. The sound of country gospel is similar to traditional country, the primary difference being the subject matter. Like other country styles, the sound changed with the times. However, country gospel is closely identified with simple arrangements, small vocal ensembles, and twangy instrumentation.

White gospel has had more influence on country music than black gospel, because the genre features a more emotional, exhortative singing style than is the case with country. Gospel-influenced singers had a hand in changing country vocals completely.

For many years, country performers included at least one sacred tune in their concerts, usually at the conclusion. These sentimental, emotional expressions of the Southern religious experience often concentrate on a better life in the hereafter. Bluegrass legend Bill Malone explains: "By in large, the southern protestant tradition has been Calvinistic and has taught people that life is a 'veil of tears.' Death should be sought and welcomed, because the better lies beyond the grave; life on earth is a very short, sad, brutal existence, and the world is something to be rejected" (Horstman).

Many famous country performers were raised on the gospel songs of the rural camp meeting tradition.

Country gospel songs, like bluegrass, remain popular with their audiences year after year. As a matter of fact, these next few songs are still sung today.

Albert E. Brumley wrote "I'll Fly Away" in 1932 as he was dreaming of flying away from the cotton fields where he was working. The song has become one of the most famous of all gospel songs, but particularly in the country market. The song was named by RIAA and NEA as one of its *Songs of the Century* and was listed for the Chuck Wagon Gang's 1948 recording.

"Will the Circle Be Unbroken?" as we know it today, came from a song by Ada R. Habershon, later rearranged by A. P. Carter, of the Carter Family. First published in 1907, the song has become one of America's most beloved and most often recorded songs. Its lyrics speak of loss, grief, salvation, and hope.

One of the classic country gospel songs is Hank Williams's "I Saw the Light," which was used on the soundtrack of his movie biography, *Your Cheatin' Heart* (1964).

"Precious Memories" is a traditional Gospel hymn credited to J. B. F. Wright in 1925. However, records indicate the song may have been around as early as 1877. It has been performed by a wide variety of famous recording artists, including Johnny Cash and Emmylou Harris.

Other country gospel numbers include Red Foley's recordings of "Steal Away" (1950), "Just a Closer Walk With Thee" (1950), and "Peace In The

Valley" (1951), which all became million-sellers, and Ferlin Husky's "Wings of a Dove," which was a big country hit in 1959.

SINGING COWBOYS

Cowboy music actually originated in the Old West with the cowpokes out on the open range who sang to pass the time on cattle drives. That's where the "western" part of "country and western" originated. Long after the West became civilized and most cattle ranches used modern methods of getting their beef to market, the cowboy mythology lingered. There were a plethora of western and cowboy full-length movies and serial episode films. The era of singing cowboys like Roy Rogers and Gene Autry was the heyday of those films, which needed songs that thematically celebrated the cowboy's life-style. One important group that produced several songs of this type was the Sons of the Pioneers.

Because many country performers adopted the dress of the movie cowboy, the "western" designation was added to "country" in the late forties.

Gene Autry became the first major singing cowboy movie star. His film debut was in Ken Maynard's *In Old Santa Fe* in 1934. The following year, he starred in a thirteen-part serial, *Phantom Empire*. His first starring movie role came in the 1935 film *Tumbling Tumbleweeds*. His own company produced his TV series *The Gene Autry Show*, plus *The Adventures of Champion* and *Annie Oakley* in the fifties. In addition, he was the star of the radio show *Melody Ranch* from the early forties through the early fifties.

Autry recorded extensively and made several hit records, particularly several Christmas hits, including "Rudolph the Red-Nosed Reindeer" (number one in 1949, and it also charted the next four holiday seasons), "Here Comes Santa Claus" (charted in 1947, 1948, and 1950), and "Frosty the Snowman" (charted in 1950 and 1952).

He was also the writer or cowriter of over 200 songs. "Back in the Saddle Again" is one example of his writing. His recording of the song was inducted into the Grammy Hall of Fame in 1997. He was also the composer or co-composer of several hits in the country-western market, some of which also became national hits. His most famous compositions include "That Silver-Haired Daddy of Mine," "At Mail Call Today," "Have I Told You Lately That I Love You?," and "Here Comes Santa Claus."

In his latter years, Gene Autry was less active in show business, concentrating instead on his considerable business empire, which included radio and television stations, recording and publishing firms, movie studios, and the California (or Anaheim) Angels baseball team.

Autry's many honors and awards include being inducted into the Country Music Hall of Fame in 1969. The Country Music Association presented him with the Pioneer Award in 1973 in recognition of his contributions to films and music since the early thirties.

Roy Rogers, known as "The King of the Cowboys," was a major western film star between the late thirties and the early fifties. Rogers, whose birth name was Leonard Slye, used the name Dick Weston when he first appeared in films. He became known as Roy Rogers with his first starring role in *Under Western Skies* in 1938. He, his horse Trigger, and Dale Evans, whom he married in 1947, starred in a succession of western films. Rogers became Gene Autry's chief rival, starring in more than a hundred films and in his own television series in the early fifties. He became a member of the Country Music Hall of Fame in 1988.

One of RIAA and NEA's *Songs of the Century* was Dale Evans's "Happy Trails." She wanted to write a song for her husband that he could use on his personal appearances and on their Saturday night radio show. When Roy gave autographs, he signed them "Many Happy Trails, Roy and Trigger." That gave Evans the idea for the song, which she wrote in a couple of hours. She took it to the show's orchestra leader, and they closed the show with the song. Their audiences loved the song and it became their closing theme.

Elected to the Country Music Hall of Fame in 1980, the Sons of the Pioneers, America's premier western singing group, was formed in 1933 as the Pioneer Trio by Leonard Slye, Bob Nolan, and Tim Spencer. They soon added country fiddler Hugh Farr and Hugh's guitarist brother, Karl. That quintet became the most famous incarnation of the Sons of the Pioneers. When Slye left the group to sign with Republic Pictures and become Roy Rogers in 1937, comedian–bass player Pat Brady was his replacement.

The songs composed by Bob Nolan and Tim Spencer were often inspired by their participation in western films, including several Roy Rogers films. Some of their most famous recordings include "Tumbling Tumbleweeds" (1934 and 1948), "Cool Water" (1941 and 1948), and "Room Full of Roses" (1949).

"Cool Water" was written in 1941 by Bob Nolan. The Sons of the Pioneers' 1948 recording with Vaughn Monroe was a pop crossover hit. Their original 1941 recording of the song was inducted into the Grammy Hall of Fame in 1986.

"Riders in the Sky," a haunting western number (not country), subtitled "A Cowboy Legend," was written by Stan Jones, a park ranger. Once Jones shared the song with Bob Nolan of the Sons of the Pioneers, the group recorded it for RCA Victor, but their version didn't catch on with the public. It wasn't until Vaughn Monroe's dramatic version was released that the song became a major hit. His recording was named by RIAA and NEA as one of its *Songs of the Century*. To read about the song's origin, see http://www.westernmusic.org/HallOfFamefiles/StanJones.html.

Woodward Maurice "Tex" Ritter took his nickname from his home state. After studying law at the University of Texas and Northwestern, Ritter tried the Broadway stage, appearing in some thirty productions, including "Green Grow the Lilacs," the play that became the basis for Rodgers and Hammerstein's classic musical *Oklahoma!* While in New York City, he also appeared on radio's *Cowboy Tom's Round-Up* and cohosted the WHN *Barn Dance* with Ray Whitley. Ritter moved to California in the mid-thirties and starred in sixty cowboy films. He became the first country artist signed by the new Capitol label. He performed the theme song from the 1952 film *High Noon* on the movie's soundtrack. The song won the Academy Award for Best Song, and Ritter's recording of it was particularly popular on the country chart, but his and Frankie Laine's version made *Billboard*'s pop chart. Tex was the father of television star John Ritter (*Three's Company*). Tex was inducted into the Country Music Hall of Fame in 1964.

"Cattle Call" was written by Tex Owen in 1934, but it is most remembered for Eddy Arnold's recording of the song in 1945. It is a classic western song, and the yodel-like "cattle call" is very distinctive. RIAA and NEA's *Songs of the Century* included Eddy Arnold's "Cattle Call."

WESTERN SWING

When "swing" was the thing, during the Big Band era, young people across the nation were dancing to the music of Benny Goodman, Tommy Dorsey, Glenn Miller, and other popular dance bands. But "swing" wasn't limited to urban ballrooms or to "city" bands. The country bands that played the dance halls of Texas, Oklahoma, and other western states began to combine traditional country with swing to create what became known as "western swing."

Bob Wills and Milton Brown popularized the genre in the late thirties and early forties. Wills became known as the father of the genre since he and his band remained popular for several decades, during which he had a remarkable string of hit singles.

The birth of western swing can be traced to "The Light Crust Dough-boys," a group named for the sponsor of their radio show, the Burris Mill and Elevator Company, which produced "Light Crust Flour." Fiddler Bob Wills and vocalist Milton Brown were original members of that band, but they soon left to form their own western swing groups.

It was Milton Brown and his Musical Brownies and Bob Wills and his Texas Playboys that first included the amplified steel guitar and other elec-trified instruments into their traditional string bands. In the late thirties, Wills also added some horns. When the World War II draft took most of his players, Wills reorganized his band and moved to California, where they found many transplanted Texans and Okies eager for the western swing sound. Bob Wills was inducted into the Country Music Hall of Fame in 1968. However, many of his most famous recordings were between 1939 and 1944, a period not covered by this book.

While the genre draws from country music for much of its instrumenta-tion and lyrics, it differs with respect to its rhythms and sophisticated dance-orchestra arrangements. A vocal version of Bob Wills's 1935 instru-mental "Spanish Two Step," called "New Spanish Two-Step," became Wills's biggest hit, tying "Guitar Polka" for weeks at the top of the country chart in 1946.

"Sugar Moon," a song about a woman marking the days until she can see her man again, was another chart-topping hit in 1947 for Bob Wills and his Texas Playboys.

"Oklahoma Hills" was written by Woody and Jack Guthrie. Woody's cousin, Leon, recorded a 1945 western swing version of the song that became one of the year's biggest country hits. In 2001, the Oklahoma State Legislature declared the Guthries' "Oklahoma Hills" the Official State Folk Song.

By the mid-fifties, the zenith of western swing had passed, but the style found new life in the seventies in bands like Asleep at the Wheel and, later again, in the music of George Strait.

HONKY-TONK

During the forties and early fifties, a unique institution sprang up in the oil-booming farming communities of Texas and Louisiana—the honky-tonk.

These tiny rural taverns provided the itinerant, hardworking laborers a place to drink and socialize. It was inevitable that a distinctive style of music would develop for these rather low-class, uncultured, drinking-and-carousing hangouts. What developed was a style of country music called "honky-tonk," with its heavy beat, electrified instruments, and bold lyrics. The honky-tonk and its music became major ingredients of the country lifestyle, and a major factor in country music.

The honky-tonk spawned a rash of songs about the lifestyle: songs about heartbreak, infidelity, pain that could only be numbed with alcohol, morning-after remorse, and religious guilt. Honky-tonk lyrics tend to be emotionally simple and direct.

Many country performers got their training by playing music in honky-tonks. Beginning with Al Dexter, Jimmy Skinner, and Floyd Tillman during the forties, a distinct honky-tonk style developed further with stars like Lefty Frizzell, Hank Williams, and Webb Pierce in the fifties.

The basic honky-tonk sound features acoustic guitar, fiddle, and string bass, while the vocals are often the same "high lonesome" sound of traditional country and bluegrass. As the movement progressed, the steel guitar, which was imported from Hawaii, drums, and eventually amplified instruments were added to the honky-tonk bands so they could be heard over the din of a barroom jammed with dancing couples.

The performers had to find appropriate music to play for the honky-tonk crowd. Generally, the music became livelier and some of the lyrics got more raucous and off color.

The music initially became popular during World War II, but the style's golden era came after the war.

Ted Daffan's "Headin' Down the Wrong Highway" is a classic honky-tonk number from 1945. Daffan confessed that the song was inspired by his own personal experiences with heavy drinking. One hangover morning in Los Angeles, he went to the nearest bar for another drink to ease the pain of the previous night. Seeing two seedy customers in the bar at that time of day convinced Daffan he was definitely on the wrong road. The lyrics to the song began to materialize, so he left the bar immediately to write them down and, in just a few minutes, the song—with music and lyrics—was done.

Hank Thompson's "The Wild Side of Life" became a number-one country hit in 1952. Thompson's recording with his Brazos Valley Boys became a classic honky-tonk song. When Thompson's wife of less than a year asked for a divorce, he couldn't understand why, but he agreed. He and a buddy went to a dance and saw his former wife drinking and having a good time with another guy. Thompson told his buddy she had left him to go back to "the wild side of life." That comment gave him the idea for the song. Thompson was inducted into the Country Music Hall of Fame in 1989.

One day, Jay Miller heard "The Wild Side of Life" on his car radio. One line in the song, "I didn't know God made honky-tonk angels," inspired him to write "It Wasn't God Who Made Honky-Tonk Angels," which became a Kitty Wells number-one country hit. Inducted into the Country Music Hall of Fame in 1976, Kitty Wells became the first female solo artist to score a number-one hit on the *Billboard* country charts with Miller's song in 1952. The song forever changed how women were seen, both in song and professionally.

William Orville "Lefty" Frizzell grew up in the area of Corsicana, Texas. He earned his nickname when he fought and won several amateur fights. By his early twenties, Frizzell had learned to play guitar and sing and was performing in the honky-tonks in the Corsicana area. A Dallas agent took Lefty's demo recording of "If You've Got the Money" to Nashville and secured him a recording contract. Released in 1950, the song became Frizzell's first chart single, his first number-one single, and launched his country music career. Lefty said the idea for the song came when a friend visiting from Oklahoma wanted to go out on the town. Lefty's reply was, "Well, if you got the money, I got the time!" Frizzell collected three number-one hits in 1951: "Always Late (with Your Kisses)," "I Want to Be with You Always," and "I Love You a Thousand Ways." For a couple of years in the early fifties, Lefty and Hank Williams toured together. Hank was instrumental in getting Lefty an invitation to join the *Grand Ole Opry*. In 1952, Lefty's "Give Me More, More, More (Of Your Kisses)" was his last number-one hit on the country chart during the period covered by this book. Frizzell was inducted into the Country Music Hall of Fame in 1982.

Jimmy Wakely's recording of "One Has My Name (the Other Has My Heart)" was one of the first "cheating songs." This song was so daring for this era that it was banned in some places. The lyrics were written by Hal Blair. Eddie Dean wrote the music, and his wife came up with the title. Blair had been engaged to marry a girl when he returned from overseas after the war, but due to a misunderstanding they called off the wedding. On the rebound, Blair married someone else. The song's lyrics comment about his being married to one person, but his former intended still has his love.

Country singer and songwriter Floyd Tillman wrote "Slipping Around," one of the classic "cheating songs." It was first popularized on the country charts by Tillman and by Ernest Tubb. When Jimmy Wakely and pop singer Margaret Whiting recorded a duet version, it became a number-one hit on both the country and pop charts.

Tillman also wrote "I Love You So Much It Hurts." One day, shortly after his discharge from the military following World War II, Tillman was just sitting around, fooling with his guitar. He played four notes which made him think of the words "I love you so," and then simply improvised "much it hurts me." He said the rest of the song followed almost automatically. He was concerned that the song wasn't country enough, so he didn't record it until 1948. Jimmy Wakely's version of the song was the biggest hit on the country chart, and it also made the pop charts. In 1949, the song was popularized further in the pop market in a recording by the Mills Brothers. Singer and songwriter Floyd Tillman was inducted into the Country Music Hall of Fame in 1984.

"There Stands the Glass," practically the epitome of country drinking songs, was written and popularized by Webb Pierce in 1953. Jim Denny of the *Grand Ole Opry,* and publisher Fred Rose. told Pierce the song would ruin his career because it condoned drinking. But instead, it became a classic honky-tonk song.

Ray Price was born on an East Texas farm but grew up in Dallas. After high school and serving in the armed forces, he returned to civilian life in 1946 and attended college to study veterinary medicine. During his stay in college, he began playing and singing for college events and in local clubs, which led to performing on *Big D Jamboree* in Dallas. In the early fifties, Price began recording for Nashville's Bullet Records but soon moved to Columbia. In 1952, he earned an Opry invitation, but it really wasn't until the later fifties that he really began to achieve star status. His first big hit came in 1956 with "Crazy Arms," followed in 1957 by "My Shoes Keep Walking Back to You." His recording of "City Lights" spent thirteen weeks at number one in 1958. Bill Anderson, the writer of "City Lights," was a nineteen-year-old college student working as a part-time disc jockey in Commerce, Georgia, when he wrote the song. One night, he went out on top of the hotel, looked at the lights of the town and then looked up at the stars. The idea for "City Lights" began to materialize. He said he "was asking could that same God who made the stars that were so beautiful and clean make the lights of the town which sometimes tended to be kind of dirty?" (Horstman).

His most famous recordings evidencing the Nashville-sound influence came after the mid-sixties, like "For the Good Times" in 1966. Price was inducted into the Country Music Hall of Fame in 1996.

Hank Williams became one of the most famous country singers and songwriters of all time. He was a charismatic figure and the leading exponent of the honky-tonk style of country music. After his early death in 1953, he became a country legend.

"Lovesick Blues" was written by lyricist Irving Mills and composer Cliff Friend after World War I and was first recorded in 1922 without much success. When Hank Williams recorded it with his Drifting Cowboys, he added some personal touches, including a yodel-like swoop at the end of the first phrase ("I got a feelin' called the blues [swoop]; Oh, oh, Lawd, since my baby said goodbye"). When his recording was released in 1949, it shot to the top of the charts. Its success got him an invitation to join the *Grand Ole Opry*. Williams's recording of "Lovesick Blues" was named by the Library of Congress to the National Recording Registry. In addition to "Lovesick Blues," Williams also had success with "Mind Your Own Business," and "My Bucket's Got a Hole in It" in 1949.

When Williams's movie biography *Your Cheatin' Heart* was released in 1964, "I'm So Lonesome I Could Cry," from 1949, was used on the soundtrack. This Williams song was one of the songs on RIAA and NEA's list of

Hank Williams, Sr. (Courtesy of Photofest)

Songs of the Century, and *Rolling Stone* magazine named it to their "500 Greatest Songs of All Time." It was one of the oldest songs on the list, and one of only two from the forties. The song was about the depression Hank felt due to his troubled relationship with his wife, Audrey. The opening lines, "Hear that lonesome whippoorwill/He sounds too blue to fly," vividly paint his lonesomeness.

Hank Williams and his Drifting Cowboys had a string of hit singles in 1950, including the "Long Gone Lonesome Blues," "Why Don't You Love Me," and "Moanin' the Blues." "Long Gone Lonesome Blues" is another example of Williams's semiyodels interspersed into the song's lyrics. "Long Gone Lonesome Blues" was used on the soundtrack of Williams's movie biography. The lyrics claim he "ain't had no lovin' ... in a long, long while" because his sweetheart won't get "nearer or further than a country mile." "Moanin' the Blues" is another song of lost and unrequited love—a constantly recurring theme in country music.

Also in 1950, Hank Williams began recording a series of spiritual records under the name Luke the Drifter. Luke the Drifter was a character who preached the gospel and performed good deeds while the real Williams was a drunkard who cheated on the women of his life.

Williams continued to rack up hits in 1951, beginning with the number-one hit "Cold, Cold Heart." Fred Rose, Williams's publisher, thought the song had potential on the pop market. After several "no, thanks" from recording companies who thought it was "too hillbilly," Columbia's A&R director, Mitch Miller, was willing to gamble on it. He had an aspiring young singer, Tony Bennett, record it, and it became Bennett's second number-one hit. Hank also began experiencing more crossover success himself, and he appeared on the Perry Como television show and toured with Bob Hope, Jack Benny, and Minnie Pearl.

In the summer of 1951, Williams toured with the "Hadacol Caravan," a tour promoting the patent medicine Hadacol, which was marketed as a vitamin supplement but was twelve percent alcohol, which helped it sell in counties that prohibited the sale of alcohol. During that tour, Williams wrote "Hey, Good Lookin'," which became almost as popular as "Cold, Cold Heart." The song, a moderate boogie, is an upbeat number that capitalized on a slang expression then in vogue ("Hey, good lookin', what-cha got cookin'?").

Next, Williams scored with another self-pitying, unrequited love song, "I Can't Help It (If I'm Still in Love With You)." This song, like "Cold, Cold Heart," was directly related to his deteriorating marriage.

Even though his professional career was soaring, Williams's personal life was spinning out of control. He'd had a drinking problem for many years, but now his drinking markedly increased. In the fall of 1951, he was on a hunting trip on his farm near Franklin, Tennessee, when he tripped, fell, and aggravated a back injury. Williams quickly became addicted to the morphine and other pain killers he took to ease the pain.

In January of 1952, Williams and his wife separated for a final time. Despite all his success, his life continued its downward spiral. A major blow came in October, when he was fired from the *Grand Ole Opry*.

He then joined Shreveport's *Louisiana Hayride*. It was there that he came into contact with the Cajun culture of south Louisiana. The resulting song, "Jambalaya (On the Bayou)" became a big hit on the country and pop charts. Read more about "Jambalaya" in the **Country Covers** section (above).

"Kaw-Liga," a song written by Hank Williams and Fred Rose, was another number-one hit for Williams in 1953, and the song was used on the soundtrack of Williams's biopic *Your Cheatin' Heart*. It was about a wooden Indian named "Kaw-Liga" (pronounced Kuh-lie-juh) that never got a kiss from the lovely Indian maid with coal-black hair.

Billie Jean Eshlimar, Williams's second wife, says "Your Cheatin' Heart" came about during their engagement, when they drove to her south Louisiana home to tell her parents they were going to get married. As Hank was telling her about the problems with his previous marriage, he said that, some day, his ex-wife's cheatin' heart would have to pay. He immediately thought the idea would make a good song, so he composed the lyrics in a matter of minutes and had Billie Jean write them down. Once recorded, Williams's version became a number-one hit in 1953. It was also, of course, featured on the soundtrack of *Your Cheatin' Heart*. RIAA and NEA named it one of their *Songs of the Century*.

Williams was scheduled to play a concert in Canton, Ohio, on New Year's Day 1953. He was to fly out of Knoxville, Tennessee, on New Year's Eve, but the weather was so poor, he hired a chauffeur to drive him in his new Cadillac. Before they left, a doctor injected Williams with shots of vitamin B-12 and morphine. With Hank and a bottle of whiskey in the back seat, the chauffeur headed out for Ohio. When they were later stopped for speeding, the policeman noticed the passenger looked like he was dead. Williams was taken to the Oak Hill, West Virginia, hospital and, at age twenty-nine, he was officially declared dead on January 1, 1953. Controversy surrounds his exact cause of death. Ironically, one of the last songs he recorded was "I'll Never Get Out of This World Alive." Williams died but a legend was born.

Hank Williams's recording of "Take These Chains from My Heart," a song written by Fred Rose and Hy Heath, was released after his death and became his fourth number-one hit of 1953.

In the years following his death, Williams's songs would be covered countless times by numerous singers. Performers and songwriters lauded his influence, and his son, Hank Williams, Jr., became a country music star. Hank Williams, Sr., was inducted into the Country Music Hall of Fame in 1961.

THE NASHVILLE SOUND

The Nashville sound, or what is sometimes called "countrypolitan," emerged in the fifties in an attempt to make country music appeal to a broader market. The movement was led by legendary guitarist Chet Atkins, who was the head of RCA Records' country division in Nashville. Atkins produced recordings for a large roster of country talent, and the result—using the same type of instrumental arrangements and the same stable of musicians—became rather predictable and standardized. (Generally, recording companies did not, and still do not, allow individual performers to use their own bands. They use session musicians made up of a selected stock of

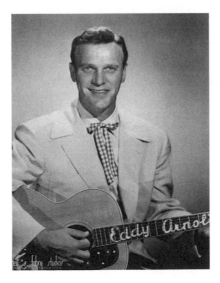

Eddy Arnold, the Tennessee Plowboy.
(Courtesy of Photofest)

quality players.) The Nashville sound was slick and sophisticated, especially compared to honky-tonk. Atkins designed a smooth, commercial product that eliminated a lot of the hillbilly sounds that noncountry listeners detested. His productions were pop-oriented country.

Eddy Arnold is greatly responsible for bringing country music out of its hillbilly roots into popular music's mainstream. He became one of the chief exponents of the Nashville sound and the most popular country performer of his era.

So what made Eddy Arnold a country superstar? He was managed by Tom Parker, later famous as Col. Tom Parker—Elvis Presley's manager. Arnold never wore gaudy rhinestones or embroidered outfits, like most of the country stars of the era, and he also avoided honky-tonk songs, so his image and recordings were more palatable to those who had never listened to country music before. The most important factor, however, was his voice, which was much more round and polished than the nasal twang of most of his country contemporaries. Steve Sholes, who produced his early hits, called him a natural singer and compared him to Bing Crosby.

Born in Henderson, Tennessee, Arnold left his sharecropper past when he turned eighteen to seek fame and fortune in the music business. His first success came as the lead male vocalist for the Pee Wee King band in 1940. He became a solo act in 1943 and was soon a *Grand Ole Opry* star. He signed with RCA Victor and cut his first record in 1944. Almost all of the country and western singers of the era had a title or nickname. Arnold was known as "The Tennessee Plowboy," which he dropped to appeal to a broader fan base.

Although his early records sold well, his first number-one hits did not come until 1947, with "It's a Sin," "What Is Life Without Love," and "I'll Hold You In My Heart (Till I Can Hold You In My Arms)," which became the biggest country hit of the decade and confirmed that Arnold was now a country superstar. He branched out by appearing on several radio and television variety shows, which broadened his fan base considerably. In 1948, his "Bouquet of Roses," "Anytime," "Just a Little Lovin' (Will Go a Long, Long Way)," "Texarkana Baby," and "A Heart Full of Love" were number-one country hits. All of those 1948 singles also charted on *Billboard*'s pop chart. His success continued in 1949 with "Don't Rob Another Man's Castle," "I'm Throwing Rice (At the Girl I Love)," and "One Kiss Too Many." His only number-one country hit of 1950 was "Take Me in Your Arms and Hold Me," followed in 1951 with "I Wanna Play House With You," "There's Been a Change in Me," plus "Kentucky Waltz." "Easy on the Eyes" and "A Full Time Job" were his top-ranked country hits in 1952, with only "Eddy's Song" hitting the top in 1953. His famous "I Really Don't Want to Know" was a country chart topper in 1954. In 1955, he upset many in the country music establishment by going to New York to record with the Hugo Winterhalter Orchestra. The pop-oriented arrangement of "Cattle Call" helped to expand his appeal beyond its country base.

As rock 'n' roll took hold, Arnold's record sales dipped, but he continued to try to court a wider audience by using pop-sounding, string-laced arrangements, the style known as the Nashville sound. That wasn't the end for Eddy Arnold, however. His rendition of "Make the World Go Away" became an international hit in the mid-sixties. Arnold was honored with induction into the Country Music Hall of Fame, in 1966, and was voted Entertainer Of The Year. He also received the Pioneer Award. Over his career, he sold more than 85 million records and had twenty-eight number-one hits on *Billboard*'s country singles chart.

Texan Jim Reeves found fame in both the country and pop venues. After an injury ended his minor-league baseball career in the St. Louis Cardinals farm system, his musical break came while working as an announcer on KWKH Radio in Shreveport, Louisiana. One evening, Hank Williams failed to make his performance on the *Louisiana Hayride*, and Reeves substituted. The owner of Abbott Records was in the audience and signed Reeves to a recording contract. Reeves's first recording success came in 1953 with a number-one country hit called "Mexican Joe," followed by "Bimbo" in 1954, both novelty songs. In 1955, he signed with RCA Victor and joined the *Grand Ole Opry*. In 1957, he and his record producer, Chet Atkins, softened his volume, pitched his vocals lower, and moved him closer to the microphone to produce more of a "crooner" sound. The first recording using this technique was "Four Walls," a song of lost love, actually written for a female singer. "Four Walls" earned him a number-one country hit again and also charted on *Billboard*'s pop chart. He helped establish the Nashville sound, with its use of orchestral arrangements instead of the more common country band. Reeves's most popular hit on the pop chart came with "He'll Have to Go" in 1960. It peaked at number two on *Billboard*. Reeves tragically died in a private airplane crash in 1964. He was posthumously voted into the Country Music Hall of Fame in 1967.

Don Gibson has been responsible for writing three of the most famous songs in country music history: "Sweet Dreams," mostly associated with

Patsy Cline (her movie biography was titled *Sweet Dreams*); "Oh, Lonesome Me;" popularized by Gibson himself; and "I Can't Stop Loving You," which became a number-one hit on the pop charts for Ray Charles. As a singer, he released more than eighty charted records on a range of labels. Gibson began his career in local radio broadcasts and live performances in his native North Carolina. After he left school, he got a job at a Knoxville radio station where he performed on the *Tennessee Barn Dance*. Even though his early recordings were not commercially successful, he began to discover his songwriting talents. "Sweet Dreams" (1955) won a songwriter's contract with Acuff-Rose Publications and a recording deal with MGM. Then, in 1957, while living in a trailer park north of Knoxville, he wrote "Oh Lonesome Me" and "I Can't Stop Loving You" on the same day. Gibson recorded "Oh Lonesome Me" the same year. He and producer Chet Atkins decided to abandon the traditional honky-tonk instrumental background and use a new sound featuring only guitars, a piano, a drummer, upright bass, and background singers. It was one of the first examples of what became known as the Nashville sound, and it won Gibson a number-one country hit. It also set the pattern for other hits, including "Blue Blue Day" (1958) and "Who Cares" (1959). He was inducted into the Nashville Songwriters Hall of Fame in 1973 and was elected to the Country Music Hall of Fame in 2001.

George Morgan joined the *Grand Ole Opry* in 1948 and was inducted into the Country Music Hall of Fame in 1998. Morgan began performing on some small Ohio radio stations, and it was there that he wrote "Candy Kisses." The song experienced enough success that WWVA in Wheeling, West Virginia, hired Morgan for their *Wheelin Jamboree* program. When Eddy Arnold left the *Grand Ole Opry* in 1948, Morgan, whose singing style was similar, was invited to replace him, even though he had never had a hit record. Columbia Records had signed Morgan, but due to the 1948 musicians' strike, he didn't record until early 1949. Recorded at his first session, "Candy Kisses" was finally released on Columbia early the following year, and it hit number one, Morgan's only chart-topper. The idea for the song came from some candy kisses that Morgan's mother brought home when she went grocery shopping. They were not the Hershey variety. The April 30, 1949, *Billboard* Country Top Ten was dominated by Morgan, who had three singles on the chart plus covers of "Candy Kisses" by Elton Britt and by Red Foley. Morgan's youngest daughter, Lorrie, is also an accomplished country artist.

Patsy Cline became the most popular female country singer in recording history. She has become a legend since her tragic death in an airplane crash at age thirty in 1963. Her brief career produced the biggest jukebox hit of all time, "Crazy" (1961), which was written by Willie Nelson.

This Virginia native was born Virginia Patterson Hensley in 1932. Her last name, Cline, came from an ill-fated marriage in 1953. She didn't make much of an impact in the music world until 1957, when she won an *Arthur Godfrey Talent Scout* show performing "Walkin' After Midnight." Her first releases didn't sell well, but after winning the televised talent contest, "Walkin' After Midnight" climbed to number two on the country chart and made the pop chart. A second marriage in 1957 resulted in a tumultuous relationship that was dramatized in *Sweet Dreams*, the 1985 film of Cline's life, starring Jessica Lange.

All other Cline hits came after the period covered by this book, but some of the most noteworthy were "I Fall to Pieces" (1961), "Crazy" (1961), and "She's Got You" (1962). Posthumously, Patsy's "Sweet Dreams" made the Top Ten. She was inducted into the Country Music Hall of Fame in 1973. A musical play, *Always . . . Patsy Cline*, about her life and music, has been performed around the country since the 1990s.

Red Foley's first recording was "Old Shep," a song he had written in 1933 about a dog he had owned as a child. Foley became the first modern country performer to record in Nashville and was one of the first to avail himself of Nashville's cadre of professional studio musicians. His first chart success came in 1945, with the patriotic wartime song "Smoke on the Water," and with "Shame on You." In April 1946, Foley became a regular member of the *Grand Ole Opry*. During the next eight years, Foley established himself as one of the most respected and versatile performers in country music. He acted as master of ceremonies, the straight man for *Opry* comedians like Minnie Pearl, and proved himself a vocalist who could handle all types of material. "New Jolie Blonde" was a hit for him in 1947.

A round dance is a folk dance where the dancers are arranged in a circle. "Tennessee Saturday Night," popularized by Red Foley and the Cumberland Valley Boys in 1949, is an example of a round dance. Foley had a great year in 1949 with four number-one country hits: "Chattanoogie Shoe Shine Boy," "M-I-S-S-I-S-S-I-P-P-I," a duet of "Goodnight Irene" with Ernest Tubb, and "Birmingham Bounce." "Chattanoogie Shoe Shine Boy" was not only a country hit, it crossed over to become a number-one pop hit as well. "M-I-S-S-I-S-S-I-P-P-I" is a spelling song. In it, the lyrics spell "Mississippi" this way: "M-I-crooked letter-crooked letter-I-crooked letter-crooked letter-I-humpback-humpback-I." Read more about "Goodnight, Irene" in the

"From Swing to Sing" chapter. In addition to hitting the top of the country chart, Foley's recording of "Birmingham Bounce" made the pop chart.

In 1953, Foley topped the country chart with recordings of "Midnight" and "Shake a Hand." In 1954, he and Kitty Wells' duet of "One By One" climbed to the top of the country chart. Also in 1954, he moved to KWTO Springfield, Missouri, to host the *Ozark Jubilee*, which became one of the first successful network television country shows in 1956.

Foley's daughter, Shirley, married Pat Boone. Red Foley was elected to the Country Music Hall of Fame in 1967.

Famed guitarist Chet Atkins became an immense musical influence on country, rock, and jazz. As A&R director for RCA's Nashville division, he produced many hit records that are now considered classics. A Country Music Hall of Fame member since 1973, Chet Atkins may be best known for his instrumental prowess, which earned him six Grammy Awards between 1967 and 1976. Behind the scenes, he was perhaps the person most responsible for the Nashville sound.

ROCKABILLY

Change is inevitable, and as country music evolved, the once-prominent fiddle was supplemented with guitars, mandolins, and the dance-band bass fiddle, used for percussive effects. Next, electric instruments and the drums—first introduced by the western swing bands—were added. As rhythm and blues influenced country, a hybrid known as "rockabilly" emerged.

The genesis of rockabilly dates back to the early fifties, when country performer Bill Haley started fusing country with rhythm and blues. Bill Haley and his Comets' "(We're Gonna) Rock Around the Clock" brought rockabilly into the big time in 1955.

With his mid-fifties recordings for Sun Records, Johnny Cash began his trek to superstar status, but he had to exorcise several personal demons along the way. His recordings have found favor in both the country and rock communities. As evidence, he was elected to the Country Music Hall of Fame (1980) and the Rock and Roll Hall of Fame (1992).

While he was serving in the air force in Germany in the early fifties, Cash wrote the future classic "Folsom Prison Blues." When he returned home in 1954, he married, settled in Memphis, became an appliance salesman, and performed gospel music on a local radio station.

He and his band auditioned for Sun owner-producer Sam Phillips in 1954 and, once signed, became the label's most promising talent (Phillips was willing to sell Elvis Presley's contract to RCA because he felt his other talent was sufficient). Cash's first releases were "Cry, Cry, Cry," and "Hey Porter" in 1955. The year 1956 was highlighted by "I Walk the Line," one of his most famous songs. Other country chart toppers include "There You Go" (1957), "Ballad of a Teenage Queen" (1958), "Guess Things Happen That Way" (1958), and "Don't Take Your Guns to Town" (1959). He joined the *Grand Ole Opry* cast in 1956.

In 1958, Cash left the *Opry* and went to Hollywood to try films. He also left Sun to sign with Columbia. Hit singles continued, but Cash turned his attention increasingly to recording albums.

Many people are much more familiar with Johnny Cash, his life, and his music since the 2005 film *Walk the Line*. Reese Witherspoon won the Oscar for Best Performance by an Actress in a Leading Role for her portrayal of June Carter Cash, and Joaquin Phoenix was excellent as Johnny Cash, some of whose most well-known songs were featured on the soundtrack, including "Cry, Cry, Cry," "I Walk the Line," "Ring of Fire," and "Folsom Prison Blues."

Elvis Presley started his music career as a country artist, recording at first for Sam Phillips at Sun Records in Memphis. He toured with country performers like Hank Snow and Johnny Cash, made one appearance on the *Grand Ole Opry*, where he was told he shouldn't quit his truck-driving job, and appeared regularly on *The Louisiana Hayride*. It wasn't until Col. Tom Parker became his manager, and Phillips sold his contract to RCA, that Elvis became the "King of Rock 'n' Roll." Elvis's recordings did well on the country chart, however. His Sun recordings of "Blue Moon of Kentucky" and "That's All Right, Mama" charted well, but "Heartbreak Hotel" and "Don't Be Cruel/Hound Dog" became giant country hits in 1956. Other Elvis hits that made number one on the country chart include "I Forgot to Remember to Forget" (1956), "I Want You, I Need You, I Love You" (1956), "All Shook Up" (1957), "(Let Me Be Your) Teddy Bear" (1957), and "Jailhouse Rock" (1957). Read more about Elvis Presley in the "The Top Recording Artists of the Postwar Years" chapter.

Jerry Lee Lewis became known for his frantic piano style—greatly influenced by Moon Mullican's honky-tonk piano playing—and for his wild singing, which came from his Assembly of God heritage. Two of his 1957 Sun Record releases have become rock 'n' roll classics: "Whole Lot of Shakin'

Going On" and "Great Balls of Fire." Both topped the country chart and peaked at number three and two, respectively, on the *Billboard* pop chart. When it was revealed that Lewis had married his second wife before the divorce from his first wife was final, and that his third wife was his thirteen-year-old cousin, his career suffered irreparable damage. In addition, he experienced a great deal of drug and alcohol problems. The 1998 film *Great Balls of Fire*, with Dennis Quaid, chronicled Lewis's life as that of one of the wildest music personalities of the fifties. Lewis was inducted into the Rock and Roll Hall of Fame in 1986.

Carl Perkins became famous as one of the rockabilly artists that came out of Sun Records in Memphis in the mid-fifties. Although he wrote and recorded other songs, he is primarily known for "Blue Suede Shoes," which he popularized to a number-one hit on the country chart and to number two on the *Billboard* pop chart (although Elvis Presley is also often associated with the song, Presley's version peaked at number twenty). Perkins never really got to capitalize on the success of "Blue Suede Shoes" due to spending a year in recovery from being hurt in an automobile accident. The accident also marked the start of his struggle with alcoholism.

Sonny James is most famous for his 1957 country and crossover number-one hit "Young Love," but he had considerably more success on the country chart. However, most of that success was in the seventies, a period not covered by this book.

The Everly Brothers' success on the country chart paralleled their hits on the pop charts in the late fifties. Read more about the Everly Brothers in "The Top Recording Artists of the Postwar Years" chapter.

As rock 'n' roll evolved very quickly in the mid- to late fifties, rockabilly largely disappeared from the charts after 1958.

9

The Most Noteworthy Composers and Lyricists of the Postwar Years

The songwriters who were most productive during the postwar years include Irving Berlin, Felice and Boudeleaux Bryant, Sammy Cahn, Sammy Fain, Jerry Leiber and Mike Stoller, Frank Loesser, Johnny Mercer, Richard Rodgers and Oscar Hammerstein II, and Jule Styne. The majority of number-one hits of the era were written by songwriters who had only one number-one hit on the combined charts. Other multiple top-of-the-chart writers that might easily be included in the list above include Paul Francis Webster, Jack Lawrence, Al Hoffman, and Carl Sigman.

IRVING BERLIN

Birth name: Israel Baline (or Beilin)
Born: May 11, 1888, Mogilyov, Russia
Died: September 22, 1989, New York, New York

Irving Berlin became arguably the greatest writer of popular songs in the history of America's popular music industry. His career stretches from just after the turn of the century into the sixties. He was elected to the Songwriters Hall of Fame when it was organized in 1970 and was inducted into the Popular Music Hall of Fame in 2000.

He came to the United States as a youngster when his family immigrated and settled in New York City in 1893. When his father died, Berlin, just thirteen years old, left home to earn a living. He worked as a busker singing for pennies, then as a singing waiter. Part of his early music career was spent as a song plugger for publishing firms. He changed his name to Irving Berlin and began his composing career shortly before 1910. His first monster hit, song "Alexander's Ragtime Band," came in 1911.

Over the next fifty years, Irving Berlin produced an amazing abundance of hit songs, including ballads, dance numbers, novelty tunes, and love songs. He was equally at home writing for Broadway revues and musicals as for Hollywood films.

Berlin's hit list is extensive. A few from the early ones, which were revived during the postwar years, include "Alexander's Ragtime Band" (1911, revived in 1947), "Play a Simple Melody" (1914, a top hit in 1950), "I've Got My Love to Keep Me Warm" (1937, a top hit in 1949), and the incredibly famous "White Christmas" (1942, which charted every Christmas season for many years).

By the mid-forties, most people probably thought Berlin was through writing hit songs and shows, but *Annie Get Your Gun* proved his critics vastly wrong. If "There's No Business Like Show Business" had been the only remembered song from the score, it would have been noteworthy, but the musical boasted a number of memorable songs, including "Doin' What Comes Natur'lly," "The Girl That I Marry," "You Can't Get a Man with a Gun," "They Say It's Wonderful," "I Got the Sun in the Morning," and "Anything You Can Do."

Berlin's last well-known songs came in the mid-fifties from the movie musical *White Christmas*. "Count Your Blessings Instead of Sheep" and "Sisters" are from that film. Berlin's last composing venture was the Broadway musical *Mr. President* in 1962. As late as 1983, Berlin's song "Puttin' on the Ritz" was revived and charted.

Berlin's personal favorites among his hit songs were "Easter Parade" (1933), "Always" (1926), "God Bless America" (written in 1918, most popular in 1940), "There's No Business Like Show Business" (1946), and "White Christmas" (1942). Even if that had been all, he would still be considered one of the best songwriters ever.

When ASCAP (American Society of Composer, Authors, and Publishers) selected its *All-Time Hit Parade* on the organization's fiftieth anniversary in 1963, Berlin was honored with three songs on the list of only sixteen songs: "Alexander's Ragtime Band," "God Bless America," and "White Christmas."

Berlin was a cofounder of ASCAP, founder of his own extremely successful publishing company, and he built, with producer Sam Harris, his own Broadway theater, The Music Box.

Berlin died at age 101.

FELICE AND BOUDLEAUX BRYANT

Felice Bryant

Birth name: Matilda Genevieve Scaduto
Born: August 7, 1925, Milwaukee, Wisconsin
Died: April 22, 2003, Gatlinburg, Tennessee

Boudleaux Bryant

Birth name: Diadorius Boudleaux Bryant
Born: February 13, 1920, Shellman, Georgia
Died: June 25, 1987, Knoxville, Tennessee

One of the most productive songwriting partnerships of the 1955–1959 years was the husband-and-wife writing team of Felice and Boudleaux Bryant. Boudleaux was playing country fiddle with Hank Penny and His Radio Cowboys in the cocktail lounge of the Schroeder Hotel in Milwaukee in 1945. He had quit drinking, so he'd walk over to the water fountain by the elevator. Matilda Genevieve Scaduto was the nineteen-year-old elevator operator. Five days after striking up a conversation with this visiting musician from Georgia, Matilda and Boudleaux ran off together (at first, unmarried, later married). Matilda soon became Felice, Boudleaux's pet name for her.

Boudleaux was a trained classical violinist who had studied since the age of five. He played violin on radio station WSB in Atlanta and with the Atlanta Philharmonic for the 1937–38 season. In the early forties, he worked as a western-swing fiddler. Although Felice had no musical training, she and her entire family sang and played instruments by ear. In her quiet hours, unknown to anyone else, she wrote song lyrics to traditional Italian tunes, and in World War II sang and directed shows at the local USO.

In their early years together they bounced around quite a bit. Eventually, they moved back to his hometown where they began to dabble in songwriting.

Their first published song was in 1946. A couple of years later, they signed a publishing-and-recording contract with the famous Acuff-Rose Publishing Company in Nashville, recording as Bud and Betty Bryant.

Arthur Godfrey liked their song "Country Boy" but wanted half the songwriting credit and the publishing rights. They refused. Their first hit came on the country chart when Little Jimmie Dickens recorded their "Country Boy" on Columbia Records in 1949.

With the backing of publisher Fred Rose, they were soon writing hits for other country stars like Carl Smith and Eddy Arnold. The rise of rock 'n' roll in the mid-fifties left many traditional country artists devastated, but Felice and Boudleaux became even more prosperous.

The Bryants' most famous musical affiliation was with two brothers from Kentucky whose talents assimilated the best of Southern music: the Everly Brothers. In 1957, Boudleaux pitched an oft-rejected tune called "Bye Bye Love" to the two aspiring young rockers named Don and Phil Everly. In 1958, the Bryants wrote the Everly Brothers the hit that was to become their signature song. "All I Have To Do Is Dream" became a number-one hit on the country, pop, and R&B charts. Felice and Boudleaux wrote most of the Everly Brothers' early hits. In addition to these two songs, they also contributed "Bird Dog," "Devoted to You," and "Wake Up Little Susie" to the brothers' hit list.

Other well-known compositions by the Bryants include "Love Hurts," popularized by Roy Orbison; and one of five state songs of Tennessee, and the fight song for the University of Tennessee, "Rocky Top."

Their amazing output includes more than 6,000 songs, with over 1,500 recordings, which have sold over 300 million copies. They became one of the most successful songwriting teams ever. The couple has been inducted into the Country Music Hall of Fame, the National Songwriters Hall of Fame, and the Nashville Songwriters Hall of Fame.

SAMMY CAHN

Birth name: Samuel Cohen
Born: June 18, 1913, New York, New York
Died: January 15, 1993, Los Angeles, California

Samuel Cohen was born into a Jewish immigrant family from Polish Galicia. His childhood was spent on the Lower East Side of New York City, where he learned to play the violin. By age fourteen, he was playing for local Bar Mitzvahs.

While still in his teens, Cohen began playing in burlesque-house pit bands. He became friends with a fellow band member, pianist Saul Chaplin. Cohen changed his name to Cahn and they became a songwriting partnership turning out specialty numbers for vaudeville acts. Their first big success came in 1935 when they wrote "Rhythm Is Our Business," which Jimmy Lunceford and his band popularized. Another famous Cahn success of the period was "Bei Mir Bist Du Schoen" (1938).

In 1940, Cahn and Chaplin moved to Hollywood to write for films, but they soon parted ways. In 1942, Cahn began writing with Jule Styne. For the next decade, Cahn and Styne wrote songs for nineteen films.

Among Cahn and Styne's most popular songs were "It's Been a Long, Long Time" (1945), "Saturday Night Is The Loneliest Night Of The Week" (1945), "Five Minutes More" (1946), "Let It Snow, Let It Snow, Let It Snow" (1946), "Day By Day" (1946), "It's Magic" (1948), and the title song of the film *Three Coins in the Fountain* (1954), which won the Oscar for Best Song.

In 1947, Styne and Cahn wrote the successful Broadway musical *High Button Shoes*.

Cahn wrote "Be My Love" with composer Nicholas Brodszky (1951). He also wrote the lyrics for "Teach Me Tonight" (1954) with composer Gene DePaul.

In 1955, longtime friend Frank Sinatra introduced Cahn to composer Jimmy Van Heusen. Cahn and Van Heusen began collaborating and wrote the title song for the 1955 Sinatra film *The Tender Trap*. They also wrote a TV musical version of *Our Town*, starring Sinatra, which included "Love and Marriage." In 1957, Cahn and Van Heusen wrote "All The Way" for the Sinatra film *The Joker Is Wild*. It won Cahn his second Oscar.

A Hole in the Head, another Sinatra film, came out in 1959. For that film, they wrote "High Hopes," which won Cahn his third Oscar. With a revised lyric, the song became John F. Kennedy's campaign song. Cahn won his fourth Oscar, and Van Heusen his third, in 1963 for "Call Me Irresponsible" from *Papa's Delicate Condition*.

Sammy Cahn was nominated for more than thirty Oscars and won four times. He became a member of the Songwriters Hall of Fame in 1972.

SAMMY FAIN

Birth name: Samuel Feinberg
Born: June 17, 1902, New York, New York
Died: December 6, 1989, Los Angeles, California

American popular-music composer Sammy Fain was a Jewish cantor's son. Although he was born in New York City, the family soon moved to the southern part of the state near the Catskill Mountains. After he taught himself to play the piano, Sammy began composing popular songs, but publishers rejected his early efforts. After high school, he returned to the big city to pursue a songwriting career.

He got a job as a stockroom boy for Mills Music Publishing, but was soon promoted to song plugger. During this time, he and singer Artie Dunn also formed a popular vaudeville act.

Fain's first published song came in 1925. He soon met lyricist Irving Kahal, with whom he worked until Kahal's death in 1942. In 1930, they signed with Paramount Pictures. For the remainder of their partnership, Hollywood was their base of operation and where they wrote for several movie studios. They focused on providing one or two songs for each film instead of producing entire scores.

Fain and Kahal also wrote for the Broadway stage. Their 1938 Broadway musical *Right This Way* included two of their most famous songs: "I'll Be Seeing You," which was a chart topper for Bing Crosby in 1944, and "I Can Dream, Can't I?" which became a number-one hit for the Andrews Sisters in 1950.

After Kahal's death, Fain collaborated with several other writers. In 1949 he and Bob Hilliard wrote "Dear Hearts and Gentle People," which became a number-one hit for Bing Crosby in 1950.

Fain collaborated on the scores for the Walt Disney animated feature films *Alice in Wonderland* and *Peter Pan*. In 1954, he and Paul Francis Webster wrote the Academy Award winner "Secret Love" for *Calamity Jane*, which was popularized to a number-one hit by the film's star, Doris Day. In 1955, they won another Academy Award for Best Song for the title tune for *Love Is a Many-Splendored Thing*, which became a top hit for the Four Aces. Another movie song from the team included the title song sung by Pat Boone from *April Love* (1957).

Fain continued to write for the movies for the next two decades. His last effort was for the 1977 Disney animated feature *The Rescuers*.

Fain was inducted into the Songwriters Hall of Fame in 1972.

JERRY LEIBER AND MIKE STOLLER

Jerry Leiber

Birth name: Jerry Leiber
Born: April 25, 1933, Baltimore, Maryland

Mike Stoller

Birth name: Mike Stoller
Born: March 13, 1933, Belle Harbor, New York

Two of the truly talented songwriters of the early rock years were Jerry Leiber and Mike Stoller. This songwriting team arrived on the music scene at a time when authentic rhythm and blues was beginning to be embraced by the record-buying public.

Jerry Leiber, the son of Polish–Jewish immigrants, grew up on the edge of Baltimore's African-American neighborhoods. Mike Stoller was raised in Queens, learning the basics of blues and boogie-woogie from African-American friends at summer camp. Leiber and Stoller met in Los Angeles in 1950 and quickly formed a songwriting partnership. Leiber served as the sharp-witted lyricist, while the classically trained but jazz- and R&B-loving Stoller wrote the music.

In 1951, one of their early songs, "That's What the Good Book Says," was recorded by the Robins on Modern Records (the Robins later became the

Songwriting team of Jerry Leiber (left) & Mike Stoller (right) with Elvis Presley (center) at MGM Studios, Culver City, California, during the filming of *Jailhouse Rock* (Spring 1957). (Courtesy of Photofest)

Coasters). Willie Mae "Big Mama" Thornton was the first to record their "Hound Dog" in 1952.

In 1953, Leiber and Stoller formed their own label, Spark. Two years later, Atlantic Records signed Leiber and Stoller to one of the industry's first independent production deals. For the next decade, Leiber and Stoller had hit songs. Their record productions were often at or near the top of the charts. Some of the most popular were "Searchin'," "Yakety Yak," "Charlie Brown," "Poison Ivy," "Stand By Me," "On Broadway," "Love Potion #9," "Kansas City," and "There Goes My Baby," which premiered the use of strings on an R&B record.

Leiber and Stoller are most famous for the hit songs they wrote that Elvis Presley made famous, including "Hound Dog," "Loving You," "Don't," and "Jailhouse Rock."

After their successful Atlantic production work in the late fifties and early sixties, the team made their final and most successful attempt at running their own record label in 1964. Red Bird Records spotlighted the girl-group sound. The company's very first release—"Chapel of Love" by the Dixie Cups—became a number-one hit. Red Bird's commercial success continued with such classics as the Shangri-La's "Leader of the Pack." Of Red Bird's first thirty singles, eleven made the Top Forty—an outstanding percentage in the music industry.

Leiber and Stoller were inducted into the Songwriters Hall of Fame in 1985, the Record Producers Hall of Fame in 1986, and the Rock and Roll Hall of Fame in 1987. In 1991, they were presented with the prestigious ASCAP Founders Award, and in 2000 were honored with the prestigious Johnny Mercer Award from the Songwriters Hall of Fame. *Smokey Joe's Cafe* (1995) is a musical theatrical revue showcasing thirty-nine Leiber and Stoller songs. The musical was nominated for seven Tony Awards, and the original Broadway cast album won a Grammy Award in 1995. When it closed on Broadway in 2000, it had become the longest-running musical revue in Broadway history.

FRANK LOESSER

Birth name: Frank Henry Loesser
Born: June 29, 1910, New York, New York
Died: July 28, 1969, New York, New York

In the early part of his career, Frank Loesser was primarily a lyricist. He later wrote both words and music. His five Broadway musicals are wonderful contributions to the American musical theater.

Before he wrote his first Broadway musical, *Where's Charley?*, in 1948, he was already famous for songs that had become enormously popular from his Hollywood career. He supplied lyrics to the music of such greats as Jule Styne, Hoagy Carmichael, Burton Lane, Jimmy McHugh, Victor Schertzinger, and Arthur Schwartz.

Loesser was born in New York City. His father was a German-born classical piano teacher, and his older brother, Arthur, became a well-known concert pianist, musicologist, and music critic. Frank never studied music formally.

Loesser wrote his first song at the age of four. As a child, he taught himself to play the harmonica and the piano. When he left college because of the Great Depression, he found diverse jobs in newspaper advertising, as a process server, and as a newspaper editor until he began to write songs and sketches for radio scripts.

By the mid-thirties, he had tried his hand at singing and playing piano in nightclubs, when Universal Pictures offered Loesser a contract to write songs for film musicals. For Universal and later for Paramount Pictures, Loesser wrote songs for more than sixty films over the next thirty years.

When World War II intervened, Loesser was assigned to Special Services, providing lyrics for camp shows with such composers as Harold Rome and Alex North.

The wartime hit "Praise the Lord and Pass the Ammunition" was the first song for which Loesser wrote both the words and music.

After the war he returned to Hollywood, but he was soon lured east to create the score for the musical version of the hugely successful play *Charley's Aunt*. His *Where's Charley?* opened in 1948, and Loesser's songs were very well received. Ray Bolger was the musical's star, and his performance of "Once in Love with Amy" became a classic. Also from the score was "My Darling, My Darling," which became a number-one hit in a duet by Jo Stafford and Gordon MacRae in 1949.

Other hits from the late forties include "I Wish I Didn't Love You So" from *The Perils of Pauline*, "On a Slow Boat to China," and the 1949 Academy Award–winning song "Baby, It's Cold Outside" from *Neptune's Daughter*.

In the fifties, he continued writing famous Broadway musicals, including *Guys and Dolls* (1950), which won the Tony Award for Best Musical. That score included "A Bushel and a Peck," which became a hit duet recording for Perry Como and Betty Hutton.

In addition to his Broadway and Hollywood songs, he also wrote the lyrics for "Hoop-Dee-Doo" with composer Milton DeLugg, which was popularized by Perry Como in 1950.

After *Guys and Dolls*, Loesser returned to Hollywood and created the score for the movie musical *Hans Christian Andersen* (1952), which featured "Thumbelina" and was nominated for an Academy Award.

His next Broadway musical, *The Most Happy Fella*, premiered in 1956. Even though it was more of an operatic musical with almost everything sung and very little dialogue, "Standing on the Corner" was popularized by the Four Lads in 1956.

His next Broadway project in 1960, *Greenwillow*, was nominated for seven Tony Awards, but was not very successful at the box office. In 1961, Loesser's *How to Succeed in Business Without Really Trying* won the Pulitzer prize and seven Tony Awards, including Best Musical.

Loesser died of lung cancer at the age of fifty-nine. He was elected a member of the Songwriters Hall of Fame at its inception in 1970.

JOHNNY MERCER

Birth name: John Herndon Mercer
Born: November 18, 1909, Savannah, Georgia
Died: June 25, 1976, Los Angeles, California

Johnny Mercer was a famous lyricist, composer, singer, recording artist, and record company executive.

John Herndon Mercer was born in Savannah, Georgia, in 1909. His father was a wealthy Southern attorney with a flourishing real estate business, so Johnny could easily afford to attend a fashionable prep school in Virginia. However, when Johnny was in his late teens, his father's business ventures failed because of the Great Depression. Suddenly Mercer couldn't afford to go to college, so he headed for New York City to try his luck at becoming an actor.

His first break came when one of his song lyrics was sung on Broadway in *The Garrick Gaieties of 1930*, but an even bigger break came when he won

Johnny Mercer, circa 1950. (Courtesy of Photofest)

a singing contest sponsored by Paul Whiteman, who hired him as his vocalist. During his Whiteman days, in addition to his singing, he often wrote material for the group. It was Whiteman who introduced Mercer to Hoagy Carmichael. Soon Mercer and Carmichael had a hit with "Lazybones," and his career as a popular song lyricist had begun.

After Whiteman, he sang with Benny Goodman and Bob Crosby. By this time, Mercer had created enough attention as a lyricist to procure a contract to write for Hollywood films. At first he served as lyricist for other composers, but sometimes wrote both lyrics and music. Mercer was a leading lyricist from the thirties into the sixties and remained active until his death in the mid-seventies. He also appeared on radio frequently and recorded often.

As president and cofounder of Capitol Records, Mercer was instrumental in the early recording careers of such musicians as Peggy Lee, Stan Kenton, Nat "King" Cole, Jo Stafford, and Margaret Whiting. By the mid-forties, Capitol was responsible for one sixth of all records sold in the United States.

He wrote lyrics for several Broadway musicals, including *St. Louis Woman* (1946) with Harold Arlen and *Li'l Abner* (1956) with Gene DePaul. In 1954, he wrote the lyrics to DePaul's music for the classic Hollywood movie musical *Seven Brides for Seven Brothers*.

Mercer wrote hit songs in four different decades, from the thirties through the sixties. He wrote more than 1,500 songs, 750 of which are published, and had nearly 100 hit songs. Those figures make him, along with

Irving Berlin and Oscar Hammerstein II, one of the most prolific song-writers of all time.

His hit songs of the postwar era were "Ac-Cent-Tchu-Ate the Positive" (1945); "Dream" (1945); "Laura" (1945); the Academy Award winner of 1946 "On the Atchison, Topeka and the Santa Fe" from *The Harvey Girls*; "Come Rain or Come Shine" from the Broadway musical *St. Louis Woman* (1946); and "In the Cool, Cool, Cool of the Evening" from *Here Comes the Groom*, which won the Oscar for Best Song in 1951. Publisher Edward Marks signed Johnny Mercer to write new lyrics for "The Glow Worm," which the Mills Brothers recorded and popularized in 1952. Other Mercer successes include the English lyrics for "Autumn Leaves" (1950) and "Something's Gotta Give" from *Daddy Long Legs* (1955).

Johnny Mercer was not only a songwriter, but also a popular recording artist in the mid- to late-forties. He wrote both the words and music to "Dream." A recording by the Pied Pipers backed by Paul Weston's orchestra became particularly popular. He had big hit recordings of "On the Atchison, Topeka and the Santa Fe" (1945), "Ac-Cent-Tchu-Ate the Positive" (1945), "Candy" (1945), with Jo Stafford and the Pied Pipers, "Personality" (1946), and "Baby, It's Cold Outside" in a duet with Margaret Whiting (1949).

Mercer became the first songwriter to win the Best Song Oscar four times. He won Academy Awards for "Atchison, Topeka and Santa Fe" from *The Harvey Girls*, "In The Cool, Cool, Cool Of The Evening" from *Here Comes the Groom*, "Moon River" from *Breakfast at Tiffany's* (1961), and "Days Of Wine And Roses" from the film of the same name (1962).

Away from music, Mercer painted watercolors and played golf.

He was the founding president of the Songwriters Hall of Fame and was honored as an inductee in 1971. Mercer's writing continued its influence even after his death, when his widow allowed Barry Manilow to set music to one of his lyrics in 1984. It wasn't a giant hit, but "When October Goes" was a beautiful song and lyric.

RICHARD RODGERS AND OSCAR HAMMERSTEIN II

Richard Rodgers

Birth name: Richard Charles Rodgers
Born: June 28, 1902, New York, New York
Died: December 30, 1979, New York, New York

Oscar Hammerstein II

Birth name: Oscar Hammerstein II
Born: July 12, 1895, New York, New York
Died: August 23, 1960, Doylestown, Pennsylvania

Richard Rodgers became one of the most famous and most prolific composers of popular songs. He collaborated with lyricist Lorenz "Larry" Hart from 1919 until 1943, when he began his association with Oscar Hammerstein II. Rodgers and Hammerstein wrote together until Hammerstein's death in 1960. Rodgers continued to write, as composer and lyricist for some songs. He wrote more than 900 published songs and forty Broadway musicals.

Most of Rodgers's songs were written in a dramatic context for movies and especially for the Broadway stage. In the first decade of their collaboration, Rodgers and Hart averaged two new shows every season.

The most productive period for Rodgers and Hart—and golden age for the American musical—was 1936 to the beginning of America's

Richard Rodgers and Oscar Hammerstein II. (Courtesy of Photofest)

involvement in World War II (1942). Rodgers and Hart produced one gem after another during this period. The Rodgers and Hart partnership came to an end in 1943 just prior to Hart's death. The 1948 film *Words and Music* was based on Rodgers and Hart's partnership.

Rodgers then joined forces with lyricist Oscar Hammerstein II. The first Rodgers and Hammerstein collaboration was *Oklahoma!* in 1943, which was a new genre of Broadway musical, the musical play.

Other than Irving Berlin, Oscar Hammerstein II is the most prolific lyricist of all time. Hammerstein collaborated with several excellent composers, but his association with Richard Rodgers from the early forties until his death is the best known. He had previously collaborated with Jerome Kern, Sigmund Romberg, Rudolf Friml, George Gershwin, and Vincent Youmans.

Hammerstein was born into a show business family. His father was manager of the historic Victoria vaudeville theater in New York City, and his grandfather had been an important opera impresario and theater builder.

The list of hit songs credited to Oscar Hammerstein II is filled with some of the greatest lyrics written from the twenties through the fifties.

The Rodgers and Hammerstein partnership marked the beginning of the most successful songwriting team in Broadway musical history. After *Oklahoma!* came *Carousel* (1945), *South Pacific* (1949), *The King and I* (1951), *Me and Juliet* (1953), *Flower Drum Song* (1958), and *The Sound of Music* (1959). The team wrote one movie musical, *State Fair* (1945), and one for television, *Cinderella* (1957).

Collectively, the Rodgers and Hammerstein musicals earned thirty-five Tony Awards, fifteen Academy Awards, two Pulitzer prizes, two Grammy Awards, and two Emmy Awards.

Hammerstein also collaborated with Jerome Kern on "All Through the Day" for the movie musical *Centennial Summer* (1946).

Despite Hammerstein's death in 1960, Rodgers continued to write for the Broadway stage, collaborating with Stephen Sondheim and Martin Charnin in the sixties and seventies. *No Strings*—Rodgers's only project as both composer and lyricist—earned him two Tony Awards in 1962. He continued to write until the end of the seventies.

Rodgers and Hammerstein's most famous songs from postwar musicals include "If I Loved You" (1945); "You'll Never Walk Alone" (1945), from *Carousel*; and the wonderful songs from *South Pacific*, including "Some

Enchanted Evening" (1949). Rodgers and Hammerstein also collaborated on the songs for the Hollywood movie musical *State Fair*, including "It Might As Well Be Spring" (1945).

Their most memorable songs from Broadway musicals of the fifties include "Hello, Young Lovers" and "We Kiss in a Shadow" from *The King and I* (1951), "I Enjoy Being a Girl" from *Flower Drum Song* (1958), and "Climb Every Mountain" from *The Sound of Music* (1959).

Both men are Songwriters Hall of Fame members.

JULE STYNE

Birth name: Julius Kerwin Stein
Born: December 31, 1905, London, England
Died: September 24, 1994, New York, New York

Jule Styne became a leading composer of music for movies and Broadway from the forties through the sixties. He wrote some 1,500 songs during a seven-decade career.

Styne began studying piano with a teacher at the London Conservatory of Music when he was only six years old. His family emigrated to the United States and settled in Chicago when he was eight. He studied piano at the Chicago College of Music and played with the Chicago, Detroit, and St. Louis Symphony orchestras before his teen years. Because his hands were small and he injured the second finger on his right hand in a factory accident, his classical career never materialized.

At age thirteen, he played in a burlesque house band without his parents' knowledge, and as a teenager played piano in bands and for stage productions. He joined the Ben Pollack Band in 1926. In 1932, he formed his own dance band, Jule Stein and His Society Orchestra, but he soon changed his name to Jule Styne to avoid confusion with Dr. Julius Stein, who was head of Music Corporation of America. His band performed with Fanny Brice for four weeks at the 225 Club in Chicago (years later, Styne would collaborate on the musical about Brice, *Funny Girl*).

Around the mid-thirties, Styne moved to New York City. He played piano in a number of bands and began to work as a vocal coach for such singers as Tony Martin, Alice Faye, Shirley Temple, and Mary Martin.

In the late thirties, he became musical director for Alice Faye's radio show and, after a few years at Twentieth Century Fox, moved to Republic Pictures, where he became songwriter-in-residence. By 1943, he had teamed up with Sammy Cahn. They wrote songs together for three Columbia Pictures films.

Most composers worked on Broadway shows before being called to Hollywood. Not Styne. He teamed with Sammy Cahn to write the following famous postwar songs: "It's Been a Long, Long Time" (1945); "Saturday Night Is the Loneliest Night of the Week" (1945); "Five Minutes More" (1946); "Let It Snow, Let It Snow, Let It Snow" (1946); "It's Magic" from *Romance on the High Seas* (1948); and "Three Coins in a Fountain" from the film of the same name, which won the Academy Award for Best Song (1954).

In 1947, they wrote their first Broadway musical, *High Button Shoes*, which starred Nanette Fabray and Phil Silvers. The most famous song from the score was "Papa, Won't You Dance with Me." In 1949, they had another Broadway success with *Gentlemen Prefer Blondes*, starring Carol Channing. The most famous song from that production was "Diamonds Are a Girl's Best Friend."

In 1956, Styne composed the music for *Bells Are Ringing*, with lyrics by Betty Comden and Adolph Green. The show was a smash hit and premiered the songs "The Party's Over" and "Just in Time." The film version was released in 1960.

The reasonably unsuccessful *Say Darling* came in 1958, followed by the blockbuster *Gypsy*, in 1959, based on the early life of stripper Gypsy Rose Lee. The most memorable songs from the score were "Everything's Coming Up Roses" and "Let Me Entertain You." The film version came out in 1959, and a TV version was made in 1993.

His next Broadway smash hit, *Funny Girl*, in 1964, starred Barbra Streisand as Fanny Brice. The most famous songs from that score include "People" and "Don't Rain on My Parade."

Styne has been a member of the Songwriters Hall of Fame since 1972.

10

The Top Recording Artists of the Postwar Years

During the postwar years, there were 145 number-one hit singles on *Billboard*, with seventy-eight different artists claiming at least one top-hit recording. Thirty-two recording artists managed multiple number ones, which leaves the huge majority with only one. Perry Como was the most dominant recording personality with more than twice the number of top hits as his next closest competitors, Frank Sinatra, Vaughn Monroe, and Bing Crosby. In the next plateau were Sammy Kaye and his orchestra, Nat "King" Cole, Patti Page, Rosemary Clooney, Jo Stafford, and Eddie Fisher.

Of the seventy-eight recording artists listed in the 1955–1959 charts, seventy-four percent had only one number-one hit on the list. Elvis Presley, on the other hand, accounted for fifteen percent of the hits during this five-year period. Two artists—Pat Boone and the Platters—collected four top hits each, while the McGuire Sisters, Perry Como, and the Everly Brothers managed three each. The only others with multiple number ones were Tennessee Ernie Ford, Pérez "Prez" Prado, the Four Aces, Les Baxter, Frank Sinatra, Georgia Gibbs, Guy Mitchell, the Diamonds, David Seville, the Coasters, Frankie Avalon, Paul Anka, the Fleetwoods, and Lloyd Price.

The artists below are in alphabetical order.

PAT BOONE

Birth name: Charles Eugene Boone
Born: June 1, 1934, Jacksonville, Florida

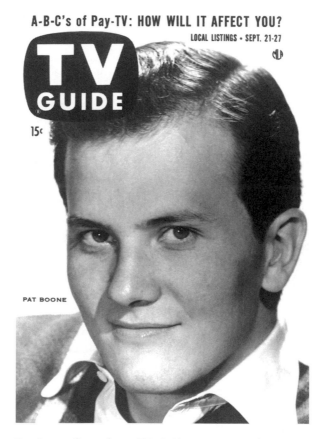

Pat Boone featured on TV Guide Cover, circa late 1950s.
(Courtesy of Photofest)

Pat Boone is the only performer who rivaled the chart dominance of Elvis Presley. Even though he performed soft rock or covers of R&B tunes, parents didn't object to Boone like they did to the blatant sexuality and greasy-haired black-leather-jacket image of Presley. Even during these early years of his recording and film careers, he was still attending college, earning his master's degree in English *and* he was a family man. Boone married country legend Red Foley's daughter, Shirley, and was the father of four daughters. Pat Boone is a descendent of American frontier hero Daniel Boone.

While he was in college at North Texas State, Pat Boone won the semifinal round on *Ted Mack's Original Amateur Hour*. Before he reached the finals, Boone appeared on *Arthur Godfrey's Talent Scouts* program and won. Godfrey's show was a professional engagement, which disqualified him from further competition on Mack's amateur show.

On the way back from New York, Pat Boone stopped in Nashville to visit his parents. While there, a friend introduced him to Randy Wood, the owner of Dot Records. He had seen his Godfrey and Mack appearances and felt Boone had potential. A few months later, Wood signed Boone to a recording contract.

Although Boone was not thrilled with the idea, he did as his boss instructed and covered Fats Domino's "Ain't That a Shame" and Ivory Joe Hunter's "I Almost Lost My Mind," both number-one hits, plus the El Dorados' "At My Front Door (Crazy Little Mama)," the Flamingos' "I'll Be Home," and Little Richard's "Long Tall Sally" and "Tutti-Frutti." He admitted he felt pretty silly singing lyrics like "a wop-bop-a-loo-bop awop-bam-boom," but he was happy when the songs became hits.

Boone was heavily criticized for singing homogenized, sanitized versions of R&B songs. He was recording these R&B songs in his own smooth style, which was quite different from the way they had been done originally. But the formula worked and the records sold.

Finally in 1956, he recorded something original, the title song for the Hollywood film *Friendly Persuasion*.

Known for wearing white buck shoes, Boone's singing style was much more in the tradition of Bing Crosby's than that of other rockers. He was much better suited to ballads like "Don't Forbid Me," which hit number one on *Billboard* in early 1957 for one week.

Pat Boone signed a seven-year movie contract with 20th Century Fox and starred in *Bernadine* in 1957. The producers realized it would be foolish for their youthful, handsome star not to sing, so they added a couple of songs: a title song, written by Johnny Mercer, and "Love Letters in the Sand" (1931), which Boone had recorded earlier. One of the key ingredients connected with the sound of the early years of rock is present in Boone's recording of this song. The song is in four-four time, but the accompaniment, especially the piano, is playing triplets, repeating the chord three times in each beat. "Love Letters in the Sand" became Boone's fourth number-one single.

Boone also scored in 1957 with the title song for his next film *April Love*, which was written by the Academy Award–winning writing team of Sammy Fain and Paul Francis Webster. Boone's recording of the song became a number-one hit on *Billboard* and the song also topped the *Your Hit Parade* chart.

In 1957, television producers came calling. From 1957 to 1960 he hosted his own prime time variety television series, *The Pat Boone/Chevy Showroom*. He became the youngest person to date to be awarded his own (weekly) musical variety show on ABC.

All during this time, Boone never stopped attending college. While he was in New York City for his television show, he graduated *magna cum laude* with his degree in speech and English from Columbia University. His wife and his four daughters attended his graduation.

After 1957, Pat Boone's recording career faded a bit, so he concentrated more on his Hollywood career. His most famous film from this period was *State Fair* in 1962.

With over forty-five million units sold and thirty-eight Top 40 hits, he was recognized by *Billboard* as the number twenty-one recording artist of the second half of the twentieth century. He was also inducted into the Gospel Music Association Hall of Fame in 2003.

Boone's advice book for teenagers, *Twixt Twelve and Twenty*, was the top nonfiction best seller for two years.

One of Pat and Shirley's daughters, Debbie, practically topped all her Dad's achievements in one fell swoop in 1977. Her recording of the title song from the film *You Light Up My Life* was a *Billboard* number-one hit for ten weeks, the top hit of the entire decade of the seventies.

ROSEMARY CLOONEY

Birth name: Rosemary Clooney
Born: May 23, 1928, Maysville, Kentucky
Death: June 29, 2002, Beverly Hills, California

Rosemary Clooney became one of the most popular female singers of the fifties. Rosemary, Betty, and her brother Nick all became entertainers (her brother's son, George Clooney, became a famous actor).

In 1945, Rosemary and Betty, as the Clooney Sisters, began singing on a Cincinnati radio station. A year later, the Clooney Sisters signed on with Tony Pastor's band, with whom they recorded. Three years later, Rosemary became a soloist when Columbia's A&R man, Mitch Miller, helped her toward a career in records, television, nightclubs, and films.

Her first number-one single, "Come on-a My House," was her third chart single. Other number-one hits include "Half as Much" (1952), "Hey There" (1954), and "This Ole House" (1954). Clooney also reached Gold status with "Botch-a-Me (Ba-Ba-Baciami Piccina)" in 1952.

She appeared in several films, but she is most famous for appearing in *White Christmas* (1954) with Bing Crosby. She and her sister Betty recorded Irving Berlin's clever duet "Sisters," and she released a single version of "Count Your Blessings (Instead of Sheep)" from *White Christmas*.

Clooney was married three times, twice to José Ferrer (from 1953 until 1961 and again from 1964 to 1967). They had five children, including Gabriel Ferrer—who married Pat Boone's daughter Debby—and actor Miguel Ferrer. Clooney married Dante DePaolo in 1997.

Rosemary Clooney was inducted into the Popular Music Hall of Fame in 2000. A longtime smoker, she died from lung cancer in 2002.

NAT "KING" COLE

Birth name: Nathaniel Adams Coles
Born: March 17, 1919, Montgomery, Alabama
Death: February 15, 1965, Santa Monica, California

Nat "King" Cole, circa 1950s. (Courtesy of Photofest)

Nat Coles's mother, a church organist, taught him to play the piano. She saw to it that he learned a wide range of music from jazz and gospel to

European classics. When the family lived in the Bronzeville section of Chicago, Nat was exposed to many famous African American artists who performed in the clubs of his neighborhood.

In the mid-thirties, while he was still in his teens, Nat began performing and adopted "Cole" as his stage name. Nat's older brother, Eddie, joined Nat's group as bassist and they made their first recording in 1936 under Eddie's name.

Nat toured as pianist with Eubie Blake's revue, *Shuffle Along*. When the tour suddenly folded out West, Nat decided to stay in California. He married one of the dancers in the cast. In 1939, he formed a trio with guitarist Oscar Moore and bassist Wesley Prince (Johnny Miller later replaced Prince). He added the "King" to his name in 1940, undoubtedly from the obvious relation to the nursery rhyme "Old King Cole." Although he sang with the trio occasionally, Cole considered himself a jazz pianist and was rather shy about his voice. His singing career actually started almost by accident. On a particular evening, an overly enthusiastic, drunk patron insisted that he sing "Sweet Lorraine." At first he refused, but after he complied, his relaxed style and velvet voice became a major asset. The trio signed with Capitol Records in 1943, and Nat "King" Cole began to emerge as a solo attraction.

Cole's most famous recordings of the postwar years were "(I Love You) For Sentimental Reasons" (1946), "Nature Boy" (1948), "Mona Lisa" (1950), and "Too Young" (1951). In addition to those four number-one hits, he collected Gold Records for "The Christmas Song" (1946), "Pretend" (1953), and "Answer Me, My Love" (1954). His recording of "Nature Boy" was inducted into the Grammy Hall of Fame in 1999. His 1957 single "When I Fall in Love" was more popular in England than in the U.S., but it has become one of his signature recordings in the years since. He continued to have chart hits into the sixties.

As albums became more important in the mid-fifties, Cole also released several LPs that became popular sellers.

In the fifties, he became the first African American performer to have his own radio program and later his own television series. Unfortunately, both were canceled because companies were reticent to sponsor black artists. Nat faced a significant amount of racial discrimination during his career. He refused to perform for segregated audiences and, in 1956, was physically attacked while performing in Birmingham, Alabama.

He appeared in several Hollywood films, but his only starring role in films was as W. C. Handy in *St. Louis Blues* (1958).

At the time of his death from lung cancer, Cole had sold 50 million dollars worth of records for Capitol, which had twenty-nine of his albums on the market at once. The Capitol Records building is sometimes referred to as "the house that Nat built."

Nat's daughter, Natalie, has also had a very successful recording career. Twenty-seven years after her father's death, she recorded a duet of "Unforgettable" with an edited version of her father's performance of the song. Even though the song was written in 1951, it won the Song of the Year Grammy Award in 1992. Cole was elected to the Big Band and Jazz Hall of Fame in 1993 and was inducted into the Popular Music Hall of Fame in 2003.

PERRY COMO

Birth name: Pierino Roland Como
Born: May 18, 1912, Canonsburg, Pennsylvania
Death: May 12, 2001, Jupiter Inlet, Florida

Perry Como, late 1950s. (Courtesy of Photofest)

Perry Como became one of the most dominant performers in the recording field from the mid-forties through the fifties. His amazingly popular career extended into the seventies, but his prime popularity came from the end of the big band era into the early years of rock.

After high school, he opened a barbershop in his hometown and married his hometown sweetheart. Perry Como had always loved singing, so he finally decided if his vocal idol Bing Crosby could make it, so could he. In 1933, he successfully auditioned as singer for Freddie Carlone's band. After touring with that group for three years, he moved to Ted Weems's band. When Weems dissolved his orchestra in 1942, Como worked for CBS for a couple of years. Just as he was about to return to Canonsburg and his barbering career, NBC offered him a spot on the *Supper Club*.

In 1943, he signed a solo recording contract and had his first hit with "Till the End of Time" in 1945. He collected 100 *Billboard* chart singles in the pre-rock era and twenty-nine more during the rock era. Perry Como's biggest hit recordings include "Till the End of Time" (1945), "If I Loved You" (1945), "Prisoner of Love" (1946), "Surrender" (1946), "They Say It's Wonderful" (1946), "Chi-Baba, Chi-Baba" (1947), "Some Enchanted Evening" (1949), "A – You're Adorable" (1949), "Hoop-Dee-Doo" (1950), "A Bushel and a Peck" with Betty Hutton (1950), "A Dreamer's Holiday" (1950), "If" (1951), "Don't Let the Stars Get in Your Eyes" (1953), "No Other Love" (1953), "Wanted" (1954), "Hot Diggity" (1956), "Round and Round" (1957), and "Catch a Falling Star" (1958), which became the first "Gold Record" certified by RIAA.

Como appeared in several Hollywood films, including *Something for the Boys* (1944), *Doll Face* (1945), *If I'm Lucky* (1946), and *Words and Music* (1948), but he was much more successful on television. He hosted an extremely successful weekly hour-long variety show from 1955 to 1963. Also, his annual Christmas show became a holiday tradition. His relaxed singing style and his informality with his audience—on TV or in live performances—became his trademark. Even though Como was not a rock 'n' roll singer, he was not a critic of it either. He welcomed many rock guest stars on his television series.

His collective disc sales by the end of the sixties were estimated at more than fifty million. Como was elected to the Big Band and Jazz Hall of Fame in 2004 and was inducted into the Popular Music Hall of Fame in 2004. His final Top 40 hit was a cover of Don McLean's "And I Love You So" in 1973.

BING CROSBY

Birth name: Harry Lillis Crosby
Born: May 3, 1903, Tacoma, Washington
Death: October 14, 1977, Madrid, Spain

Bing Crosby, 1947. (Courtesy of Photofest)

Bing Crosby had the most successful career of any artist in the twentieth century. According to Joel Whitburn's *Pop Memories* and his *A Century of Pop Music*, Crosby was the number-one recording artist of the thirties and the forties, the top-recording artist of the 1890–1954 pre-rock era, and the top recording artist of the first half of the twentieth century. However, he became a chart topper not only in popular music, but also at the movie box office. His smooth, rich baritone voice became instantly recognizable and his expertise with lyrics was unmatched. When Frank Sinatra became Tommy Dorsey's male vocalist, Dorsey told him, "there is only one singer you ought to listen to, and his name is Crosby. All that matters to him is the words" (Kelly). Crosby became the nation's favorite crooner, recording everything from ballads to swing to blues, and his affable personality shone brightly over the radio, then later on television and on the silver screen.

He received his nickname, "Bing," during his childhood because of his attachment to the comic strip *The Bingville Bugle*.

While studying law at Gonzaga College, he started a jazz band with a friend, Al Rinker, in which he was the vocalist and drummer. When the group broke up in the mid-twenties, Crosby and Rinker quit school and headed for Los Angeles. They hoped Rinker's sister Mildred Bailey could help them get started in show business. After several jobs on the West Coast, Paul Whiteman hired them to sing with his famous orchestra and took them to New York City. There, Harry Barris was added to the duo forming The Rhythm Boys.

Crosby's fun-loving ways eventually began to irritate Whiteman, who fired the Rhythm Boys after Crosby was arrested for drunk driving during the filming of the movie *The King of Jazz* (1930), which featured Whiteman and his orchestra. They soon found a job with Gus Arnheim's band at the Coconut Grove in Los Angeles, where Bing began to emerge as a soloist. In early 1931, Bing recorded his first solo hit, "I Surrender Dear," and began his CBS radio career, which eventually brought him a film contract.

Bing Crosby collaborated with Roy Turk and Fred Ahlert on the song that became his theme song, "Where the Blue of the Night (Meets the Gold of the Day)" in 1931.

At about the same time, movie producer Max Sennett (of Keystone Kops fame) hired Crosby to star in six comedy shorts with music, which led to a contract with Paramount. The first of his fifty-five feature films was *The Big Broadcast* in 1932. Between 1944 and 1948, Bing became the top money-making box office star five times. In 1948, he won an Oscar for Best Actor for his performance as a Catholic priest in *Going My Way*. He also won the Oscar for Best Supporting Actor for his role as an ex-alcoholic actor in *The Country Girl* (1954). Bing Crosby is one of only five actors to have a number-one single and an Oscar for best actor. The others are Barbra Streisand, Frank Sinatra, Cher, and Jamie Foxx.

Some of his most popular films were the "road" films with Bob Hope and Dorothy Lamour. Other Crosby movie musicals of the postwar years include *The Bells of St. Mary's* (1945), *Blue Skies* (1946), *A Connecticut Yankee in King Arthur's Court* (1949), *Here Comes the Groom* (1951), *White Christmas* (1954), and *High Society* (1956).

Bing Crosby made more than 2,600 recordings during his career, most of them on the Decca label, with whom he was under contract from 1934 to 1955. His total disc sales by 1975 was four hundred million. Twenty-three of his recordings became Gold Records, and "White Christmas" and "Silent Night" were awarded Platinum certification in 1960 and 1970, respectively. He also had one Gold Album. Bing Crosby was inducted into the Popular Music Hall of Fame in 2000 and was elected to the Big Band and Jazz Hall of Fame in 2004.

Crosby had 154 chart hits in the thirties and only slightly less in the early forties. Hit recordings of the postwar years include "I Can't Begin to Tell You" (1945); "It's Been a Long, Long Time" (1945); "Now Is the Hour" (1948); his 1942 recording of "White Christmas" was a number-one hit again in 1945 and 1946; and "Dear Hearts and Gentle People" in 1950. His last chart hit was "True Love" with Grace Kelly from *High Society* in 1956.

No other artist managed to parlay his multiple talents in film, radio, concerts, and recordings into the earnings that Bing Crosby experienced during 1945. He was the hottest commodity in the entertainment industry, reflected by the unprecedented royalties he received from his recordings. Add his radio and personal appearances, his motion pictures, and he was emerging as a one-man show business industry.

Through the electronics lab he funded, he was heavily involved in the initial development of audiotape recording in the late forties. One of the very first commercial uses of audiotape in the United States was the recording and editing of his radio program on ABC.

Bing Crosby was married to singer and actress Dixie Lee (from 1930 until her death in 1952) and actress Kathryn Grant (from 1957 until his death). Crosby had seven children, six sons and a daughter. His brother Bob was a successful bandleader and singer.

Bing Crosby loved sports. From the forties to the sixties, he owned fifteen percent of the Pittsburgh Pirates baseball team. He was also quite fond of horse racing and golf. He suffered a heart attack and died while playing golf in Spain.

THE EVERLY BROTHERS

Don Everly

Birth name: Isaac Donald Everly
Born: February 1, 1937, Brownie, Kentucky

Phil Everly

Birth name: Philip Everly
Born: January 19, 1939, Chicago, Illinois

At the ages of eight and six, Don and Phil Everly began to perform on their parents' live radio show. Ike, their father, instilled a love for music in the boys and taught them to play guitar. By 1950, the radio show had become known as *The Everly Family Show.*

Soon after they moved to Knoxville, Tennessee, Ike gave up his music career, so Don and Phil went to Nashville to try to sell some of the songs they had written. Archie Bleyer auditioned the brothers for his label, but when he turned them down, Columbia Records signed them for a two-record deal. When their Columbia option expired, their father asked his friend, legendary country guitarist Chet Atkins, to introduce the boys to publisher Fred Rose, who became their manager. Rose then convinced Archie Bleyer to reconsider and he signed them.

Felice and Boudleaux Bryant's "Bye Bye Love" had been making the Nashville rounds but nobody had recorded it. Don and Phil took it. Their recording of the song enjoyed a twenty-two week run on the *Billboard* pop chart, peaking at number two, where it stayed for four weeks. It went number one on the country chart and number five on the R&B chart. That hit established a formula for the brothers: Boudleaux Bryant's tunes and rhythms, Felice Bryant's lyrics, Don Everly's guitar introductions, and Phil Everly's harmonies. The Bryant songwriting team began composing songs tailored to the brothers' harmonizing capabilities while providing a solo for Don somewhere in the middle. "Bye Bye Love" began a string of twenty-six Top 40 singles for the Everly Brothers, whose worldwide record sales have now topped 40 million. Their next hit, "Wake Up Little Susie" (1957), hit number one and stayed there for four weeks.

"All I Have To Do Is Dream," another Boudleaux and Felice Bryant creation, was recorded in 1958. Don and Phil premiered the song on *American Bandstand*, and Dick Clark introduced it as "their next number-one record." "All I Have To Do Is Dream" did reach number one and stayed at the top of the *Billboard* chart for five weeks. That single was quickly followed by the release of their first album, simply called "The Everly Brothers."

Later in 1958, the brothers took Boudleaux's "Bird Dog" to number one. Their last number-one hit, in 1960, was "Cathy's Clown," which was written by Don and Phil Everly. Eleven years later, they parted company to pursue solo careers.

Don and Phil Everly influenced a generation of country and rock singers, and they have received numerous awards and accolades. In 1986, the Everly Brothers were among the first ten inductees into The Rock and Roll Hall of Fame, and they received a star on Hollywood's Walk of Fame that year. In February 1997, the brothers received a Lifetime Achievement Award from The Recording Academy.

EDDIE FISHER

Birth name: Edwin John Fisher
Born: August 10, 1928, Philadelphia, Pennsylvania

Eddie Fisher became one of the nation's singing idols of the early fifties. His vocal talent was evident at an early age, and he appeared in numerous local amateur contests. He also performed on local radio and later on *Arthur*

Godfrey's Talent Scouts. In the mid-forties, he acquired band vocalist jobs with Buddy Morrow and Charlie Ventura.

In 1949, Fisher became the protégé of Eddie Cantor, who had heard him at Grossinger's, the New York Catskills resort. Cantor featured him on his radio show and promoted him toward a successful singing career.

Fisher signed a recording contract with RCA Victor and had his first chart single in 1950. His popularity climbed for about a year, but his career was interrupted when he was drafted into the Army in 1951 and served a year in Korea. During his military service, he was also a tenor in the United States Army Chorus in Washington, DC After his discharge, he began his climb to stardom again.

According to his autobiography, Fisher admits he was ill equipped to cope with his celebrity status. He claims the press practically forced his first marriage to actress and singer Debbie Reynolds. A daughter, Carrie, who starred as Princess Leia in the *Star Wars* films, was a product of that marriage. When Fisher divorced Debbie Reynolds to marry actress Elizabeth Taylor, the public never forgave him; his career never recovered. Fisher later married Connie Stevens. Eddie Fisher attempted several comebacks but was not able to regain the popularity he had in the early fifties.

Fisher's number-one hits were "Wish You Were Here" (1952), "I'm Walking Behind You" (1953), "Oh! My Pa-Pa" (1954), and "I Need You Now" (1954).

SAMMY KAYE

Birth name: Samuel Zarnocay, Jr.
Born: March 13, 1910, Lakewood, Ohio
Death: June 2, 1987, Ridgewood, New Jersey

Bandleader Sammy Kaye led a very successful sweet-style band. They had 103 chart recordings between 1937 and 1953. "Swing and Sway with Sammy Kaye" is one of the most memorable tag lines of the big band era.

After high school, he attended Ohio University in Athens, where he began playing clarinet. Sammy Kaye also played saxophone, but was never a super soloist on either instrument.

In the early thirties, he organized his own orchestra that played at the Statler Hotel in Cleveland. Later he performed at many of the best hotels in New York City and starred in his own radio program, which moved to television during the fifties.

Kaye's postwar major hits include "Chickery Chick" (1945), "The Old Lamp-lighter" (1946), "I'm a Big Girl Now" (1946), "Harbor Lights" (1950), and "It Isn't Fair" (1950) with vocalist Don Cornell, which became his only Gold Record.

Sammy Kaye also helped Don Reid compose the music for the World War II hit "Remember Pearl Harbor."

Kaye was known for an audience participation gimmick called "So You Want To Lead A Band?" where he would bring audience members on stage to conduct the orchestra.

He eventually retired to Southern California, though his orchestra carried on under the direction of trumpeter Roger Thorpe and is still performing.

Kaye died from cancer in 1987. He was inducted into the Big Band and Jazz Hall of Fame in 1992.

He is mentioned in the lyrics of the song "Kids" from the Broadway musical *Bye Bye Birdie*, and also in the song "Opus One."

FRANKIE LAINE

Birth name: Francesco Paolo Lo Vecchio
Born: March 30, 1913, Chicago, Illinois
Death: February 6, 2007, San Diego, California

Frankie Laine had two *Billboard* number-one hits in 1949, the only year he accomplished that feat, and one in 1950.

Singer and songwriter Hoagy Carmichael "discovered" Laine and per-suaded him to Anglicize his name. His first chart single was "That's My Desire" in 1947. His tenth chart single was his first *Billboard* number one, "That Lucky Old Sun," in 1949.

Before the year ended, he had claimed the top spot on *Billboard* a second time with "Mule Train," a rugged, western-flavored number. By September 1951, Laine's version of the song had sold over two million records. The song provided the title for and was sung by Gene Autry in a 1950 film. Vaughn Monroe sang it in *Singing Guns*, also in 1950. Even though it was not specifically written for the film in which it appeared, which broke the Academy's rules, it was nominated for the Academy Award for Best Song from a Film for its appearance in *Singing Guns*.

Laine managed another *Billboard* number one, "The Cry of the Wild Goose," in 1950, but collected several other million-sellers by 1953.

Frankie Laine's voice was also heard singing the main themes of several films.

THE MCGUIRE SISTERS

Phyllis McGuire

Birth name: Phyllis McGuire
Born: February 14, 1931, Middletown, Ohio

Dorothy McGuire

Birth name: Dorothy McGuire
Born: February 22, 1928, Middletown, Ohio

Christine McGuire

Birth name: Christine McGuire
Born: July 30, 1926, Middletown, Ohio

The McGuire Sisters began singing in the church where their mother was the pastor when they were young children. They often sang together at church functions, weddings, and funerals. They quickly learned that their voices blended naturally—they had that "family harmony" that is difficult to come by except in a filial way.

In the late forties and early fifties, they toured military bases and veterans' hospitals around the country for the USO. In 1950, when an agent and bandleader happened to hear them sing on a church service radio broadcast, he encouraged them to become a pop trio. Very soon the girls were singing with that agent's band in Dayton, Ohio.

They began to receive national attention when they performed for eight weeks on Kate Smith's radio show in 1952 and won *Arthur Godfrey's Talent Scouts*. Godfrey asked them to replace the Chordettes on his morning show for a week. The McGuire Sisters stayed for six years.

By the end of 1952, they had signed a recording contract and had their first single release. It wasn't until 1954 that they made the Top Ten with their cover version of the R&B song "Goodnight Sweetheart, Goodnight." Their eleventh single was a cover of another R&B song, the Moonglows' "Sincerely," which became their first number one. The McGuire Sisters' version became a number-one hit on *Billboard* and *Cash Box*, and number eight for the year on *Variety*. For more on "Sincerely," see **Payola** in the "How Was Popular Music Dispensed?" chapter.

After a couple of other chart singles, "Something's Gotta Give" hit the top of *Your Hit Parade* in 1955. The year 1958 opened with their last number-one hit, "Sugartime." Their recording rose to the top of the *Billboard* chart and remained on top for four weeks and was a number-one hit on *Your Hit Parade* for two weeks.

By the late sixties, the sisters decided to call it quits. Phyllis had been a soloist since the early sixties and Dorothy and Christine wanted to devote more time to their growing families. The sisters were inducted into the Vocal Group Hall of Fame in 2001.

VAUGHN MONROE

Birth name: Vaughn Wilton Monroe
Born: October 7, 1911, Akron, Ohio
Death: May 21, 1973, Stuart, Florida

Singer and bandleader Vaughn Monroe's greatest period of popularity was from the mid-forties into the early years of rock 'n' roll.

Throughout high school and for a couple of years following graduation, Monroe earned money by playing in neighborhood bands. In 1931, he enrolled in college to study engineering, but later studied at the New England Conservatory of Music in Boston. After wavering between engineering and music, he quit school and devoted all his energies to a music career.

His first band job was with Austin Wiley's group. After a couple of years, the band broke up and Monroe landed a job as trumpeter in Larry Funk's orchestra. After a tour of exhausting one-nighters, Monroe decided to settle down in the Boston area as trumpeter and vocalist with bandleader Jack Marshard's society-style orchestra. Soon Marshard convinced Monroe to take over leadership. The group continued to play in society clubs in the Boston area and at hotels in Boston and Miami.

In 1940, Vaughn Monroe disbanded the Marshard group to organize his own band. He also married his high school sweetheart.

The new Monroe band debuted at and made their first radio broadcast from Siler's Ten Acres in New England. RCA Victor executives soon heard one of the band's broadcasts and signed Monroe to a recording contract. His first chart single, "There I Go," made it to number one in 1940.

Monroe's fame began to spread as his orchestra played hotels, theaters, ballrooms, and nightclubs all over New England and the Midwest.

Monroe's most popular recordings of the postwar years were "There! I've Said It Again" (1945), "Let It Snow! Let It Snow! Let It Snow!" (1946), "Ballerina" (1947), "Riders in the Sky" (1949), and "Someday" (1949). Vaughn Monroe sang "Mule Train" in the movie *Singing Guns* in 1950.

Monroe was a man of many hobbies, enjoying photography, motorcycling, miniature trains, carpentry, swimming, golf, and especially flying.

PATTI PAGE

Birth name: Clara Ann Fowler
Born: November 8, 1927, Claremore, Oklahoma

Patti Page became a nightclub, television, and recording star, who was particularly popular during the fifties. Page had 111 hits on the pop, country, and R&B charts, with fifteen certified Gold Records. She also recorded over one hundred albums. According to her official Web site at http://www. misspattipage.com, she "sold approximately 100 million plus recordings, making her one of the biggest, if not the biggest selling female recording artist in history."

She began life as Clara Ann Fowler, the second from the youngest of eleven children. The Fowler Sisters began singing in church and later on a local radio station. A Tulsa radio station executive heard her sing at a high school function. He was looking for a girl to replace the current Patti Page on his "Meet Patti Page Show," sponsored by the Page Milk Company. So Clara Ann became Patti Page and began her professional career as a country singer on a fifteen-minute radio program at age eighteen.

In 1946, Jack Rael, a band manager, heard her on the radio and asked her to join the Jimmy Joy band, which he managed. Eventually both left the band and Rael became her personal manager and orchestra leader on many of her recordings (taking the name "Patti Page" with her).

In 1948, she signed with Mercury Records and recorded a song called "Confess," which needed one singer to answer another, so Rael suggested she sing both parts. After recording "Confess" as a duet, Page liked the result so much that she asked for permission to do an entire song as a quartet. Mitch Miller, A&R director at Mercury and later more famous at Columbia, was skeptical until Page recorded and played a short demo in four different voices for him. He decided to allow the multitrack (or overdubbing) experiment and the song, "With My Eyes Wide Open I'm Dreaming" (1950), became a hit, her first million seller. On some of her multitrack recordings, especially in the case of "With My Eyes Wide Open I'm Dreaming," she was billed as "The Patti Page quartet: Patti Page, Patti Page, Patti Page and ... Patti Page."

Her first number-one hit was "All My Love" (1950), based on Maurice Ravel's *Bolero*. Her biggest hit was "The Tennessee Waltz," which became the biggest hit song in fifty years, selling over six million records, over two million in Patti's version alone. Her recording of the song was concurrently number one on the pop, country, and R&B charts. It also became the largest selling record by a female artist in recording history. Other number-one hit singles include "I Went to Your Wedding" (1952) and "(How Much Is) That Doggie in the Window?" (1953). Other singles that reached Gold status were "Would I Love You (Love You, Love You)" (1951), "Mockin' Bird Hill" (1951), "Mister and Mississippi" (1951), "Detour" (1951), "Changing Partners" (1953), and "Cross Over the Bridge" (1954).

Her biggest hits of the rock era were "Allegheny Moon" (1956) and "Old Cape Cod" (1957). In addition to her singing, she appeared in the film *Elmer Gantry* (1960). Patti Page was inducted into the Popular Music Hall of Fame in 2004.

THE PLATTERS

Tony Williams

Birth name: Samuel Anthony "Tony" Williams (lead vocalist)
Born: April 15, 1928, Roselle, New Jersey
Death: August 14, 1992, Manhattan, New York

David Lynch

Birth name: David Lynch (tenor)
Born: July 3, 1930, St. Louis, Missouri
Death: January 2, 1981, Long Beach, California

Paul Robi

Birth name: Paul Robi (baritone)
Born: August 20, 1931, New Orleans, Louisiana
Death: February 1, 1989, Los Angeles, California

Herbert Reed

Birth name: Herbert Reed (bass)
Born: August 7, 1931, Kansas City, Missouri

Zola Taylor

Birth name: Zola Taylor (alto)
Born: 1934, Los Angeles, California

The Platters became the most successful vocal group of the early years of rock 'n' roll. They were different from the other groups of the period and, thanks to Buck Ram, their manager and record producer, featured some innovations that gave the group great appeal. Lead singer Tony Williams had sung in gospel groups and had a polished voice. The group was often accompanied by strings, and having a woman as part of the assembly was not common in a doo-wop group at the time. Their songs were particularly popular at parties when it came time to play a slow dance number.

The Platters were a quartet when Buck Ram met them in 1953. He signed the group to a management contract and added a female to make a quintet. The act went through many personnel changes, but the most popular and successful incarnation included the names listed above.

The Platters had earlier released "Only You" on Federal Records, but it didn't do particularly well. Mercury Records was interested in signing another Buck Ram group, the Penguins, who had been successful with "Earth Angel." Ram told Mercury they could have the Penguins if they also signed the Platters. The Platters' first Mercury release was a rerecording of "Only You," which was their first chart single. Their recording shot up to number one on the R&B chart and crossed over to the pop chart, where it reached number five. The Platters' recording of "Only You" was inducted into the Grammy Hall of Fame in 1999.

Their next release was "The Great Pretender." Even though some of the group thought it was "a hillbilly song," it became their first *Billboard* number-one hit. Ram, in addition to being the group's manager, was also the writer of "The Great Pretender."

Music video may well have been born with the Platter's "Twilight Time." In the mid-July issue of *Billboard*, Mercury announced it was producing a film of the Platters performing the song, which would be made available to almost 200 television disc jockeys for use on their television record shows. In 1944, Buck Ram, with the help of the Three Suns, had written "Twilight Time." The Three Suns were the first to record it, but theirs, and other recordings of the period, were only marginally successful. However, the Platters' recording of the song sold 105 million copies in 1958 and was a *Billboard* number-one hit.

The Platters specialized on reviving oldies. For their next single, Ram pulled out a 1939 song, "My Prayer," a French song written by Georges Boulanger as "Avant de Mourir." British songwriter Jimmy Kennedy had written the English lyrics. "My Prayer" became the Platters' second chart topper.

In 1959, they resurrected Jerome Kern and Otto Harbach's "Smoke Gets in Your Eyes" from the 1933 Broadway musical *Roberta*. It became their last number-one hit. Jerome Kern's widow threatened to get an injunction to prevent the Platters' recording of the song from being released, however, she never followed through with the threat.

The Platters were inducted into the Rock and Roll Hall of Fame in 1990 and into the Vocal Group Hall of Fame in its inaugural year of 1998.

ELVIS PRESLEY

Birth name: Elvis Aaron Presley
Born: January 8, 1935, Tupelo, Mississippi
Death: August 16, 1977, Memphis, Tennessee

Rock 'n' roll started as a fad, and it needed a charismatic personality who would solidify rock into the nation's consciousness. That person was found in what might have been thought the unlikeliest of places.

His family lived in near poverty in his native Mississippi until after his father was released from prison on a forgery charge. The family soon moved

Elvis Presley appears on *The Ed Sullivan Show*. (Courtesy of Photofest)

to Memphis, Tennessee, where Presley graduated from Humes High School in 1953.

In late 1953, the truck-driving Elvis went to Sam Phillips's Memphis recording studio to record "My Happiness" and "That's When Your Heartaches Begin" as a gift for his mother's birthday.

Phillips had told his assistant, "If I could find a white boy who could sing like a negro, I could make a million dollars." At first, however, he was not convinced that Elvis was that person. In the spring, Phillips's secretary convinced him to call Elvis to record a demo. After many failed takes, Phillips asked Presley what other songs he knew. He sang some of the R&B, country, and gospel songs he knew and also a Dean Martin hit. Phillips became interested enough to ask guitarist Scotty Moore to work with Elvis Presley. His first Sun recording session was July 5, 1954. During a break, Elvis began playing around with the song "That's All Right, Mama." When Moore and bass player Bill Black joined in, Phillips ran into the studio and had them start again so he could get it on tape. He had found what he was looking for. Between July 1954 and November 1955, Sam Phillips issued five Elvis Presley singles on his label.

Still considered a country act, Presley appeared on the *Louisiana Hayride* and in April 1955 auditioned for *Arthur Godfrey's Talent Scouts* program— Godfrey turned him down. In September, he had his first number-one country record, "Mystery Train." At this time, Bob Neal, a Memphis disc jockey, was Presley's manager. However, Colonel Tom Parker had become increasingly involved with his career and negotiated a deal where RCA would purchase Elvis's contract from Sun Records for $35,000. Elvis used his $5,000 advance to buy a pink Cadillac for his mother.

In 1956, Elvis Presley exploded into the national spotlight. He was a breath of fresh air to the nation's youth. He was the charismatic personality that rock 'n' roll needed to solidify its position. One of this white Southerner's chief contributions was blurring the color line between black popular music and white popular music. His unique performing style—which included rebellious, hip-swiveling sexuality and a singing voice tinged with country, gospel, and R&B—endeared him immediately to the nation's young people who were seeking a new, restless identity. His soon-to-be manager, Col. Tom Parker, knew exactly how to market his unique singing and dancing style, those sideburns and that ducktail hair, and his bad boy sexuality. Elvis Presley became the first star of rock 'n' roll.

Elvis topped the *Billboard* chart four times in 1956 and held the number-one position for forty-eight percent of the weeks for the entire year. Elvis sold 10 million pop singles in one year—quite an achievement.

Songwriter Mae Axton was handling public relations for Col. Tom Parker. She told Elvis she was going to write a million-seller for him. Not long after that remark, Mae saw a newspaper article about a suicide victim who had written the following line in his suicide note: "I walk a lonely street." She thought there should be a heartbreak hotel at the end of that lonely street. In less than thirty minutes, Mae and Tommy Durden had written the song and recorded a demo version. She telephoned Elvis and asked him to meet her in Nashville to hear the million-seller she had written for him. His first RCA recording session was in Nashville, where he recorded what would become his first number-one hit, "Heartbreak Hotel."

On January 28, 1956, he made his national television debut on Tommy and Jimmy Dorsey's television program and appeared six times.

In March, Col. Tom Parker officially became Presley's manager in a deal where he would receive twenty-five percent of the earnings for Presley's lifetime and beyond.

Presley made his Las Vegas debut in April, but the two-week engagement was canceled after a week due to poor audience response. However, it was during that engagement that he first heard the song "Hound Dog," as performed in a comic version by Freddie Bell and the Bellboys.

His next coup came with the back-to-back hits "Don't Be Cruel" and "Hound Dog." Reportedly "Don't Be Cruel" sold over three million copies, while "Hound Dog" sold more than 10 million copies. However, how can back-to-back songs on the same record sell varying quantities?

In April and June of 1956, Elvis Presley appeared on the *Milton Berle Show*. Presley's version of "Hound Dog" was introduced on his June appearance, and his pelvic gyrations caused quite an uproar. In July, he appeared on Steve Allen's show performing "Hound Dog" dressed in a tux and blue suede shoes. Even though he was instructed to stand perfectly still while he sang to a basset hound, his appearance attracted such an audience that Ed Sullivan, who swore he would never have Presley on his show, was forced to reconsider and signed him for three appearances at $50,000 (the normal guest received $5,000 per appearance).

In late July, Presley's "I Want You, I Need You, I Love You" became his third number-one hit of the year.

In August, Elvis began filming his first film, *Love Me Tender*, a Civil War story. The song "Love Me Tender" from the film is basically the 1861 folk ballad "Aura Lee" with new lyrics furnished by Vera Watson, the wife of Ken Darby, the musical director for the film. Presley's recording of the song was a number-one hit on *Billboard*, *Variety*, *Cash Box*, and *Your Hit Parade* the number-two hit of the year in the combined charts.

While he was filming *Love Me Tender*, "Don't Be Cruel" and "Hound Dog" topped the charts, followed by the title song from the film. That was the first time since the birth of rock 'n' roll that an artist followed himself into the top spot on the *Billboard* chart. He had topped the *Billboard* chart four times in 1956 for a total of twenty-five weeks.

Elvis repeated the same incredible feat in 1957. His "Too Much," "All Shook Up," "(Let Me Be Your) Teddy Bear," and "Jailhouse Rock" were his four chart toppers for the year.

Lee Rosenberg, one of the cowriters of "Too Much," handed the song to Elvis as he boarded a train for Los Angeles. He premiered his version of the song on his third and last Ed Sullivan show appearance in January 1957, where he was shown only from the waist up—no pelvic shots allowed.

Otis Blackwell, the writer of "Don't Be Cruel" also penned "All Shook Up" for Elvis, which became *Billboard*'s top hit of 1957. It was the second year in a row that he had the top single of the year, a feat that no other artist has ever accomplished.

A rumor began to circulate that Elvis collected teddy bears, so his fans flooded him with the cute, cuddly toys. Kal Mann and Bernie Lowe heard about Elvis's supposed affinity and wrote "(Let Me Be Your) Teddy Bear" for him. The song was included in his next film *Loving You*. During the 1957 Christmas season, Elvis donated thousands of the teddy bears he had received to the National Foundation for Infantile Paralysis.

It was during this time that he purchased his Memphis home, Graceland. He bought the house for $100,000 from Mrs. Ruth Brown Moore, whose husband had built the house and named it after an aunt, Grace Toof. Elvis decided to retain the name, Graceland.

Elvis's third film was *Jailhouse Rock*. The highlight of the movie was the big production number in a jail where Elvis performed the title song. He also choreographed the number, which has become one of the most famous scenes from any of his films.

Three weeks after "Jailhouse Rock" hit number one, Presley received his draft notice from the U.S. Army. Paramount requested and received a deferment so he could complete the filming of his fourth movie, *King Creole*.

Elvis Presley had two number-one hits in 1958: "Don't" and "Hard Headed Woman." Not a bad year by any means, but not the same pace as he had set in 1956 and 1957. "Don't," by Jerry Leiber and Mike Stoller, became his ninth number-one single.

In 1958, he became a private in the U.S. Army. Many worried that two years out of circulation would permanently disrupt his career.

"Hard Headed Woman," from *King Creole*, was his next chart topper. That occurred while he was in basic training at Fort Hood, Texas. Logically, Elvis would have been assigned to Special Services to entertain the other soldiers. However, he became a regular GI.

When his mother became ill with acute severe hepatitis and was admitted to Methodist Hospital in Memphis, Elvis requested leave to visit her. His request was denied. Finally, he was granted a seven-day emergency leave. While he was home to visit his mother, she died of heart failure. Her death was an extreme blow for Presley, who idolized her.

He was soon transferred to the Army base at Friedberg, Germany. During his two-year Army duty, he had one recording session, a two-day session in Nashville during his first furlough. Five songs were recorded in those two days, including "A Big Hunk of Love."

Elvis had only one *Billboard* number-one hit in 1959—"A Big Hunk of Love." Col. Parker purposefully kept him away from the recording studio during his military service years. He wanted the public to be hungry for a new Elvis Presley release once he was discharged. "A Fool Such As I," which peaked at number two, and "A Big Hunk of Love" were the only single releases of 1959.

While he was stationed in Germany, Presley met Priscilla, the fourteen-year-old stepdaughter of Capt. Joseph Beaulieu. They saw each other often and fell in love. After he was discharged and returned to the states, he invited Priscilla to spend Christmas 1960 at Graceland. Later, he asked for and received her stepfather's permission for her to live at Graceland, under the supervision of his father, and finish high school in Memphis. After four years, they were married in 1967 in Las Vegas. Their daughter, Lisa Marie, was born in 1968. Elvis and Priscilla divorced in 1973.

Elvis Presley went on to star in thirty-three successful films, made history with his television appearances and specials, and knew great acclaim through his many, often record-breaking, live concert performances on tour and in Las Vegas. His record sales total over one billion globally. His American sales have earned him Gold, Platinum, or Multiplatinum awards for 150 different albums and singles. Among his many awards were three Grammys (among fourteen nominations) and the Grammy Lifetime Achievement Award, which he received at age thirty-six. RIAA named Elvis the best-selling solo artist in U.S. history. In total, Elvis Presley has received ninety-seven Gold Records, fifty-five of which have been certified Platinum, and twenty-five have gone on to Multiplatinum status.

Known the world over by his first name and also as "The King," he is regarded as one of the most important figures of twentieth century popular culture. Elvis died at Graceland in 1977. His legions of fans still flock to Graceland, especially on his birth and death dates.

FRANK SINATRA

Birth name: Francis Albert Sinatra
Born: December 12, 1915, Hoboken, New Jersey
Death: May 14, 1998, Los Angeles, California

Frank Sinatra, circa 1940s. (Courtesy of Photofest)

Frank Sinatra had been the singing idol of the bobby-soxers of the big band era, but by the mid-forties he and his former fans had matured. He was now starring in movie musicals such as *Anchors Aweigh* and *On the Town*.

His most popular recordings of the late forties included "Oh! What It Seemed to Be," which was a number-one hit; "Five Minutes More," a top hit on *Billboard, Your Hit Parade,* and *Variety* in 1946; and "Mam'selle" in 1947.

By 1952, Sinatra's career was in tatters, and when his Columbia Records deal was not renewed, he had difficulty getting a contract with any company. Finally, Capitol signed him to a one-year deal. Then, in 1953, his career blossomed again when he won an Oscar for his acting in *From Here to Eternity.*

Over the next several years, he appeared in many films, including *Young at Heart* (1954), *The Tender Trap* (1955), *Guys and Dolls* (1955), *High Society* (1956), *Pal Joey* (1957), and *The Joker Is Wild* (1957), which premiered "All the Way," a number-one hit on *Your Hit Parade.*

In 1955, his recording of "Learnin' the Blues" was a number-one hit, his first *Billboard* chart topper since 1947. The song also climbed to the top of *Your Hit Parade.*

His only other number-one hits were "Strangers in the Night" (1966) and "Somethin' Stupid" (1967), a duet with his daughter Nancy.

In 1980, Sinatra was elected to the Big Band and Jazz Hall of Fame, and he was inducted into the Popular Music Hall of Fame in 2000.

JO STAFFORD

Birth name: Jo Elizabeth Stafford
Born: November 12, 1917, Coalinga, California

Jo Stafford became one of the most popular female vocalists of the mid-forties and early fifties. She joined the Pied Pipers in 1937, and they recorded the number-one hit, "Dream" (1945). She also collected a number-one hit with "Candy" with Johnny Mercer and the Pied Pipers that same year.

Her next top hit came in 1947 as Cinderella G. Stump, a hillbilly diva, singing "Tim-Tayshun" with Red Ingle and the Natural Seven. Their recording was a spoof of Arthur Freed and Nacio Herb Brown's song, "Temptation," a beautiful song Bing Crosby had introduced in the movie musical *Going Hollywood* in 1933.

After more than two dozen chart singles, she collected another chart topper with "My Darling, My Darling" from *Where's Charley?* in a duet with Buddy Clark in early 1949.

Stafford's 1952 recording of "You Belong to Me," her biggest hit with a dozen weeks at number one, was inducted into the Grammy Hall of Fame in 1998. Her last number one was "Make Love to Me!" in 1954.

Appendix: The Combined Hits Charts for 1945–1959

(From 1945 to 1949 *Billboard*, *Your Hit Parade*, and *Variety* are used.)

THE TOP HITS OF 1945

Song Title	Artist(s)
1. "Till the End of Time" *Billboard* Nos. 2, 30, & 36; *Your Hit Parade* No. 1; *Variety* No. 2	Perry Como, Les Brown (Doris Day), Dick Haymes
2. "Sentimental Journey" *Billboard* Nos. 3, 27, & 39; *Your Hit Parade* No. 2 tie; *Variety* No. 1	Les Brown (Doris Day), Hal McIntyre (Frankie Lester), Merry Macs
3. "My Dreams Are Getting Better All the Time" from *In Society* *Billboard* Nos. 5, 28, & 35; *Your Hit Parade* No. 7 tie; *Variety* No. 7	Les Brown (Doris Day), Johnny Long & Dick Robertson, Phil Moore Four
4. "It's Been a Long, Long Time" *Billboard* Nos. 9 & 12, *Your Hit Parade* No. 2 tie, *Variety* No. 9	Harry James (Kitty Kallen) & Bing Crosby with Les Paul
5. "Rum and Coca Cola" *Billboard* No. 1, *Variety* No. 5	Andrews Sisters
6. "On the Atchison, Topeka and the Santa Fe" from *The Harvey Girls* *Billboard* Nos. 4 & 31, *Variety* No. 3	Johnny Mercer, Bing Crosby
7. "There! I've Said It Again" *Billboard* No. 6, *Variety* No. 6	Vaughn Monroe
8. "Chickery Chick" *Billboard* No. 8, *Variety* No. 8	Sammy Kaye (Nancy Norman & Billy Williams)
9. "Ac-Cent-Tchu-Ate the Positive" from *Here Come the Waves* *Billboard* Nos. 11 & 22, *Your Hit Parade* No.5 tie	Johnny Mercer, Bing Crosby, & the Andrews Sisters
10. "I Can't Begin to Tell You" from *The Dolly Sisters* *Billboard* No. 7, *Your Hit Parade* No. 11 in 1946	Bing Crosby with Carmen Cavallaro
11. "Candy" *Billboard* No. 14, *Your Hit Parade* No. 4	Johnny Mercer & Jo Stafford
12. "Dream" *Billboard* No. 15, *Your Hit Parade* No. 5 tie	The Pied Pipers

13. "I'm Beginning to See the Light"
    Billboard No. 10, *Your Hit Parade* No. 10 tie — Harry James (Kitty Kallen)

14. "I'll Buy That Dream" from *Sing Your Way Home*
    Billboard Nos. 19 & 25, *Your Hit Parade* No. 10 tie — Helen Forrest & Dick Haymes & Harry James (Kitty Kallen)

15. "Chopin's Polonaise"
    Billboard No. 26, *Variety* No. 10 — Carmen Cavallaro

16. "If I Loved You" from *Carousel* (musical)
    Billboard No. 32, *Your Hit Parade* No. 7 tie — Perry Como

17. "It Might As Well Be Spring" from *State Fair*
    Your Hit Parade No. 7 tie — Dick Haymes

18. "A Little on the Lonely Side"
    Billboard No. 37, *Your Hit Parade* No. 12 tie — Frankie Carle (Paula Allen)

19. "Laura" from *Laura*
    Your Hit Parade No. 12 tie — Woody Herman

20. "The More I See You" from *Diamond Horseshoe*
    Your Hit Parade No. 12 tie — Dick Haymes

THE TOP HITS OF 1946

Song Title	Artist(s)
1. "The Gypsy" *Billboard* Nos. 1, 5, & 34; *Your Hit Parade* No. 1 tie; *Variety* Nos. 1 & 8	Ink Spots, Dinah Shore, Sammy Kaye (Mary Marlow)
2. "To Each His Own" *Billboard* Nos. 4, 12, & 18; *Your Hit Parade* No. 1 tie; *Variety* No. 2	Eddy Howard, Freddy Martin (Stuart Wade), Ink Spots
3. "Oh! What It Seemed to Be" *Billboard* Nos. 2 & 6, *Your Hit Parade* No. 3, *Variety* No. 7	Frankie Carle, Frank Sinatra
4. "Rumors Are Flying" *Billboard* No. 3, *Your Hit Parade* No. 10, *Variety* No. 5	Frankie Carle (Marjorie Hughes)

(Continued)

Song Title	Artist(s)
5. "Five Minutes More" *Billboard* No. 10, *Your Hit Parade* No. 8, *Variety* No. 6	Frank Sinatra
6. "The Old Lamplighter" *Billboard* Nos. 7 & 31, *Variety* No. 4	Sammy Kaye (Billy Williams), Kay Kyser (Michael Douglas)
7. "Symphony" *Billboard* Nos. 14, 26, & 32; *Your Hit Parade* No. 4; *Variety* No. 10 tie	Freddy Martin (Clyde Rogers), Benny Goodman (Liza Morrow), Bing Crosby
8. "Let It Snow! Let It Snow! Let It Snow!" *Billboard* No. 9, *Your Hit Parade* No. 11, *Variety* No. 10 tie	Vaughn Monroe
9. "(I Love You) For Sentimental Reasons" *Billboard* Nos. 8 in 1946, 28, & 31 in 1947, *Your Hit Parade* No. 5	Nat "King" Cole, Dinah Shore, Eddy Howard
10. "Prisoner of Love" *Billboard* No. 11, *Variety* No. 3	Perry Como
11. "Ole Buttermilk Sky" from *Canyon Passage* *Billboard* Nos. 16 & 21, *Your Hit Parade* No. 6	Kay Kyser (Michael Douglas), Hoagy Carmichael
12. "Personality" from *Road to Utopia* *Billboard* No. 13, *Variety* No. 9	Johnny Mercer
13. "They Say It's Wonderful" from *Annie Get Your Gun* *Billboard* Nos. 25 & 39, *Your Hit Parade* No. 7	Frank Sinatra, Perry Como
14. "Laughing on the Outside (Crying on the Inside)" *Billboard* Nos. 29, 36, & 38, *Your Hit Parade* No. 12	Dinah Shore, Sammy Kaye (Billy Williams), Andy Russell
15. "All Through the Day" from *Centennial Summer* *Your Hit Parade* No. 9	Frank Sinatra
16. "Doctor, Lawyer and Indian Chief" from *Stork Club* *Billboard* No. 15	Betty Hutton
17. "I'm a Big Girl Now" *Billboard* No. 19	Sammy Kaye (Betty Barclay)
18. "White Christmas" *Billboard* No. 20	Bing Crosby

THE TOP HITS OF 1947

Song Title	Artist(s)
1. "Near You" *Billboard* Nos. 1, 30, 35, & 36; *Your Hit Parade* No. 3; *Variety* No. 1	Francis Craig, Andrews Sisters, Larry Green, Alvino Rey (Jimmy Joyce)
2. "Peg o' My Heart" *Billboard* Nos. 4, 5, & 7; *Your Hit Parade* No. 1; *Variety* Nos. 4 & 10	The Harmonicats, Buddy Clark, The Three Suns
3. "Ballerina" *Billboard* Nos. 3 in 1947 & 36 in 1948, *Your Hit Parade* No. 5, *Variety* No. 2	Vaughn Monroe, Buddy Clark
4. "Heartaches" *Billboard* No. 2, *Your Hit Parade* No. 8, *Variety* No. 3	Ted Weems
5. "Linda" from *The Story of G.I. Joe* *Billboard* No. 10, *Your Hit Parade* No. 4, *Variety* No. 7	Ray Noble with Buddy Clark
6. "Anniversary Song" from *The Jolson Story* *Billboard* Nos. 13, 20, 25, & 38; *Your Hit Parade* No. 2; *Variety* No. 9	Dinah Shore, Al Jolson, Guy Lombardo (Don Rodney), Tex Beneke
7. "Smoke! Smoke! Smoke! (That Cigarette)" *Billboard* No. 6, *Variety* No. 5	Tex Williams
8. "Chi-Baba, Chi-Baba (My Bambino Go to Sleep)" *Billboard* No. 9, *Variety* No. 6	Perry Como
9. "Mam'selle" from *The Razor's Edge* *Billboard* Nos. 12, 18, & 40, *Your Hit Parade* No. 5 tie	Art Lund, Frank Sinatra, Pied Pipers
10. "Too Fat Polka (I Don't Want Her, You Can Have Her, She's Too Fat for Me)" *Billboard* No. 19, *Variety* No. 8	Arthur Godfrey
11. "I Wish I Didn't Love You So" from *The Perils of Pauline* *Billboard* Nos. 24 & 26, *Your Hit Parade* No. 5 tie	Vaughn Monroe, Dinah Shore
12. "I Wonder, I Wonder, I Wonder" *Billboard* Nos. 22 & 37, *Your Hit Parade* No. 9 tie	Eddy Howard, Guy Lombardo (Don Rodney)
13. "I Wonder Who's Kissing Her Now" from *I Wonder Who's Kissing Her Now* *Billboard* No. 21, *Your Hit Parade* No. 11	Ted Weems with Perry Como
14. "That's My Desire" *Billboard* No. 29, *Your Hit Parade* No. 7	Sammy Kaye (Don Cornell)

Song Title	Artist(s)
15. "Managua, Nicaragua" *Billboard Nos. 8 & 14*	Freddy Martin (Stuart Wade), Guy Lombardo (Don Rodney)
16. "Gal in Calico" from *The Time, the Place and the Girl* *Your Hit Parade No. 9 tie*	Johnny Mercer
17. "Huggin' and Chalkin'" *Billboard No. 11*	Hoagy Carmichael
18. "Feudin' and Fightin'" *Your Hit Parade No. 12 tie*	Dorothy Shay
19. "You Do" from *Mother Wore Tights* *Your Hit Parade No. 12 tie*	Dinah Shore
20. "Civilization (Bongo, Bongo, Bongo)" *Billboard No. 39, Your Hit Parade No. 14*	Danny Kaye & Andrews Sisters
21. "Tim-Tayshun" *Billboard No. 15*	Red Ingle & the Natural Seven (Cinderella G. Stump)
22. "Open the Door, Richard" *Billboard Nos. 16 & 17*	Count Basie, The Three Flames

THE TOP HITS OF 1948

Song Title	Artist(s)
1. "Buttons and Bows" from *The Paleface* *Billboard Nos. 1 & 34, Your Hit Parade No. 2, Variety No. 1*	Dinah Shore, Dinning Sisters
2. "Nature Boy" *Billboard No. 4, Your Hit Parade No. 4, Variety No. 5*	Nat "King" Cole

3. "A Tree in the Meadow" — Margaret Whiting
   Billboard No. 8, Your Hit Parade No. 1, Variety No. 4
4. "Mañana (Is Soon Enough for Me)" — Peggy Lee
   Billboard No. 2, Your Hit Parade No. 11, Variety No. 3
5. "You Can't Be True, Dear" — Ken Griffin (Jerry Wayne), Ken Griffin (organ solo)
   Billboard Nos. 5 & 14, Your Hit Parade No. 5, Variety No. 8
6. "Now Is the Hour" — Bing Crosby, Margaret Whiting, Gracie Fields
   Billboard Nos. 11, 20, & 24; Your Hit Parade No. 2 tie; Variety No. 6
7. "I'm Looking Over a Four Leaf Clover" — Art Mooney
   Billboard No. 9, Your Hit Parade No. 8, Variety No. 7
8. "Woody Woodpecker" from *Wet Blanket Policy* — Kay Kyser (Gloria Wood/Campus Kids), Sportsmen, & Mel Blanc
   Billboard Nos. 7 & 15, Your Hit Parade No. 9, Variety No. 10
9. "On a Slow Boat to China" — Kay Kyser (Harry Babbitt/Gloria Wood), Freddy Martin (Glenn Hughes)
   Billboard Nos. 13 & 31, Your Hit Parade No. 9 in 1949, Variety No. 9
10. "Twelfth Street Rag" — Pee Wee Hunt
    Billboard No. 3, Variety No. 2
11. "You Call Everybody Darlin'" — Al Trace (Bob Vincent)
    Billboard No. 6, Your Hit Parade No. 10
12. "It's Magic" from *Romance on the High Seas* — Doris Day
    Billboard No. 18, Your Hit Parade No. 7
13. "How Soon (Will I Be Seeing You)" — Vaughn Monroe, Jack Owens
    Billboard Nos. 26 in 1948 & 32 in 1947, Your Hit Parade No. 6
14. "Love Somebody" — Doris Day & Buddy Clark
    Billboard No. 10
15. "All I Want for Christmas (Is My Two Front Teeth)" — Spike Jones (George Rock)
    Billboard No. 12

THE TOP HITS OF 1949

Song Title	Artist(s)
1. "Riders in the Sky (A Cowboy Legend)" *Billboard* Nos. 1 & 24, *Your Hit Parade* No. 6 tie, *Variety* No. 1	Vaughn Monroe, Peggy Lee
2. "Some Enchanted Evening" from *South Pacific* *Billboard* Nos. 7 & 26, *Your Hit Parade* No. 1, *Variety* No. 2	Perry Como, Bing Crosby
3. "Cruising Down the River" *Billboard* Nos. 4, 5, & 28; *Your Hit Parade* No. 2; *Variety* No. 6 & 10	Russ Morgan (The Skylarks), Blue Barron, Jack Smith & the Clark Sisters
4. "That Lucky Old Sun" *Billboard* No. 2, *Your Hit Parade* No. 8, *Variety* No. 5	Frankie Laine
5. "A Little Bird Told Me" *Billboard* No. 3, *Your Hit Parade* No. 5, *Variety* No. 7	Evelyn Knight
6. "You're Breaking My Heart" *Billboard* No. 8, *Your Hit Parade* No. 3, *Variety* No. 4	Vic Damone
7. "Again" from *Road House* *Billboard* Nos. 19, 21, & 35; *Your Hit Parade* No. 12; *Variety* No. 10	Gordon Jenkins (Joe Graydon), Doris Day, Mel Torme
8. "Mule Train" *Billboard* Nos. 6 & 40, *Your Hit Parade* No. 14, *Variety* No. 9	Frankie Laine, Bing Crosby
9. "Slipping Around" *Billboard* No. 10, *Variety* No. 8	Margaret Whiting & Jimmy Wakely
10. "Far Away Places" *Billboard* Nos. 18 & 20, *Your Hit Parade* No. 4	Margaret Whiting, Bing Crosby
11. "Powder Your Face With Sunshine (Smile! Smile! Smile!)" *Billboard* No. 14, *Your Hit Parade* No. 10	Evelyn Knight
12. "Rudolph, the Red-Nosed Reindeer" *Billboard* No. 17, *Your Hit Parade* No. 10 in 1950	Gene Autry (The Pinafores)
13. "Room Full of Roses" *Billboard* Nos. 23 & 38, *Your Hit Parade* No. 11	Sammy Kaye (Don Cornell), Eddy Howard
14. "Don't Cry Joe (Let Her Go, Let Her Go, Let Her Go)" *Billboard* No. 29, *Your Hit Parade* No. 6 tie	Gordon Jenkins (Betty Brewer)

15. "Forever and Ever"
    Billboard Nos. 9 & 22   Russ Morgan (The Skylarks), Perry Como
16. "Someday (You'll Want Me to Want You)"
    Billboard No. 11   Vaughn Monroe
17. "'A' – You're Adorable"
    Billboard No. 12   Perry Como (The Fontane Sisters)
18. "My Darling, My Darling" from *Where's Charley?* (musical)
    Billboard No. 13   Jo Stafford & Gordon MacRae
19. "A Dreamer's Holiday"
    Your Hit Parade No. 13   Perry Como
20. "Careless Hands"
    Billboard Nos. 15 & 32   Mel Torme, Sammy Kaye (Don Cornell)
21. "I've Got My Love to Keep Me Warm"
    Billboard No. 16   Les Brown

(From 1950 to 1954, *Cash Box* is added to *Billboard*, *Your Hit Parade*, and *Variety*.)

THE TOP HITS OF 1950

Song Title	Artist(s)
1. "Goodnight, Irene" *Billboard* No. 2, *Your Hit Parade* No. 6, *Variety* No. 1, *Cash Box* No. 2	The Weavers with Gordon Jenkins
2. "Mona Lisa" from *Captain Carey, U.S.A.* *Billboard* No. 6, *Your Hit Parade* No. 2, *Variety* No. 3, *Cash Box* No. 5 tie	Nat "King" Cole
3. "I Can Dream, Can't I?" *Billboard* No. 8, *Your Hit Parade* No. 7, *Variety* No. 3 in 1949, *Cash Box* No. 3 tie	Andrews Sisters (Patty)

(Continued)

Song Title	Artist(s)
4. "Chattanoogie Shoe Shine Boy" *Billboard* No. 7, *Your Hit Parade* No. 4, *Variety* No. 9, *Cash Box* No. 5 tie	Red Foley
5. "Harbor Lights" *Billboard* Nos. 11 & 25, *Your Hit Parade* No. 9 tie, *Variety* No. 6, *Cash Box* No. 3 tie	Sammy Kaye (Tony Alamo), Guy Lombardo (Kenny Gardner)
6. "Music! Music! Music!" *Billboard* No. 12, *Variety* No. 5, *Cash Box* No. 5 tie	Teresa Brewer
7. "The Third Man Theme" from *The Third Man* *Billboard* Nos. 3 & 4, *Variety* Nos. 2 & 7, *Cash Box* No. 1	Anton Karas, Guy Lombardo
8. "The Thing" *Billboard* No. 10, *Variety* No. 8, *Cash Box* No. 9 tie	Phil Harris
9. "Dear Hearts and Gentle People" *Billboard* Nos. 19 & 27, *Your Hit Parade* No. 3, *Cash Box* No. 9 tie	Bing Crosby, Dinah Shore
10. "Bewitched" *Billboard* Nos. 30 & 38, *Your Hit Parade* No. 5, *Cash Box* No. 5 tie	Bill Snyder, Gordon Jenkins (Bonnie Lou Williams)
11. "Rag Mop" *Billboard* No. 14, *Variety* No. 10	Ames Brothers, Ralph Flanagan
12. "If I Knew You Were Comin' (I'd've Baked a Cake)" *Billboard* No. 5, *Your Hit Parade* No. 8	Eileen Barton
13. "All My Love" *Billboard* No. 9, *Your Hit Parade* No. 7	Patti Page
14. "Play a Simple Melody" *Billboard* No. 20, *Variety* No. 4	Gary Crosby & Friend
15. "My Foolish Heart" from *My Foolish Heart* *Billboard* No. 34, *Your Hit Parade* No. 1	Gordon Jenkins (Sandy Evans)
16. "A Bushel and a Peck" from *Guys and Dolls* *Billboard* No. 29, *Your Hit Parade* No. 11 tie	Perry Como and Betty Hutton
17. "La Vie en Rose" *Your Hit Parade* No. 12	Tony Martin
18. "Nevertheless" from *Three Little Words* *Your Hit Parade* Nos. 13 & 27	Paul Weston (Norman Luboff Choir), Mills Brothers

19. "I Wanna Be Loved"
    Billboard No. 13 — Andrews Sisters (Patty)
20. "Cry of the Wild Goose"
    Billboard No. 15 — Frankie Laine
21. "Hoop-Dee-Doo"
    Billboard Nos. 16 & 24 — Perry Como, Kay Starr
22. "Sentimental Me"
    Billboard No. 17 — The Ames Brothers

THE TOP HITS OF 1951

Song Title	Artist(s)
1. "Because of You" from *I Was an American Spy* *Billboard Nos. 2 & 33, Your Hit Parade No. 1, Variety No. 1, Cash Box No. 2*	Tony Bennett, Les Baxter
2. "The Tennessee Waltz" *Billboard No. 1 in 1950, No. 40 in 1951, Your Hit Parade No. 5, Variety No. 2, Cash Box No. 4*	Patti Page, Guy Lombardo (Kenny Gardner)
3. "Too Young" *Billboard No. 8, Your Hit Parade No. 1, Variety No. 3, Cash Box No. 3*	Nat "King" Cole
4. "(It's No) Sin" *Billboard Nos. 4, 31, & 39; Your Hit Parade No. 4; Variety No. 10; Cash Box No. 1*	Eddy Howard, Four Aces, Sarah Churchill
5. "If" *Billboard No. 5, Your Hit Parade No. 3, Variety No. 7, Cash Box No. 7 tie*	Perry Como
6. "Mockin' Bird Hill" *Billboard Nos. 12 & 17, Your Hit Parade No. 6, Variety No. 4, Cash Box No. 5 tie*	Les Paul & Mary Ford, Patti Page
7. "My Heart Cries for You" *Billboard Nos. 11, 25, & 30; Your Hit Parade No. 7 tie; Variety No. 9; Cash Box No. 7 tie*	Guy Mitchell, Dinah Shore, Vic Damone

(Continued)

Song Title	Artist(s)
8. "How High the Moon" *Billboard* No. 3, *Variety* No. 4, *Cash Box* No. 9 tie	Les Paul & Mary Ford
9. "Be My Love" from *Toast of New Orleans* *Billboard* No. 9, *Variety* No. 6, *Cash Box* No. 5 tie	Mario Lanza
10. "Come on-a My House" *Billboard* No. 6, *Variety* No. 8, *Cash Box* No. 9 tie	Rosemary Clooney
11. "On Top of Old Smoky" *Billboard* No. 10, *Your Hit Parade* No. 7 tie, *Cash Box* No. 9 tie	The Weavers & Terry Gilkyson
12. "Cold, Cold Heart" *Billboard* No. 7, *Variety* No. 5	Tony Bennett
13. "Sweet Violets" *Billboard* No. 20, *Cash Box* No. 12 tie	Dinah Shore
14. "Down Yonder" *Billboard* No. 32, *Cash Box* No. 12 tie	Del Wood
15. "Jezebel" *Billboard* No. 13	Frankie Laine
16. "The World Is Waiting for the Sunrise" *Billboard* No. 14	Les Paul & Mary Ford
17. "Shrimp Boats" *Billboard* No. 15	Jo Stafford
18. "Undecided" *Billboard* No. 16	Ames Brothers & Les Brown
19. "My Truly, Truly Fair" *Billboard* Nos. 18 & 29	Guy Mitchell, Vic Damone

THE TOP HITS OF 1952

Song Title	Artist(s)
1. "Cry" *Billboard* No. 1 in 1951, *Your Hit Parade* No. 5, *Variety* No. 1, *Cash Box* No. 2 tie	Johnnie Ray & the Four Lads
2. "You Belong to Me" *Billboard* Nos. 1 & 30, *Your Hit Parade* No. 1, *Variety* No. 5, *Cash Box* No. 6 tie	Jo Stafford, Patti Page
3. "Wheel of Fortune" *Billboard* No. 2, *Your Hit Parade* No. 4, *Variety* No. 3, *Cash Box* No. 6 tie	Kay Starr
4. "Auf Wiederseh'n Sweetheart" *Billboard* Nos. 4 & 32, *Your Hit Parade* No. 7, *Variety* No. 4, *Cash Box* No. 1	Vera Lynn, Eddy Howard
5. "Blue Tango" *Billboard* Nos. 7 & 40, *Your Hit Parade* No. 11 tie, *Variety* No. 2, *Cash Box* No. 5	Leroy Anderson, Hugo Winterhalter
6. "Why Don't You Believe Me" *Billboard* No. 6 in 1952 & No. 33 in 1953, *Your Hit Parade* No. 5 tie, *Variety* No. 7, *Cash Box* No. 9 in 1953	Joni James, Patti Page
7. "The Glow Worm" *Billboard* No. 8, *Your Hit Parade* No. 12, *Variety* No. 9, *Cash Box* No. 10	The Mills Brothers
8. "Kiss of Fire" *Billboard* No. 5, *Your Hit Parade* No. 3, *Cash Box* No. 2 tie	Georgia Gibbs
9. "I Went to Your Wedding" *Billboard* No. 3, *Variety* No. 6, *Cash Box* No. 4	Patti Page
10. "Slow Poke" *Billboard* No. 11, *Your Hit Parade* No. 2, *Cash Box* No. 8 tie	Pee Wee King (Redd Stewart)
11. "I Saw Mommy Kissing Santa Claus" *Billboard* Nos. 13 & 34, *Your Hit Parade* No. 14 tie in 1953	Jimmy Boyd, Spike Jones (George Rock)
12. "Here in My Heart" *Billboard* No. 10, *Variety* No. 8	Al Martino
13. "It's in the Book" *Billboard* No. 12, *Variety* No. 10	Johnny Standley

(Continued)

Song Title	Artist(s)
14. "Wish You Were Here" from *Wish You Were Here* *Billboard* No. 14, *Your Hit Parade* No. 9 tie	Eddie Fisher
15. "I'm Yours" *Billboard* Nos. 25 & 27, *Your Hit Parade* No. 8	Eddie Fisher, Don Cornell
16. "Walkin' My Baby Back Home" *Billboard* No. 29, *Your Hit Parade* No. 9 tie	Johnnie Ray
17. "Half as Much" *Billboard* No. 9	Rosemary Clooney
18. "Delicado" *Billboard* No. 15	Percy Faith
19. "A Guy Is a Guy" *Billboard* No. 16	Doris Day

THE TOP HITS OF 1953

Song Title	Artist(s)
1. "Song from *Moulin Rouge*" from *Moulin Rouge* *Billboard* No. 2, *Your Hit Parade* No. 1, *Variety* No. 2, *Cash Box* No. 1	Percy Faith (Felicia Sanders)
2. "Vaya Con Dios" *Billboard* No. 1, *Your Hit Parade* No. 2, *Variety* No. 1, *Cash Box* No. 4 tie	Les Paul & Mary Ford
3. "Till I Waltz Again with You" *Billboard* No. 6, *Your Hit Parade* No. 6, *Variety* No. 5, *Cash Box* No. 3	Teresa Brewer
4. "Don't Let the Stars Get in Your Eyes" *Billboard* No. 8, *Your Hit Parade* No. 3, *Variety* No. 4, *Cash Box* No. 7 tie	Perry Como

5. "(How Much Is) That Doggie in the Window?"   Patti Page
   Billboard No. 5, Your Hit Parade No. 13, Variety No. 3, Cash Box No. 2
6. "You You You"   Ames Brothers
   Billboard No. 3, Your Hit Parade No. 5, Variety No. 7, Cash Box No. 1c tie
7. "Rags to Riches"   Tony Bennett
   Billboard No. 4, Your Hit Parade No. 12, Variety No. 6, Cash Box No. 4 tie
8. "I'm Walking Behind You"   Eddie Fisher
   Billboard No. 7, Your Hit Parade No. 9, Variety No. 9, Cash Box No. 4 tie
9. "Ebb Tide"   Frank Chacksfield
   Billboard No. 12, Your Hit Parade No. 4, Variety No. 10 tie
10. "No Other Love" from *Me and Juliet*   Perry Como
    Billboard No. 9, Your Hit Parade No. 8, Cash Box No. 10 tie
11. "I Believe"   Frankie Laine
    Billboard No. 14, Your Hit Parade No. 7, Variety No. 9
12. "April in Portugal"   Les Baxter
    Billboard No. 13, Your Hit Parade No. 11, Variety No. 10 tie
13. "St. George and the Dragonet"   Stan Freberg
    Billboard No. 10, Cash Box No. 7 tie
14. "Pretend"   Nat "King" Cole
    Billboard No. 18, Your Hit Parade No. 10
15. "Ricochet"   Teresa Brewer
    Billboard No. 16, Your Hit Parade No. 14
16. "Eh, Cumpari"   Julius LaRosa
    Billboard No. 20, Cash Box No. 10 tie
17. "Crying in the Chapel"   June Valli
    Billboard No. 29, Cash Box No. 7 tie

THE TOP HITS OF 1954

Song Title	Artist(s)
1. "Hey There" from *Pajama Game* *Billboard* No. 7, *Your Hit Parade* No. 1, *Variety* No. 1, *Cash Box* No. 1 tie	Rosemary Clooney
2. "Wanted" *Billboard* No. 3, *Your Hit Parade* No. 3, *Variety* No. 3, *Cash Box* No. 1 tie	Perry Como
3. "Little Things Mean a Lot" *Billboard* No. 1, *Your Hit Parade* No. 5 tie, *Variety* No. 2, *Cash Box* No. 4 tie	Kitty Kallen
4. "Mr. Sandman" *Billboard* Nos. 6 & 30, *Your Hit Parade* No. 2, *Variety* No. 6, *Cash Box* No. 10 in 1955	The Chordettes, Four Aces
5. "Secret Love" from *Calamity Jane* *Billboard* No. 8, *Your Hit Parade* No. 4, *Variety* No. 10, *Cash Box* No. 6	Doris Day
6. "I Need You Now" *Billboard* No. 10, *Your Hit Parade* No. 11, *Variety* No. 7, *Cash Box* No. 7 tie	Eddie Fisher
7. "Oh! My Pa-Pa" *Billboard* Nos. 4 & 36, *Variety* No. 4, *Cash Box* No. 1 tie	Eddie Fisher, Eddie Calvert
8. "Sh-Boom" *Billboard* Nos. 2 & 33, *Variety* No. 5, *Cash Box* No. 4 tie	Crew-Cuts, Chords
9. "Three Coins in the Fountain" from *Three Coins in the Fountain* *Billboard* No. 11 & 28, *Your Hit Parade* No. 7, *Cash Box* No. 7 tie	Four Aces, Frank Sinatra
10. "Stranger in Paradise" from *Kismet* *Billboard* Nos. 14 & 23, *Your Hit Parade* No. 5 tie, *Cash Box* No. 7 tie	Tony Bennett, Four Aces
11. "Make Love to Me!" *Billboard* No. 5, *Variety* No. 8	Jo Stafford
12. "That's Amore" from *The Caddy* *Billboard* No. 11 in 1953, *Variety* No. 9	Dean Martin
13. "Hernando's Hideaway" from *Pajama Game* *Billboard* No. 13, *Your Hit Parade* No. 10	Archie Bleyer
14. "Young at Heart" from *Young at Heart* *Billboard* No. 16, *Your Hit Parade* No. 8	Frank Sinatra

15. "Teach Me Tonight"
Billboard No. 18, *Your Hit Parade* No. 12 — Decastro Sisters

16. "If I Give My Heart to You"
Billboard No. 22, *Your Hit Parade* No. 9 — Doris Day

17. "This Ole House"
Billboard No. 9 — Rosemary Clooney

THE TOP HITS OF 1955

Song Title	Artist(s)
1. "Sixteen Tons" *Billboard* No. 4, *Your Hit Parade* No. 4, *Variety* No. 4, *Cash Box* No. 2 tie	Tennessee Ernie Ford
2. "Rock Around the Clock" from *Blackboard Jungle* *Billboard* No. 3, *Your Hit Parade* No. 8, *Variety* No. 2, *Cash Box* No. 2 tie	Bill Haley & his Comets
3. "The Yellow Rose of Texas" *Billboard* Nos. 6 & 27, *Your Hit Parade* No. 2, *Variety* No. 5, *Cash Box* No. 2 tie	Mitch Miller, Johnny Desmond
4. "The Ballad of Davy Crockett" from *Davy Crockett* (TV theme) *Billboard* Nos. 7, 33, & 37, *Your Hit Parade* No. 1, *Variety* No. 7, *Cash Box* No. 1	Bill Hayes, Tennessee Ernie Ford, Fess Parker
5. "Cherry Pink and Apple Blossom White" from *Underwater* *Billboard* No. 1, *Your Hit Parade* No. 10, *Variety* No. 1	Pérez Prado
6. "Autumn Leaves" *Billboard* No. 8, *Your Hit Parade* No. 6, *Variety* No. 3, *Cash Box* No. 8 tie	Roger Williams
7. "Love Is a Many Splendored Thing" from *Love Is a Many Splendored Thing* *Billboard* No. 5, *Your Hit Parade* No. 7, *Variety* No. 6, *Cash Box* No. 8 tie	Four Aces
8. "Unchained Melody" from *Unchained* *Billboard* Nos. 12 & 25, *Your Hit Parade* No. 3, *Variety* No. 9, *Cash Box* No. 2 tie	Les Baxter, Al Hibbler

(Continued)

Song Title	Artist(s)
9. "Let Me Go, Lover" *Billboard No. 9, Your Hit Parade No. 9, Variety No. 10, Cash Box No. 10*	Joan Weber
10. "Sincerely" *Billboard No. 2, Your Hit Parade No. 3 tie, Variety No. 8*	McGuire Sisters
11. "Melody of Love" *Billboard Nos. 19 & 26, Your Hit Parade No. 5, Cash Box No. 2 tie*	Billy Vaughn, Four Aces
12. "Learnin' the Blues" *Billboard No. 13, Your Hit Parade No. 12*	Frank Sinatra
13. "Tweedlee Dee" *Billboard No. 21, Your Hit Parade No. 11*	Georgia Gibbs
14. "Something's Gotta Give" from *Daddy Long Legs* *Billboard No. 39, Your Hit Parade No. 13*	McGuire Sisters
15. "Wallflower (Dance With Me Henry)" *Billboard No. 10*	Georgia Gibbs
16. "Hearts of Stone" *Billboard No. 11*	The Fontane Sisters
17. "Ain't That a Shame" *Billboard No. 14*	Pat Boone
18. "The Crazy Otto" *Billboard No. 15*	Johnny Maddox
19. "Moments to Remember" *Billboard No. 18*	Four Lads
20. "I Hear You Knocking" *Billboard No. 17*	Gale Storm

THE TOP HITS OF 1956

Song Title	Artist(s)
1. "Singing the Blues" *Billboard* No. 2, *Your Hit Parade* No. 1 tie, *Variety* No. 2, *Cash Box* No. 1	Guy Mitchell
2. "Love Me Tender" from *Love Me Tender* *Billboard* No. 8, *Your Hit Parade* No. 4, *Variety* No. 3, *Cash Box* No. 4 tie	Elvis Presley
3. "The Wayward Wind" *Billboard* No. 3, *Your Hit Parade* No. 10, *Variety* No. 8, *Cash Box* No. 4 tie	Gogi Grant
4. "Heartbreak Hotel" *Billboard* No. 4, *Your Hit Parade* No. 11, *Variety* No. 8, *Cash Box* No. 2 tie	Elvis Presley
5. "The Poor People of Paris" *Billboard* No. 6, *Your Hit Parade* No. 3, *Variety* No. 9, *Cash Box* No. 6 tie	Les Baxter
6. "Memories Are Made of This" *Billboard* Nos. 7 & 39, *Your Hit Parade* No. 6 tie, *Variety* No. 7, *Cash Box* No. 8 tie	Dean Martin, Gale Storm
7. "Lisbon Antiqua" *Billboard* No. 10, *Your Hit Parade* No. 5, *Variety* No. 4, *Cash Box* No. 10 tie	Nelson Riddle
8. "My Prayer" *Billboard* No. 9, *Your Hit Parade* No. 15, *Variety* No. 10, *Cash Box* No. 10 tie	The Platters
9. "Don't Be Cruel/Hound Dog" *Billboard* No. 1, *Variety* No. 1, *Cash Box* No. 2 tie and No. 6 tie	Elvis Presley
10. "Rock and Roll Waltz" *Billboard* No. 5, *Your Hit Parade* No. 8 tie, *Cash Box* No. 10 tie	Kay Starr
11. "Moonglow and Theme from *Picnic*" from *Picnic* *Billboard* Nos. 13 & 34, *Your Hit Parade* No. 8 tie, *Cash Box* No. 10 tie	Morris Stoloff, George Cates
12. "The Green Door" *Billboard* No. 12, *Variety* No. 6	Jim Lowe
13. "I Almost Lost My Mind" *Billboard* No. 11, *Cash Box* No. 10 tie	Pat Boone
14. "The Great Pretender" *Billboard* No. 14, *Cash Box* No. 8 tie	The Platters
	(Continued)

Song Title	Artist(s)
15. "Canadian Sunset" *Billboard* No. 21, *Your Hit Parade* No. 1 tie	Hugo Winterhalter with Eddie Haywood
16. "Whatever Will Be, Will Be (Que Sera, Sera)" from *The Man Who Knew Too Much* *Billboard* No. 20, *Your Hit Parade* No. 6	Doris Day
17. "Just Walkin' in the Rain" *Billboard* No. 23, *Your Hit Parade* No. 13 tie	Johnnie Ray
18. "On the Street Where You Live" from *My Fair Lady* *Billboard* No. 29, *Your Hit Parade* No. 13 tie	Vic Damone
19. "Hot Diggity (Dog Ziggity Boom)" *Billboard* No. 15	Perry Como
20. "I Want You, I Need You, I Love You" *Billboard* No. 16	Elvis Presley

THE TOP HITS OF 1957

Song Title	Artist(s)
1. "Love Letters in the Sand" *Billboard* No. 2, *Your Hit Parade* No. 1 tie, *Variety* No. 1, *Cash Box* No. 3 tie	Pat Boone
2. "All Shook Up" *Billboard* No. 1, *Your Hit Parade* No. 6, *Variety* No. 2, *Cash Box* No. 1	Elvis Presley
3. "Tammy" from *Tammy and the Bachelor* *Billboard* No. 7, *Your Hit Parade* No. 1 tie, *Variety* No. 5, *Cash Box* No. 2	Debbie Reynolds
4. "Young Love" *Billboard* Nos. 7 & 17, *Your Hit Parade* No. 4, *Variety* No. 6, *Cash Box* No. 3 tie	Tab Hunter, Sonny James

5. "Jailhouse Rock" from *Jailhouse Rock* — Elvis Presley
   Billboard No. 3, *Variety* No. 3, *Cash Box* No. 5 tie
6. "(Let Me Be Your) Teddy Bear" from *Loving You* — Elvis Presley
   Billboard No. 4, *Variety* No. 4, *Cash Box* No. 5 tie
7. "You Send Me" — Sam Cooke
   Billboard No. 10, *Variety* No. 10, *Cash Box* No. 5 tie
8. "Wake Up Little Susie" — Everly Brothers
   Billboard No. 9, *Variety* No. 9, *Cash Box* No. 9 tie
9. "Chances Are" — Johnny Mathis
   Billboard No. 15, *Your Hit Parade* No. 6 tie, *Cash Box* No. 9 tie
10. "Little Darlin'" — Diamonds
    Billboard No. 21, *Your Hit Parade* No. 11, *Variety* No. 8
11. "Bye Bye Love" — Everly Brothers
    Billboard No. 23, *Variety* No. 7, *Cash Box* No. 12 tie
12. "April Love" from *April Love* — Pat Boone
    Billboard No. 5, *Your Hit Parade* No. 3
13. "Too Much" — Elvis Presley
    Billboard No. 12, *Cash Box* No. 5 tie
14. "Round and Round" — Perry Como
    Billboard No. 13, *Your Hit Parade* No. 5
15. "Honeycomb" — Jimmie Rodgers
    Billboard No. 8, *Cash Box* No. 12 tie
16. "Party Doll" — Buddy Knox
    Billboard No. 19, *Cash Box* No. 12 tie
17. "All the Way" from *The Joker is Wild* — Frank Sinatra
    Billboard No. 30 in 1958, *Your Hit Parade* No. 12 tie
18. "Around the World in 80 Days" from *Around the World in 80 Days* — Mantovani
    Your Hit Parade No. 9
19. "Marianne" — Hilltoppers
    Billboard No. 40, *Your Hit Parade* No. 8
20. "Fascination" — Jane Morgan
    Your Hit Parade No. 10

(*Continued*)

Song Title	Artist(s)
21. "Banana Boat Song" *Your Hit Parade* No. 12 tie	Tarriers
22. "Raunchy" *Cash Box* No. 9 tie	Bill Justis
23. "Butterfly" *Billboard* Nos. 11 & 14	Andy Williams, Charlie Grace
24. "Don't Forbid Me" *Billboard* No. 16	Pat Boone
25. "Diana" *Billboard* No. 18	Paul Anka
26. "That'll Be the Day" *Billboard* No. 20	Crickets

THE TOP HITS OF 1958

Song Title	Artist(s)
1. "At the Hop" *Billboard* No. 1, *Your Hit Parade* No. 2, *Variety* No. 2, *Cash Box* No. 2 tie	Danny & the Juniors
2. "All I Have to Do Is Dream" *Billboard* No. 4, *Your Hit Parade* No. 4 tie, *Variety* No. 4, *Cash Box* No. 6 tie	Everly Brothers
3. "Tequila" *Billboard* No. 5, *Your Hit Parade* No. 3, *Variety* No. 10 tie, *Cash Box* No. 2 tie	Champs
4. "It's All in the Game" *Billboard* No. 2, *Variety* No. 3, *Cash Box* No. 2 tie	Tommy Edwards

5. "Nel Blu, Dipinto di Blu (Volare)"   Domenico Modugno
   Billboard No. 7, *Variety* No. 1, *Cash Box* No. 1
6. "The Purple People Eater"   Sheb Wooley
   Billboard No. 3, *Variety* No. 7, *Cash Box* No. 2 tie
7. "He's Got the World in His Hands"   Laurie London
   Billboard No. 9, *Your Hit Parade* No. 4 tie, *Cash Box* No. 9 tie
8. "Don't"   Elvis Presley
   Billboard No. 6, *Variety* No. 8, *Cash Box* No. 12 tie
9. "Witch Doctor"   David Seville
   Billboard No. 11, *Variety* No. 6, *Cash Box* No. 12 tie
10. "To Know Him, Is to Love Him"   Teddy Bears
    Billboard No. 12, *Variety* No. 10 tie, *Cash Box* No. 12 tie
11. "Twilight Time"   Platters
    Billboard No. 20, *Your Hit Parade* No. 7, *Cash Box* No. 12 tie
12. "Sugartime"   McGuire Sisters
    Billboard No. 8, *Your Hit Parade* No. 6
13. "The Chipmunk Song"   David Seville & the Chipmunks
    Billboard No. 10, *Cash Box* No. 6 tie
14. "Catch a Falling Star"   Perry Como
    Billboard No. 19, *Your Hit Parade* No. 1
15. "Patricia"   Pérez Prado
    Billboard No. 17, *Cash Box* No. 6 tie
16. "Tom Dooley"   Kingston Trio
    Billboard No. 18, *Variety* No. 5
17. "Get a Job"   Silhouettes
    Billboard No. 15, *Cash Box* No. 9 tie
18. "It's Only Make Believe"   Conway Twitty
    Billboard No. 14, *Cash Box* No. 12 tie
19. "Bird Dog"   Everly Brothers
    Billboard No. 22, *Variety* No. 9
20. "Yakety Yak"   Coasters
    Billboard No. 23, *Cash Box* No. 12 tie

(*Continued*)

Song Title	Artist(s)
21. "Topsy II" *Billboard* No. 34, *Cash Box* No. 12 tie	Cozy Cole
22. "Chanson d'Amour (Song of Love)" *Your Hit Parade* No. 8	Art & Dotty Todd
23. "The Stroll" *Cash Box* No. 9 tie	Diamonds
24. "Poor Little Fool" *Billboard* No. 13	Ricky Nelson
25. "Hard Headed Woman" from *King Creole* *Billboard* No. 16	Elvis Presley
26. "Little Star" *Billboard* No. 21	Elegants

THE TOP HITS OF 1959

Song Title	Artist(s)
1. "Mack the Knife" *Billboard* No. 1, *Variety* No. 1, *Cash Box* No. 2	Bobby Darin
2. "The Battle of New Orleans" *Billboard* No. 2, *Variety* No. 2, *Cash Box* No. 1	Johnny Horton
3. "Venus" *Billboard* No. 3, *Variety* No. 4, *Cash Box* No. 3	Frankie Avalon
4. "Smoke Gets in Your Eyes" *Billboard* No. 8, *Variety* No. 3, *Cash Box* No. 4 tie	Platters

5. "The Three Bells"
   Billboard No. 5, *Variety* No. 8, *Cash Box* No. 4 tie — Browns

6. "Come Softly to Me"
   Billboard No. 7, *Variety* No. 7, *Cash Box* No. 4 tie — Fleetwoods

7. "Stagger Lee"
   Billboard No. 4, *Variety* No. 9, *Cash Box* No. 7 — Lloyd Price

8. "Lonely Boy"
   Billboard No. 6, *Variety* No. 6, *Cash Box* No. 8 tie — Paul Anka

9. "Mr. Blue"
   Billboard No. 13, *Variety* No. 5, *Cash Box* No. 8 tie — Fleetwoods

10. "Heartaches By the Number"
    Billboard No. 9, *Cash Box* No. 8 tie — Guy Mitchell

11. "The Happy Organ"
    Billboard No. 15, *Cash Box* No. 8 tie — Dave "Baby" Cortez

12. "Why"
    Billboard No. 14, *Variety* No. 10 — Frankie Avalon

13. "Kansas City"
    Billboard No. 11, *Cash Box* No. 14 — Wilbert Harrison

14. "Don't You Know"
    Billboard No. 25, *Cash Box* No. 8 tie — Della Reese

15. "There Goes My Baby"
    Billboard No. 26, *Cash Box* No. 8 tie — Drifters

16. "Sleep Walk"
    Billboard No. 10 — Santo & Johnny

17. "Big Hunk o' Love"
    Billboard No. 12 — Elvis Presley

18. "Put Your Head on My Shoulder"
    Billboard No. 16 — Paul Anka

19. "Personality"
    Billboard No. 17 — Lloyd Price

20. "Charlie Brown"
    Billboard No. 18 — Coasters

Bibliography

Albert, George, and Frank Hoffmann. *The Cash Box Country Singles Chart 1958–1982*. Metuchen, NJ: Scarecrow Press, 1984.

Barnet, Richard D., Bruce Nemerov, and Mayo R. Taylor. *The Story Behind the Song, 150 Songs that Chronicle the 20th Century*. Westport, CT: Greenwood Press, 2004.

Berendt, Joachim. *The Jazz Book: From New Orleans to Rock and Free Jazz*. New York: Lawrence Hill & Co., 1975.

Bergreen, Laurance. *As Thousands Cheer: The Life of Irving Berlin*. Cambridge, MA: DaCapo, 1996.

Berlin, Irving, and Herbert and Dorothy Fields. *Annie Get Your Gun*. New York: Irving Berlin Music Corp., 1946.

Bernstein, Leonard, and Stephen Sondheim. *Vocal Selections from West Side Story*. New York: G. Schirmer and Chappelll & Co., 1957.

——. *Top Pop Singles of the Year*. New York: Billboard Publications, 1982.

Camelli, Allen. *Our Century in Music*. New Rochelle, NY: Stonehouse Press, Inc., 1974.

Castronova, Frank V., ed. *Almanac of Famous People*. Detroit, MI: Gale, 1998.

Cowden, Robert H. *Popular Singers of the Twentieth Century*. New York: Greenwood Press, 1999.

Croce, Arlene. *The Fred Astaire & Ginger Rogers Book*. New York: Galahad Books, 1972.

Csida, Joseph and June. *American Entertainment: A Unique History of Popular Show Business*. New York: Watson-Guptill Publications, 1978.

Deller, Fred, Roy Thompson, and Douglas Green. *The Illustrated Encyclopedia of Country Music*. New York: Salamander Books, 1977.

DeRemer, Leigh Ann, project ed. *Contemporary Musicians*. Detroit, MI: Thomson, 2003.

Dunning, John. *Tune in Yesterday: The Ultimate Encyclopedia of Old-Time Radio 1925–1976*. Englewood Cliffs, NJ: Prentice-Hall Inc., 1976.

Elrod, Bruce C., ed. *Your Hit Parade and American Top 10 Hits: A Week-by-Week Guide to the Nation's Favorite Music, 1935–1994*. New York: Popular Culture, Ink., 1994.

Ensign, Lynne Naylor, and Robyn Eileen Knapton. *The Complete Dictionary of Television and Film*. New York: Stein and Day, 1985.

Erlewine, Michael, Vladimir Bogdanov, Chris Woodstra, and Stephen Thomas Erlewine, eds. *All Music Guide to Country Music*. San Francisco: Miller Freeman Books, 1997

Ewen, David. *The Complete Book of Classical Music*. Englewood Cliffs, N.J.: Prentice-Hall, 1965.

Ewen, David. *All the Years of American Popular Music*. Englewood Cliffs, NJ: Prentice-Hall, 1977.

Ewen, David. *American Popular Songs*. New York: Random House, 1966.

Ewen, David. *American Songwriters*. New York: H.W. Wilson Co., 1987.

Feist, Leonard. *An Introduction to Popular Music Publishing in America*. New York: National Music Publishers' Association, Inc., 1980.

Friskics, Bill, and Warren and David Cantwell. *Heartaches by the Number: Country Music's 500 Greatest Singles*. Nashville: Country Music Foundation Press, 2003.

Furia, Philip. *Skylark: The Life and Times of Johnny Mercer*. New York: St. Martin's Press, 2003.

Gammond, Peter. *The Oxford Companion to Popular Music*. New York: Oxford Univ. Press, 1991.

Gardner, Edward Foote. *Popular Songs of the Twentieth Century, Vol. 1 – Chart Detail and Encyclopedia 1900–1949*. St. Paul, Minnesota: Paragon House, 2000.

Goldman, Albert. *Elvis*. New York: McGraw-Hill, 1981.

Green, Abel, ed. *Variety*. New York: Variety Magazine, various issues.

Green, Stanley. *Broadway Musicals: Show by Show*. Milwaukee, WI: Hal Leonard Publishing Corp., 1994.

Green, Stanley. *Encyclopedia of the Musical Theatre*. Cambridge, MA: DaCapo, 1976.

Green, Stanley. *Hollywood Musicals: Year by Year*. Milwaukee, WI: Hal Leonard Publishing Corp., 1990.

Greenfield, Thomas Allen. *Radio: A Reference Guide*. West Port, CT: Greenwood Press, 1989.

Greenwood, Earl, and Kathleen Tracy Dutton. *The Boy Who Would Be King*. New York: Signet, 1991.

Harrison, Ian. *The Book of Firsts*. Oxford, England: Past Times, 2003.

Head, Sydney W., and Christopher H. Sterling. *Broadcasting in America*. Boston: Houghton Mifflin Co., 1982.

Hendler, Herb. *Year By Year in the Rock Era*. Westport, CT: Greenwood Press, 1983.

Hirschhorn, Clive. *The Hollywood Musical*. New York: Crown Publishers, Inc., 1981.

Hischak, Thomas. *Film It With Music, An Encyclopedic Guide to the American Movie Musical*. Westport, CT: Greenwood Press, 2001.

Hischak, Thomas S. *The Tin Pan Alley Song Encyclopedia*. Westport, CT: Greenwood Press, 2002.

Hitchcock, H. Wiley, and Stanley Sadie, eds. *The New Grove Dictionary of American Music.* New York: Grove Dictionaries of Music, 1986.

Horstman, Dorothy. *Sing Your Heart Out, Country Boy.* Nashville: Country Music Foundation Press, 1975, 3rd edition 1996.

Jensen, Joli. *The Nashville Sound.* Nashville: The Country Music Foundation Press and Vanderbilt University Press, 1998.

Kelley, Kitty. *His Way: The Unauthorized Biography of Frank Sinatra.* New York: Bantam Books, 1986.

Kingsbury, Paul, ed. *The Encyclopedia of Country Music.* New York: Oxford Press, 1998.

Kinkle, Roger D. *The Complete Encyclopedia of Popular Music and Jazz 1900–1950.* New Rochelle, NY: Arlington House Publishers, 1974.

Larkin, Colin, ed. *Encyclopedia of Popular Music.* New York: Muze, 1998.

Levinson, Peter J. *Tommy Dorsey: Livin' in a Great Big Way.* Cambridge, MA: Da Capo Press, 2005.

Loesser, Frank, Jo Swerling, and Abe Burrows. *Guys and Dolls.* Boston: Frank Music Corp., 1949.

Loewe, Frederick, and Alan Jay Lerner. *Brigadoon.* New York: Sam Fox Publishing Company, Inc. 1947.

Malone, Bill C. *Country Music U.S.A.* Austin, TX: American Folklore Society & University of Texas Press, 1975.

Mattfeld, Julius. *Variety Music Cavalcade.* Englewood Cliffs, NJ: Prentice-Hall, 1962.

McClellan, Jr., Lawrence. *The Later Swing Era: 1942 to 1955.* Westport, CT: Greenwood Press, 2004.

Morath, Max. *Popular Standards.* New York, NY: Grand Central Press and National Public Radio, 2002.

Oermann, Robert K. *A Century of Country: An Illustrated History of Country Music.* New York: TV Books, 1999.

Paymer, Marvin E., ed. *Facts Behind the Songs.* New York: Garland Publishing, Inc., 1993.

Payne, Phillip W., ed. *The Swing Era – 1940–1941.* New York: Time-Life Books, 1971.

Payne, Phillip W., ed. *The Swing Era – 1941–1942.* New York: Time-Life Books, 1971.

Payne, Phillip W., ed. *The Swing Era – 1944–1945.* New York: Time-Life Books, 1971.

Payne, Phillip W., ed. *The Swing Era – Into the '50s.* New York: Time-Life Books, 1971.

Payne, Phillip W., ed. *The Swing Era–Postwar Years.* New York: Time-Life Books, 1972.

Raph, Theodore. *The Songs We Sang.* Theodore Raph Aurora, CO: Oak Tree Publications, 1964.

Rodgers, Richard, Oscar Hammerstein II, Howard Lindsay, and Russel Crouse. *The Sound of Music.* New York: Williamson Music, Inc., 1959.

Rodgers, Richard, Oscar Hammerstein II. *Carousel.* New York: Williamson Music, Inc., 1945.

Rodgers, Richard, Oscar Hammerstein II. *The King and I.* New York: Williamson Music, Inc., 1951.

Rodgers, Richard. *Musical Stages.* Cambridge, MA: Da Capo, 2002.

Romanowski, Patricia, and Holly George-Warren, eds. *The New Rolling Stone Encyclopedia of Rock and Roll.* New York: Fireside, 1995.

Sandved, K.B., ed. *The World of Music: An Illustrated Encyclopedia.* New York: Abradale Press, 1963.

Sanjeck, Russell and David. *Pennies from Heaven: The American Popular Music Business in the Twentieth Century.* New York: Da Capo Press, 1996.

Sanjeck, Russell. *American Popular Music and Its Business Vol. 3, from 1900 to 1984.* New York: Oxford Press, 1988.

Sanjeck, Russell. *From Print to Plastic: Publishing and Promoting America's Popular Music (1900–1980).* New York: Institute for Studies in American Music, Conservatory of Music, Brooklyn College of City University of New York, 1983.

Sickels, Robwert. *The 1940s.* Westport, CT: Greenwood Press, 2004.

Simon, George T. *The Big Bands.* New York: Schirmer, 1974.

Simon, William L., ed. *The Reader's Digest Merry Christmas Songbook.* Pleasantville, NY: The Reader's Digest Association, Inc., 1981.

Spaeth, Sigmund. *A History of Popular Music in America.* New York: Random House, 1948.

Tyler, Don. *Hit Songs, 1900–1955: American Popular Music of the Pre-Rock Era.* Jefferson, NC: McFarland, 2007.

Tyler, Don. *Hit Parade: An Encyclopedia of the Jazz, Depression, Swing, and Sing Eras.* New York: Quill, 1985.

Vellenga, Dirk, with Mick Farren. *Elvis and the Colonel.* New York: Delacorte Press, 1988.

Vogel, Frederick G. *Hollywood Musicals Nominated for Best Picture.* Jefferson, NC: McFarland, 2003.

Watson, Doc. *The Songs of Doc Watson.* New York: Music Sales Corporation, 1971.

Whitburn, Joel. *A Century of Pop Music.* Menomonee Falls, WI: Record Research, Inc., 1999.

Whitburn, Joel. *Pop Memories.* Menomonee Falls, WI: Record Research, Inc., 1986.

Whitburn, Joel. *Top Country Singles: 1944–2001.* Menomonee Falls, WI: Record Research, Inc. Menomonee Falls, WI, 2002.

Whitburn, Joel. *Top R & B Singles 1942–1988.* Menomonee Falls, WI: Record Research, Inc. Menomonee Falls, WI, 1988.

Whitburn, Joel. *Top 40 Hits.* Menomonee Falls, WI: Record Research, Inc., 1987.

Wilder, Alec. *American Popular Song: The Great Innovators, 1900–1950.* New York: Oxford, 1972.

Williams, John R. *This Was Your Hit Parade.* John R. Williams, 1973.

Willson, Meredith. *Vocal Selections from The Music Man.* New York: Frank Music Corp. & Rinimer Corp., 1957.

Young, William H. and Nancy K. *Music of the Great Depression.* Westport, CT: Greenwood Press, 2005.

Young, William H. and Nancy K. Young. *The 1950s.* Westport, CT: Greenwood Press, 2004.

WEB SITES

http://en.wikipedia.org/wiki
http://history.acusd.edu/gen/recording
http://home.earthlink.net/~jaymar41

http://hometown.aol.com/mgmfanatic/index.html
http://inventors.about.com/library/inventors/bljukebox.htm
http://kokomo.ca/cd_review/_perito/perito_01.htm
http://lantz.goldenagecartoons.com/profiles/woody
http://lcweb2.loc.gov/cocoon/ihas
http://lirama.net
http://lyrical.nl
http://members.aol.com/_ht_a/randypny/cashbox/50s.html
http://members.aol.com/jeff1070/mutual.html
http://musicals.net
http://nfo.net/hits
http://parentseyes.arizona.edu/msw/westernfiddle/oldtimefiddlers.html
http://parlorsongs.com/index.asp
http://songfacts.com
http://users.bestweb.net/~foosie/julestyn.htm
http://www.alamhof.org
http://www.am1070wdia.com/pages/History_.html
http://www.americanheritage.com
http://www.answers.com
http://www.authentichistory.com/audio
http://www.billboard.biz
http://www.billboard.com
http://www.bobwills.com
http://www.bookrags.com/history/popculture/juke-boxes-sjpc-02
http://www.cbs.com
http://www.centralhome.com/ballroomcountry/tango.htm
http://www.classicmoviemusicals.com
http://www.cmgworldwide.com/music
http://www.cmt.com
http://www.countrymusichalloffame.com
http://www.dannyandthejuniors.com
http://www.dumboozle.com
http://www.elvis.com
http://www.everlybrothers.com
http://www.fiftiesweb.com
http://www.folkways.si.edu/learn_discover/bluegrass
http://www.frankloesser.com
http://www.geocities.com/bernsteincandide
http://www.geocities.com/nashville
http://www.geocities.com/porterguide/cancan.html
http://www.hanksnow.com
http://www.harrywarren.org
http://www.hillbilly-music.com
http://www.history-of-rock.com
http://www.hotshotdigital.com/OldRock/PlattersBio.html
http://www.ibma.org/about.bluegrass/history
http://www.imagi-nation.com/moonstruck/albm92.html
http://www.imdb.com

http://www.jazzhall.org
http://www.johnnymercer.com
http://www.kcmetro.cc.mo.us
http://www.laventure.net/tourist/prez_bio.htm
http://www.lib.unc.edu/mss/sfc1/hillbilly
http://www.lorenzhart.org
http://www.louisjordan.com
http://www.mcguiresisters.com
http://www.misspattipage.com
http://www.monkinstitute.com/index11.html
http://www.mtishows.com
http://www.museum.tv/archives
http://www.musicalheaven.com
http://www.musicals101.com
http://www.musicweb.uk.net
http://www.nashvillesongwritersfoundation.com
http://www.nodanw.com
http://www.oldielyrics.com
http://www.opry.com/MeetTheOpry
http://www.pantheontheatre.co.uk/shows
http://www.parabrisas.com
http://www.paulanka.com
http://www.pbs.org/jazz/biography
http://www.planet-tango.com
http://www.radiohof.org
http://www.reddstewart.com/tennesseewaltz.html
http://www.redhotjazz.com
http://www.reelclassics.com
http://www.riaa.com
http://www.rockabillyhall.com
http://www.rockhall.com
http://www.roughstock.com/history/bgrass.html
http://www.soc.duke.edu/~s142tm01/history3.html
http://www.songfacts.com
http://www.songwritershalloffame.org
http://www.spaceagepop.com/chacksfi.htm
http://www.swingmusic.net
http://www.talkinbroadway.com
http://www.tamswitmark.com/musicals
http://www.thefreedictionary.com
http://www.theinkspots.com
http://www.umkc.edu/lib/spec-col
http://www.variety.com
http://www.vaughnmonroesociety.org
http://www.videouniversity.com
http://www.westernmusic.org/HallOfFamefiles
http://www.wsu.edu/~brians/love-in-the-arts/west.html

Index

Note: **Bold** page numbers indicate the location of photos.